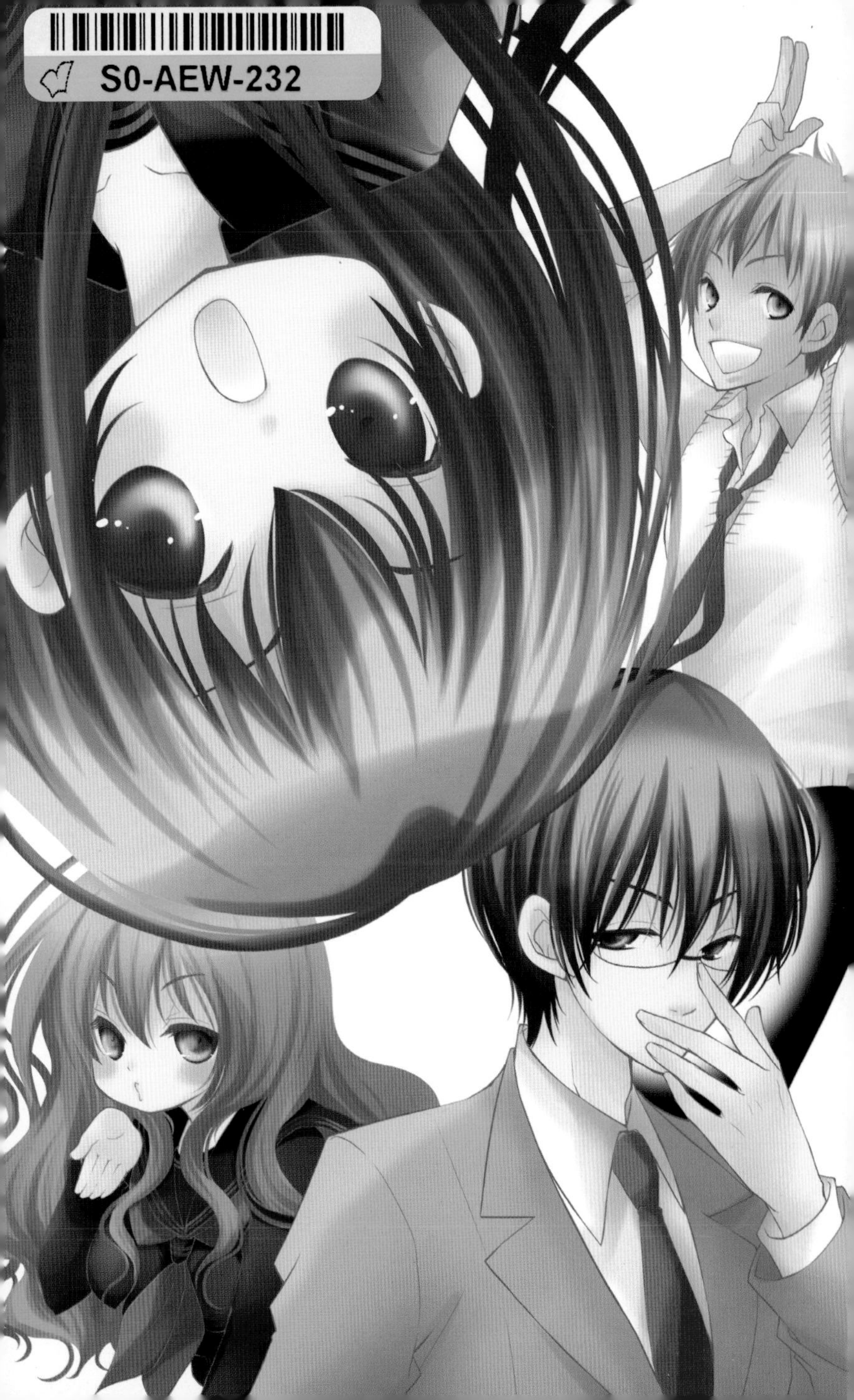

Ani-Imo

(2)

[Ani-Imo]
Big Brother becomes
Little Sister;
Little Sister becomes
Big Brother.

Haruko
Kurumatani

C H A R A C T E R S

Youta Koizumi

A first-year in high school. Outwardly appears to be Youta but is Hikaru on the inside. Her feelings for her brother are very serious and only became all the more so when they switched bodies.

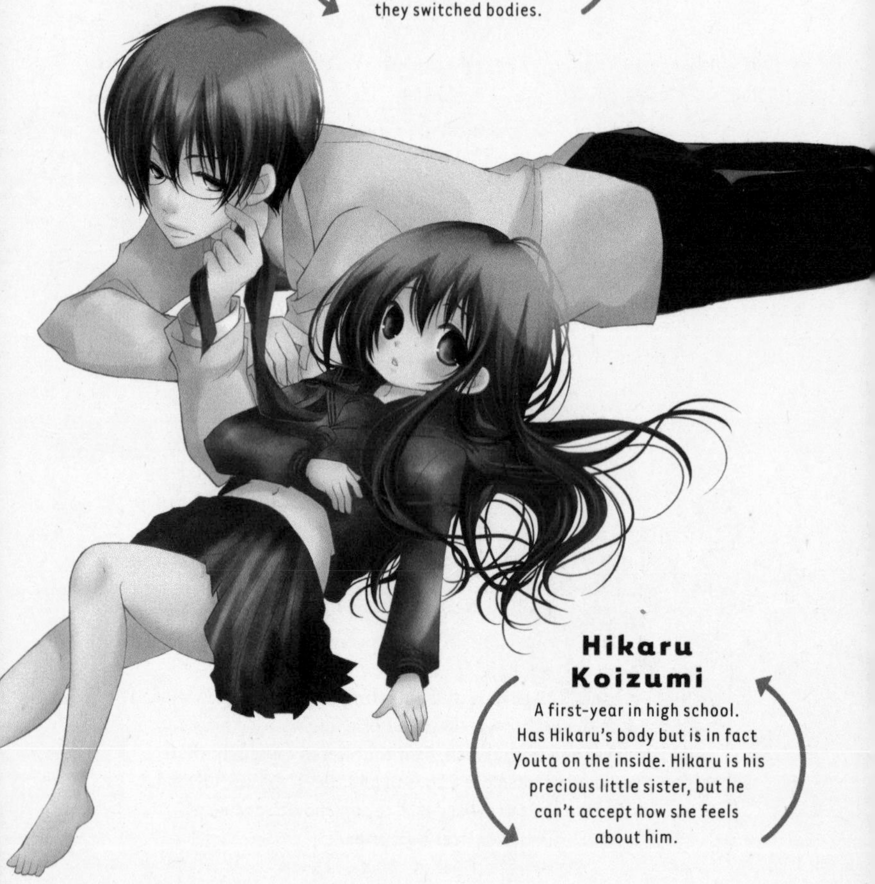

Hikaru Koizumi

A first-year in high school. Has Hikaru's body but is in fact Youta on the inside. Hikaru is his precious little sister, but he can't accept how she feels about him.

Kakeru Mayama

A showy classmate who keeps making advances toward Hikaru.

Yurika Oda

Hikaru and Youta's classmate. She likes girls.

Chisato Ichijou

Hikaru and Youta's doctor. Intensely sadistic at heart. Despite this, he has taken an interest in the Koizumi siblings.

S T O R Y

I'm Youta Koizumi.
One day, I discovered that my precious little sister, Hikaru, whom I've protected since we were very little, is not actually related to me by blood! Even though I reassured her that she'd always be my precious little sister even if we aren't technically related, Hikaru confessed that when she found out that we're not really brother and sister, she was overjoyed—and then she kissed me! But immediately following that, we were both in an accident, and somehow I ended up in Hikaru's body and she in mine!!!!! Even though I was in a near state of panic over our predicament, I tried to reassure Hikaru. But she just told me,
"I'm not giving you back your body!"
Now I'm completely exhausted adjusting to the whole new way of going to the bathroom, taking a bath, and wearing bras and tights that I have to deal with. As if that weren't enough, there's also my crush and classmate Oda-san and the frivolous Mayama... And before I even realized it, I've somehow become my little sister's girlfriend!!
Just what the hell is going on here!!?

CONTENTS

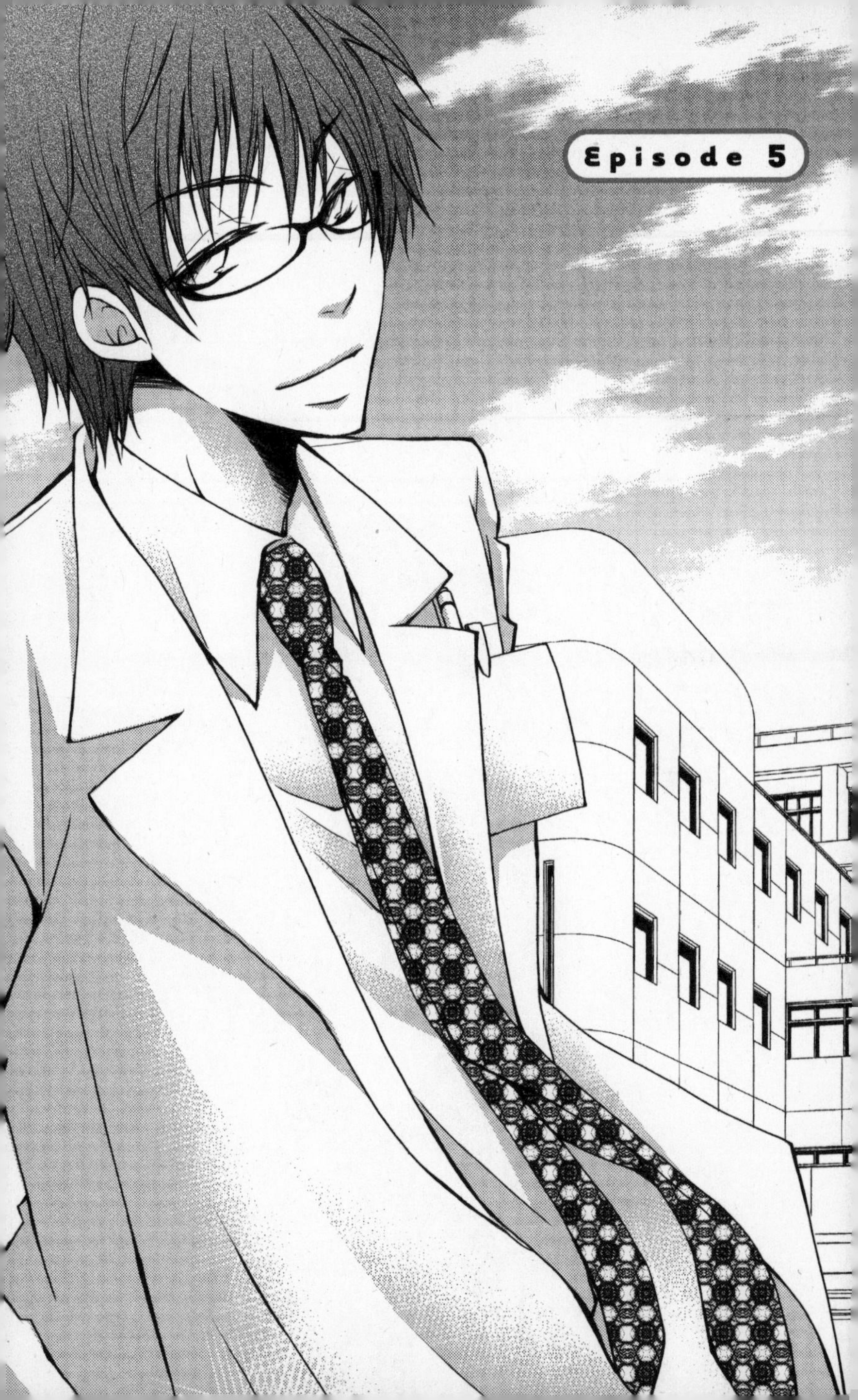
Episode 5

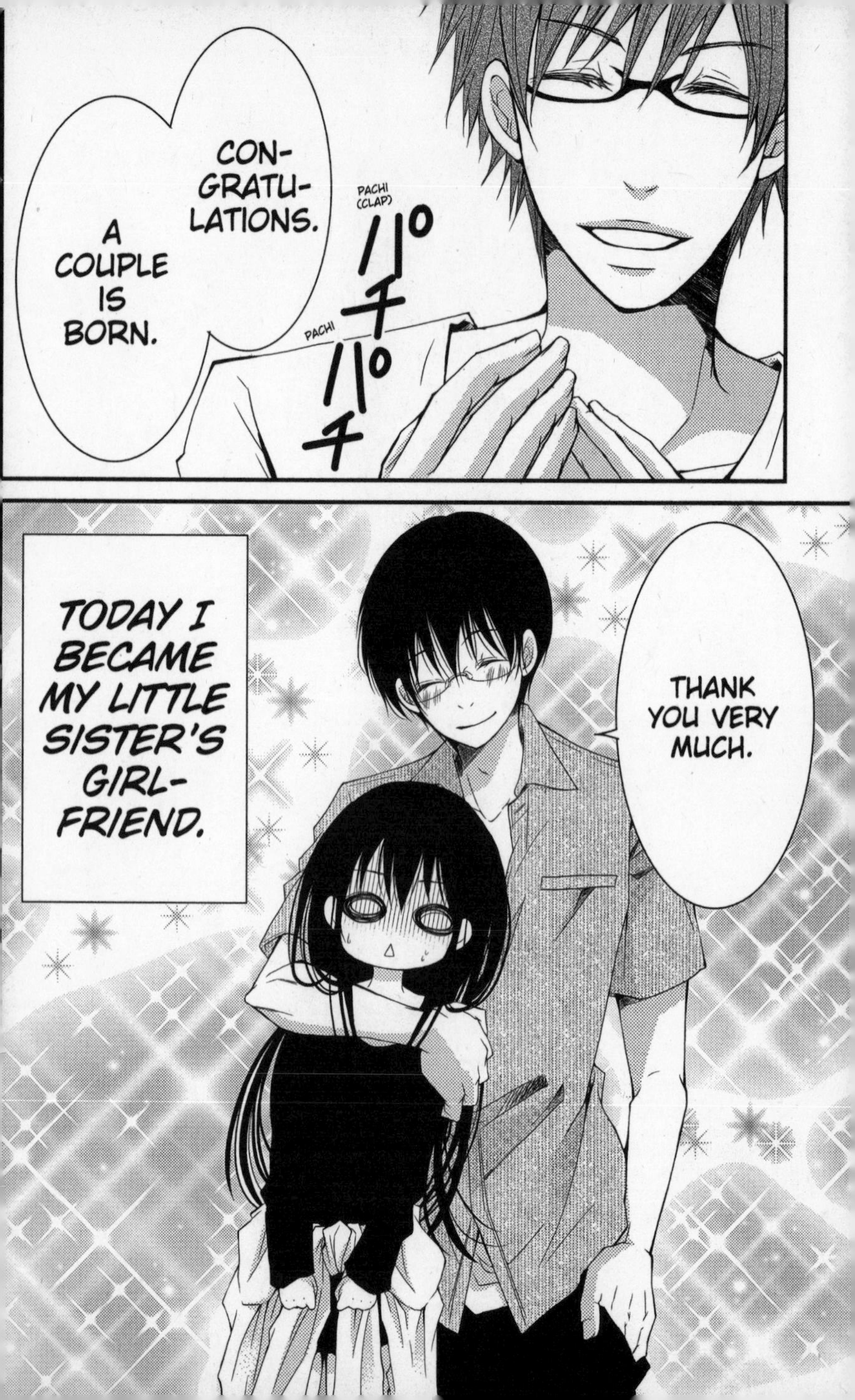
PACHI (CLAP)
PACHI
CON-GRATU-LATIONS. A COUPLE IS BORN.
THANK YOU VERY MUCH.
TODAY I BECAME MY LITTLE SISTER'S GIRL-FRIEND.

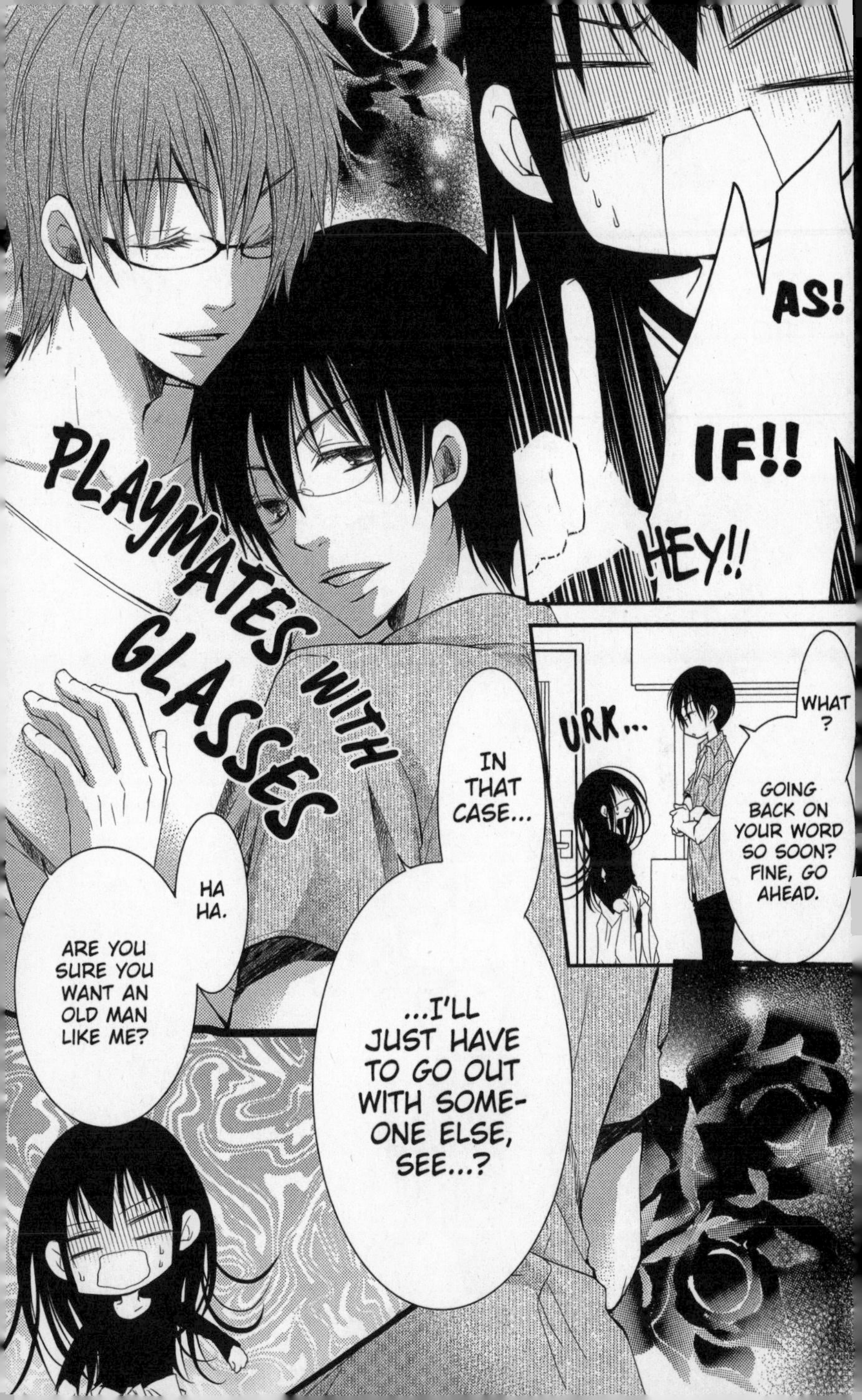
AS!
IF!!
HEY!!
WHAT?
GOING BACK ON YOUR WORD SO SOON? FINE, GO AHEAD.
URK...
IN THAT CASE...
...I'LL JUST HAVE TO GO OUT WITH SOME-ONE ELSE, SEE...?
PLAYMATES WITH GLASSES
HA HA.
ARE YOU SURE YOU WANT AN OLD MAN LIKE ME?

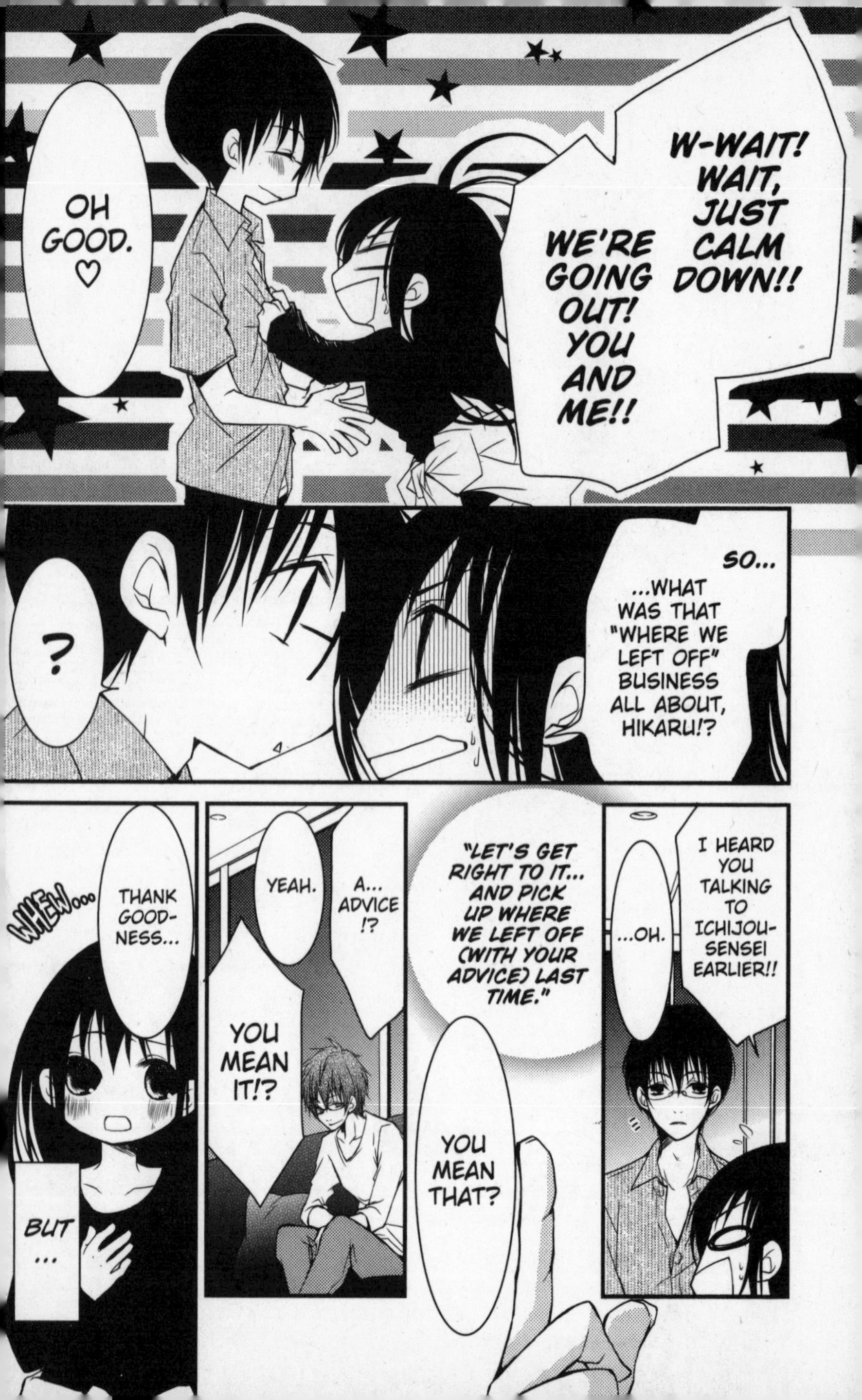
W-WAIT! WAIT, JUST CALM DOWN!!
WE'RE GOING OUT! YOU AND ME!!
OH GOOD. ♡
SO...
...WHAT WAS THAT "WHERE WE LEFT OFF" BUSINESS ALL ABOUT, HIKARU!?
?
I HEARD YOU TALKING TO ICHIJOU-SENSEI EARLIER!!
...OH.
"LET'S GET RIGHT TO IT... AND PICK UP WHERE WE LEFT OFF (WITH YOUR ADVICE) LAST TIME."
YOU MEAN THAT?
A... ADVICE!?
YEAH.
YOU MEAN IT!?
THANK GOOD-NESS...
WHEW...
BUT...

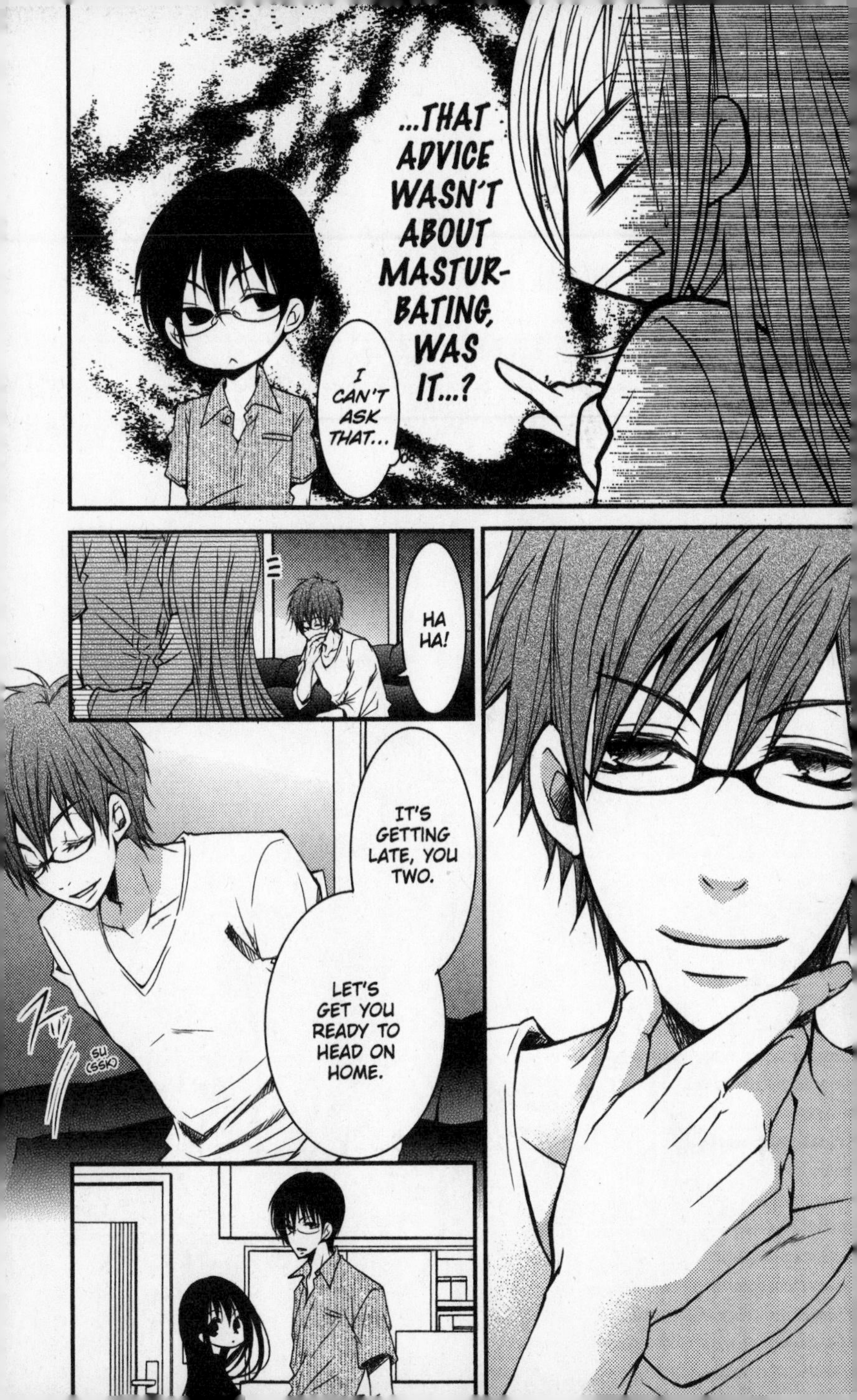
...THAT ADVICE WASN'T ABOUT MASTURBATING, WAS IT...?
I CAN'T ASK THAT...
HA HA!
IT'S GETTING LATE, YOU TWO.
LET'S GET YOU READY TO HEAD ON HOME.
SU (SSK)

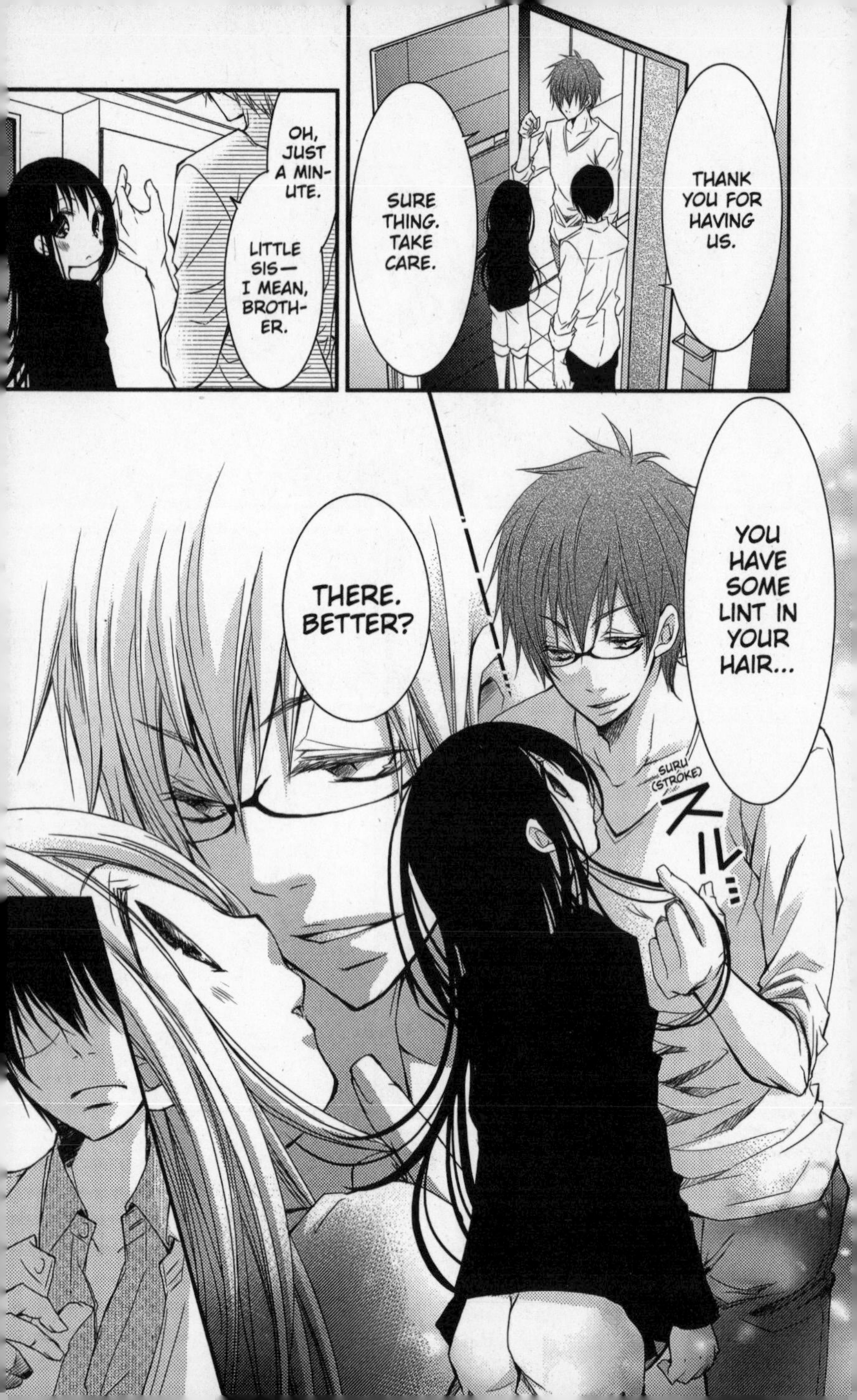
THANK YOU FOR HAVING US.
SURE THING. TAKE CARE.
OH, JUST A MIN-UTE.
LITTLE SIS— I MEAN, BROTH-ER.
YOU HAVE SOME LINT IN YOUR HAIR...
SURU (STROKE)
THERE. BETTER?

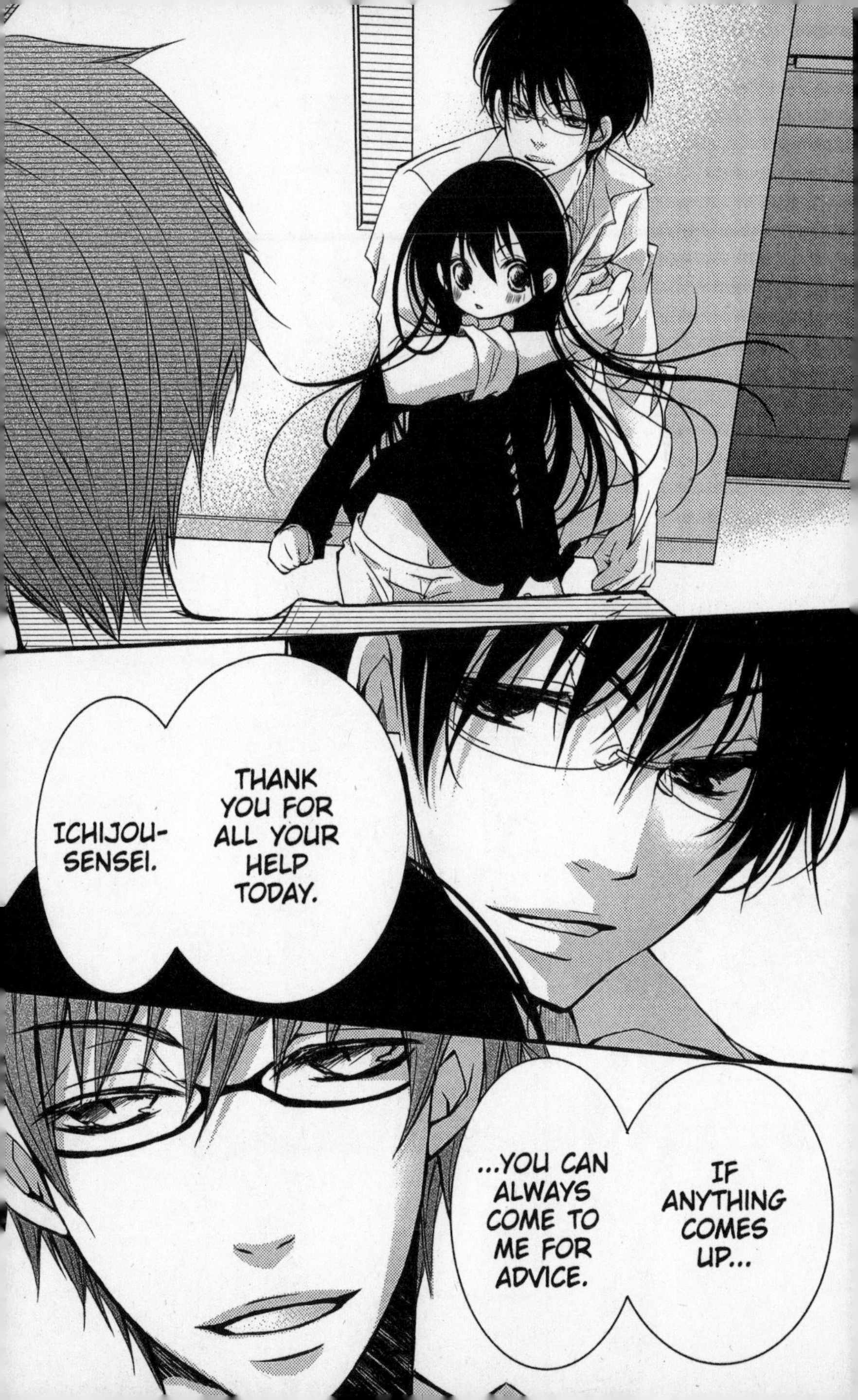
THANK YOU FOR ALL YOUR HELP TODAY.
ICHIJOU-SENSEI.
IF ANYTHING COMES UP...
...YOU CAN ALWAYS COME TO ME FOR ADVICE.

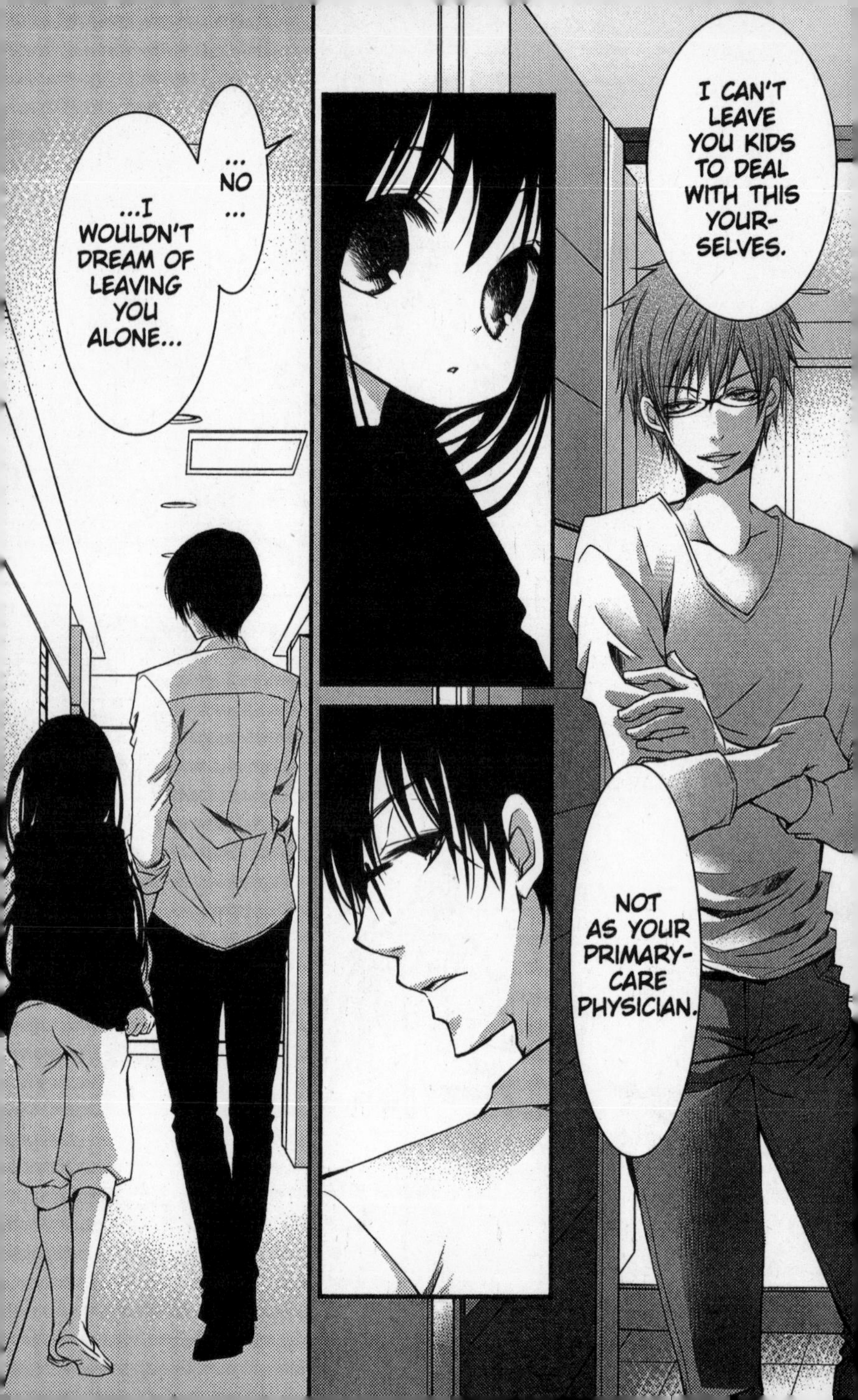
I CAN'T LEAVE YOU KIDS TO DEAL WITH THIS YOUR-SELVES.
NOT AS YOUR PRIMARY-CARE PHYSICIAN.
...NO...
...I WOULDN'T DREAM OF LEAVING YOU ALONE...

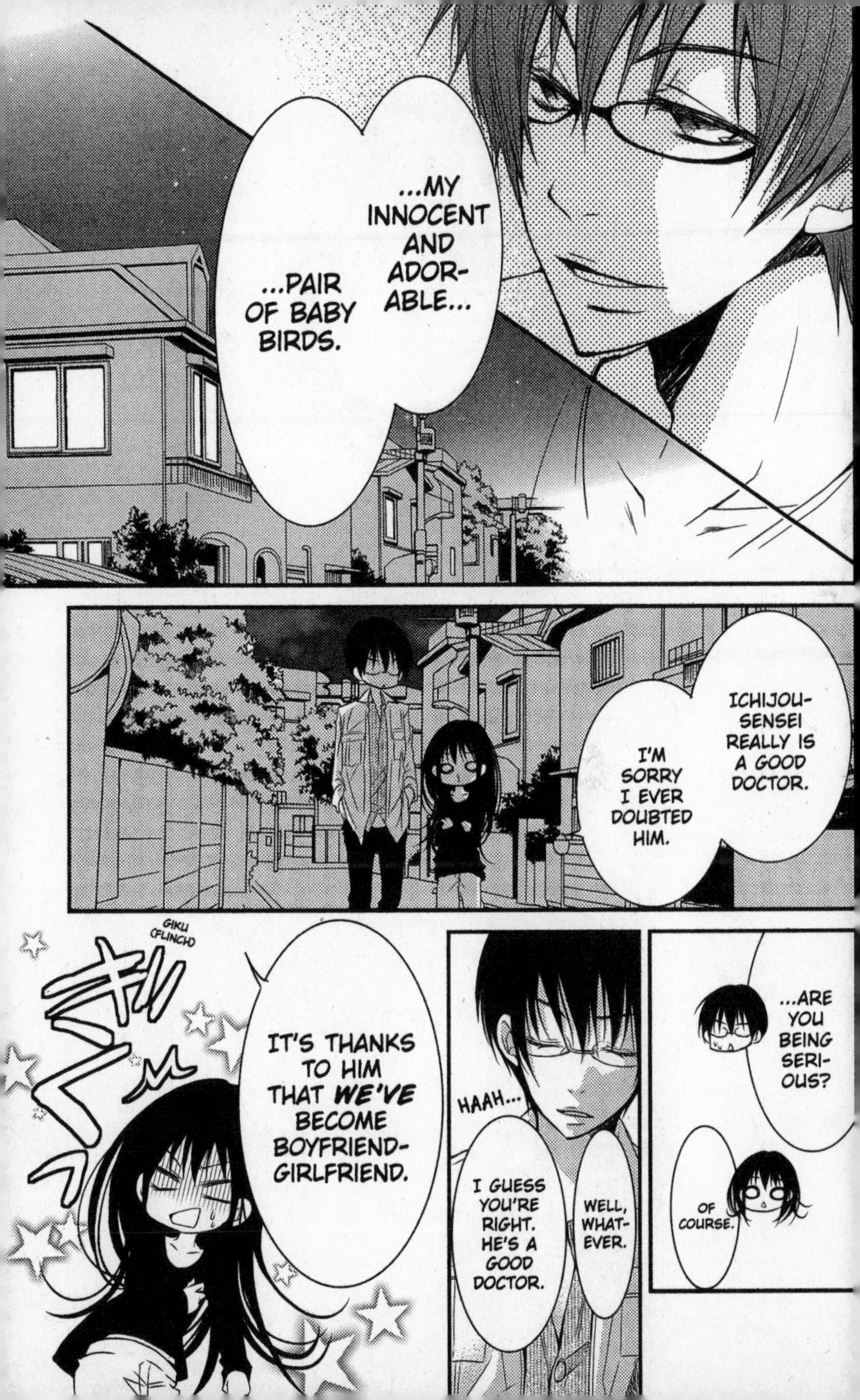
...MY INNOCENT AND ADORABLE...
...PAIR OF BABY BIRDS.
ICHIJOU-SENSEI REALLY IS A GOOD DOCTOR.
I'M SORRY I EVER DOUBTED HIM.
...ARE YOU BEING SERIOUS?
OF COURSE.
HAAH...
WELL, WHATEVER.
I GUESS YOU'RE RIGHT. HE'S A GOOD DOCTOR.
IT'S THANKS TO HIM THAT *WE'VE* BECOME BOYFRIEND-GIRLFRIEND.
GIKU (FLINCH)

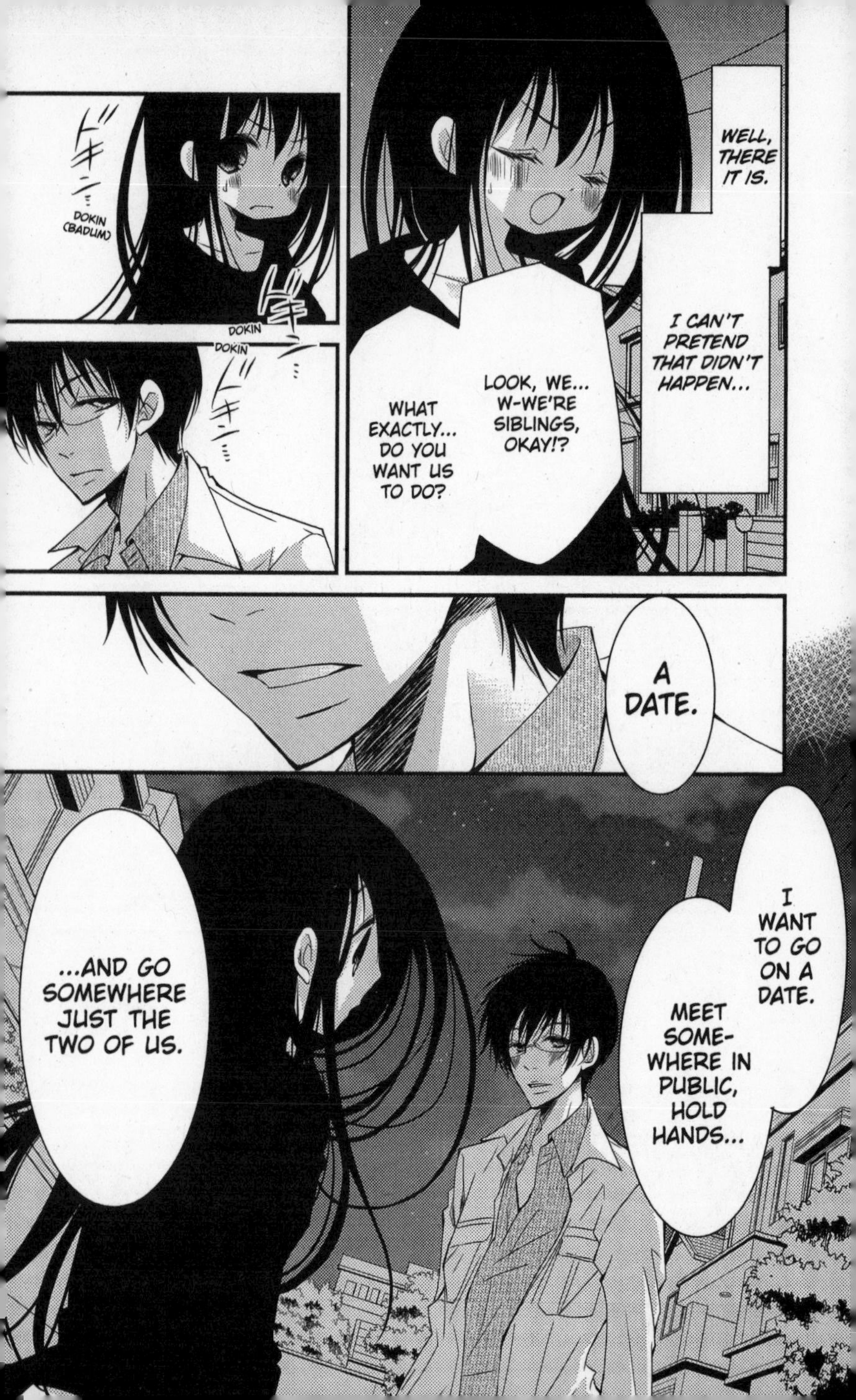
WELL, THERE IT IS.
I CAN'T PRETEND THAT DIDN'T HAPPEN...
LOOK, WE... W-WE'RE SIBLINGS, OKAY!?
WHAT EXACTLY... DO YOU WANT US TO DO?
DOKIN (BADUM)
DOKIN
DOKIN
A DATE.
I WANT TO GO ON A DATE.
MEET SOME-WHERE IN PUBLIC, HOLD HANDS...
...AND GO SOMEWHERE JUST THE TWO OF US.

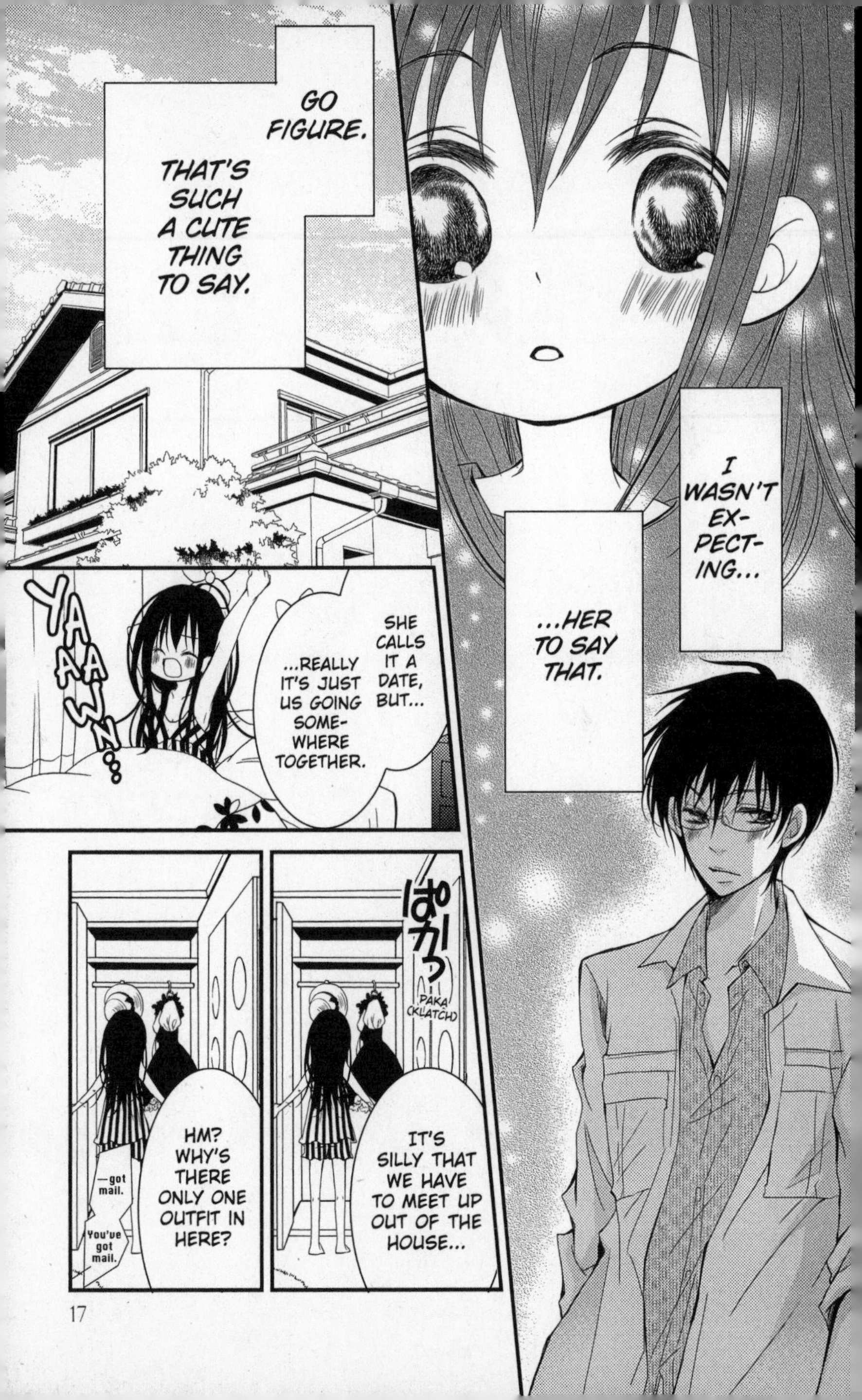
I WASN'T EXPECTING...
...HER TO SAY THAT.
GO FIGURE.
THAT'S SUCH A CUTE THING TO SAY.
SHE CALLS IT A DATE, BUT...
...REALLY IT'S JUST US GOING SOMEWHERE TOGETHER.
YAAAAWN...
ぱかっ
PAKA (KLATCH)
IT'S SILLY THAT WE HAVE TO MEET UP OUT OF THE HOUSE...
HM? WHY'S THERE ONLY ONE OUTFIT IN HERE?
You've got mail.
—got mail.

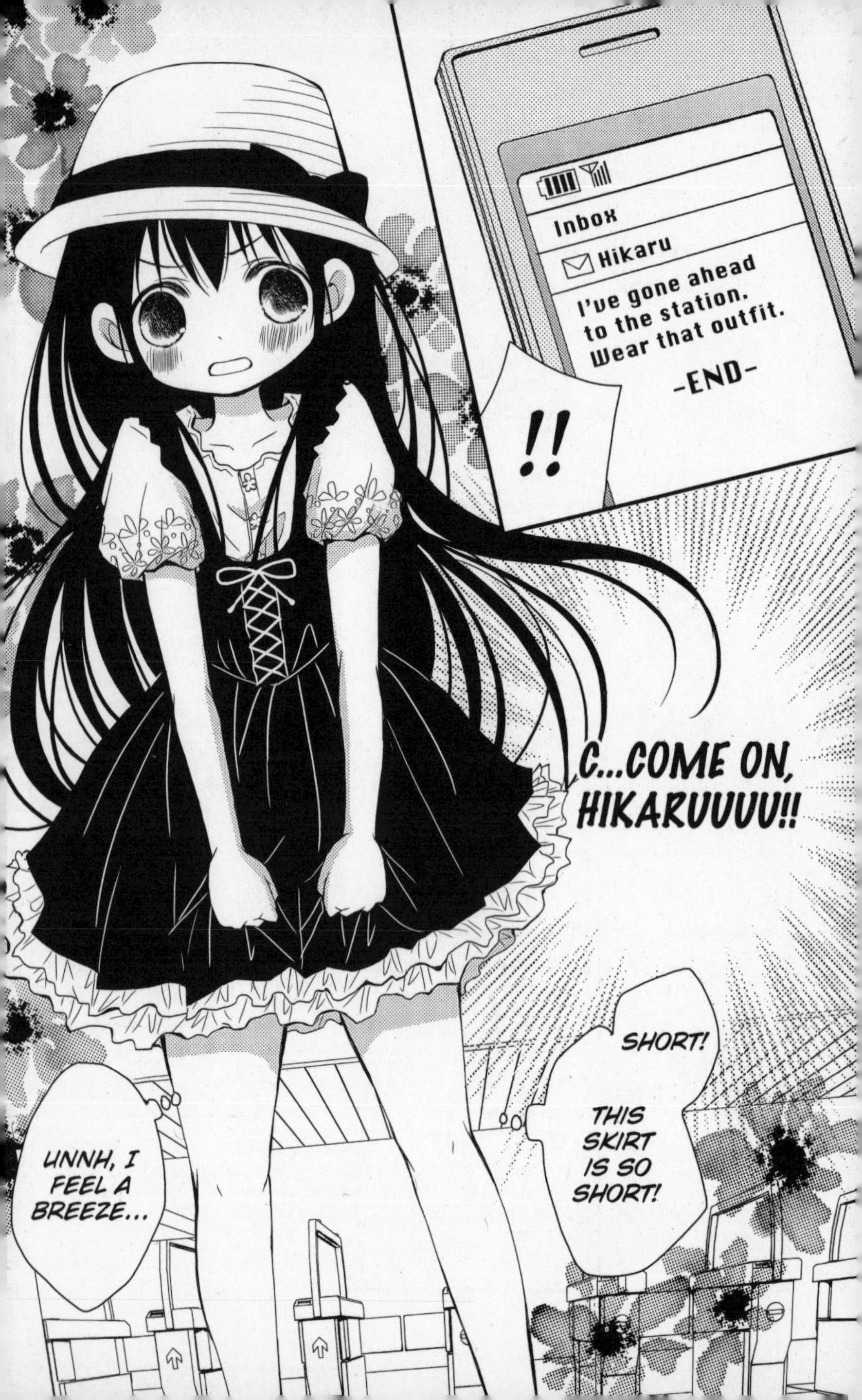
Inbox
Hikaru
I've gone ahead to the station. Wear that outfit.
-END-
!!
C...COME ON, HIKARUUUU!!
SHORT!
THIS SKIRT IS SO SHORT!
UNNH, I FEEL A BREEZE...

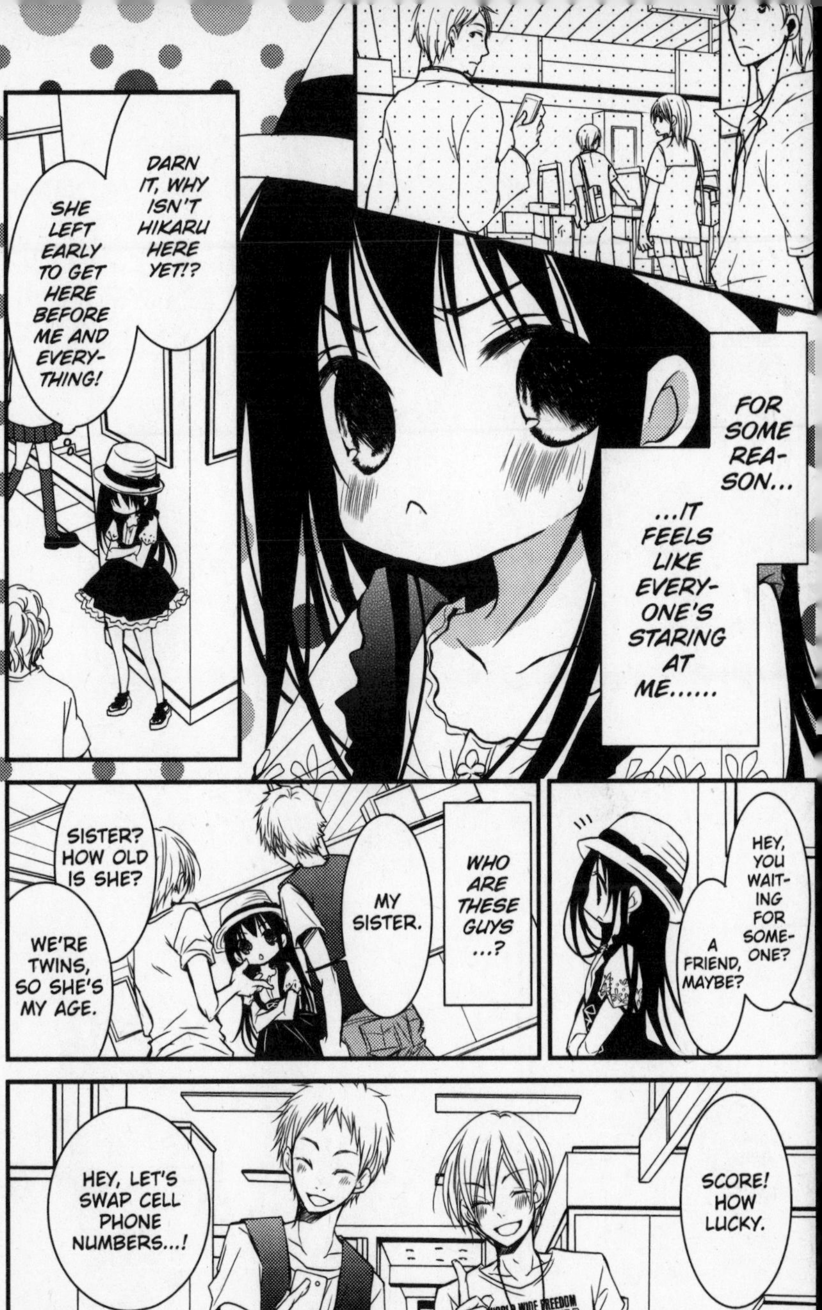
FOR SOME REASON...
...IT FEELS LIKE EVERYONE'S STARING AT ME......
DARN IT, WHY ISN'T HIKARU HERE YET!?
SHE LEFT EARLY TO GET HERE BEFORE ME AND EVERYTHING!
HEY, YOU WAITING FOR SOMEONE?
A FRIEND, MAYBE?
WHO ARE THESE GUYS...?
MY SISTER.
SISTER? HOW OLD IS SHE?
WE'RE TWINS, SO SHE'S MY AGE.
SCORE! HOW LUCKY.
HEY, LET'S SWAP CELL PHONE NUMBERS...!
WORLD WIDE FREEDOM

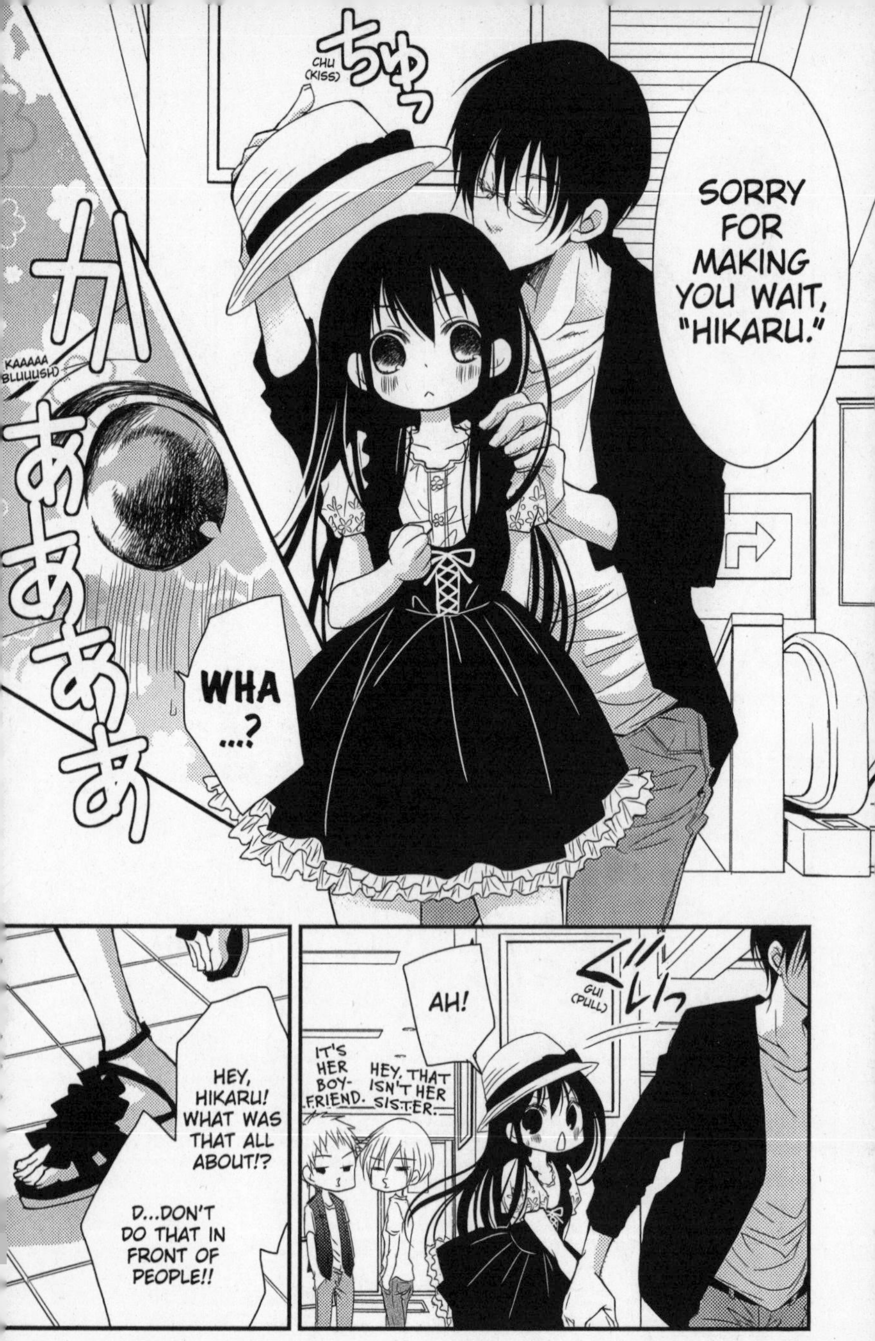
SORRY FOR MAKING YOU WAIT, "HIKARU."
ちゅっ
CHU (KISS)
かあああぁ
KAAAAA BLUUUSH
WHA ...?
ぐいっ
GUI (PULL)
AH!
HEY, THAT ISN'T HER SISTER.
IT'S HER BOY-FRIEND.
HEY, HIKARU! WHAT WAS THAT ALL ABOUT!?
D...DON'T DO THAT IN FRONT OF PEOPLE!!

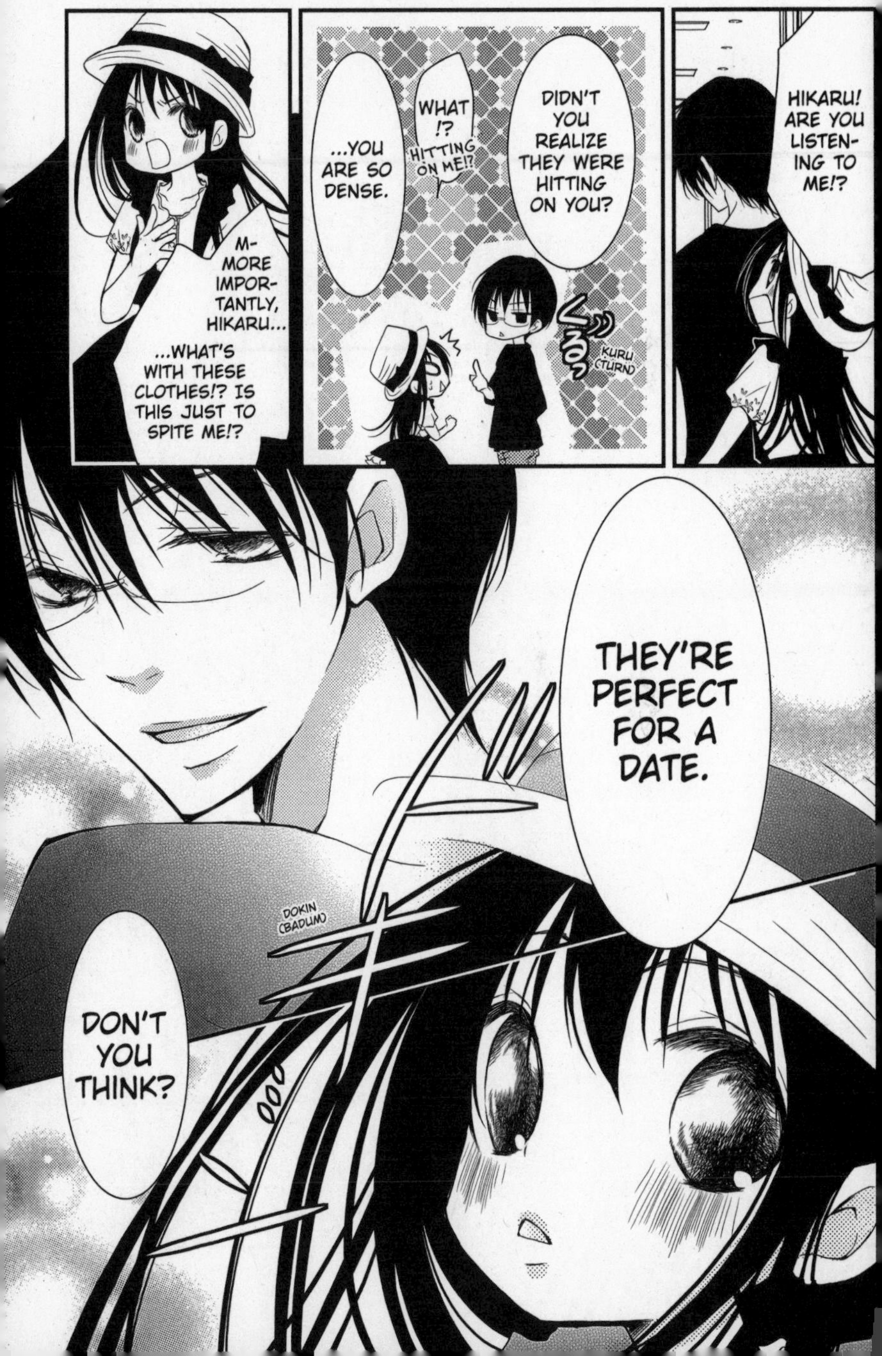
HIKARU! ARE YOU LISTENING TO ME!?
DIDN'T YOU REALIZE THEY WERE HITTING ON YOU?
WHAT!?
HITTING ON ME!?
KURU (TURN)
...YOU ARE SO DENSE.
M-MORE IMPORTANTLY, HIKARU...
...WHAT'S WITH THESE CLOTHES!? IS THIS JUST TO SPITE ME!?
THEY'RE PERFECT FOR A DATE.
DOKIN (BADUM)
DON'T YOU THINK?

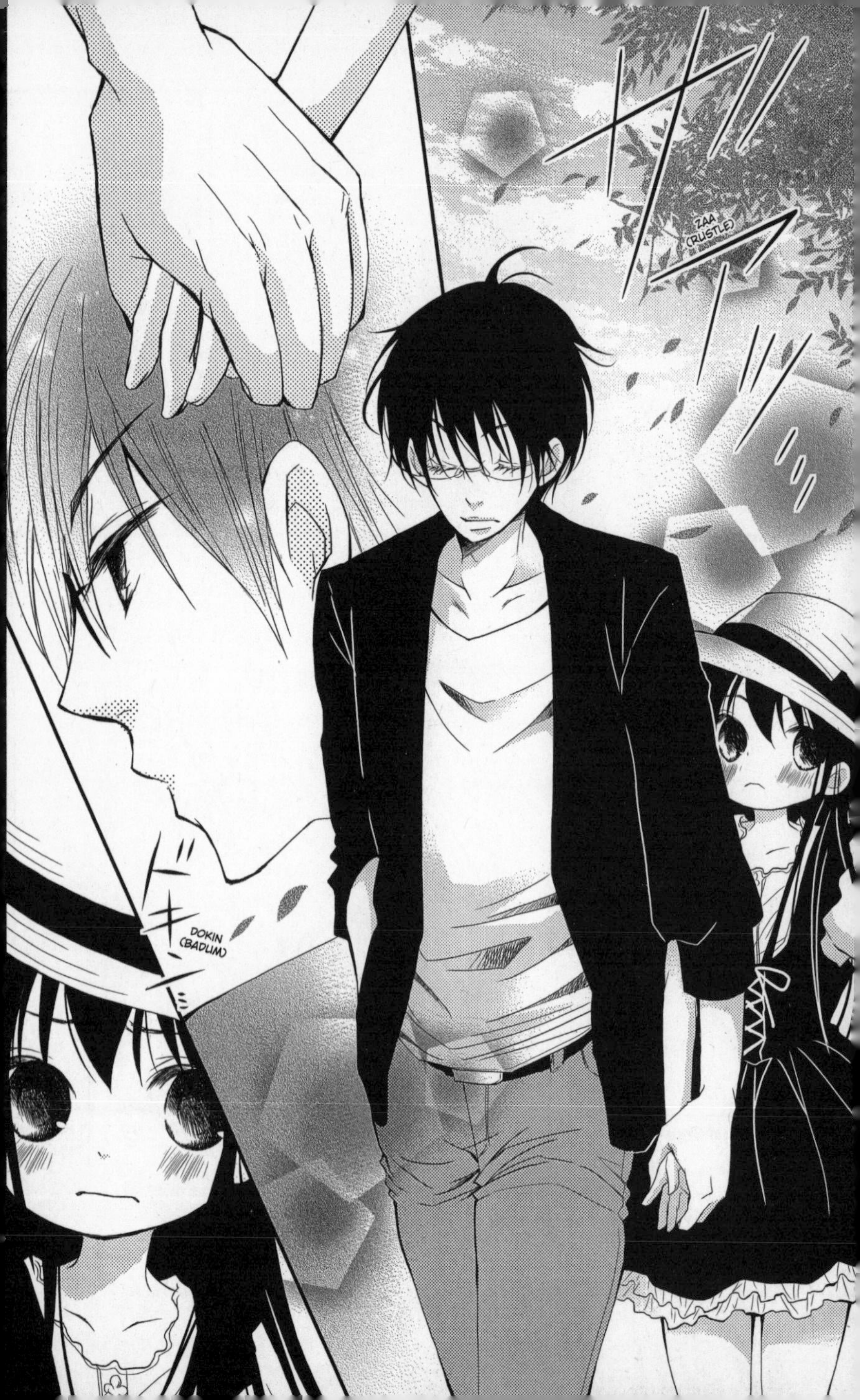
ZAA (RUSTLE)
DOKIN (BADUM)

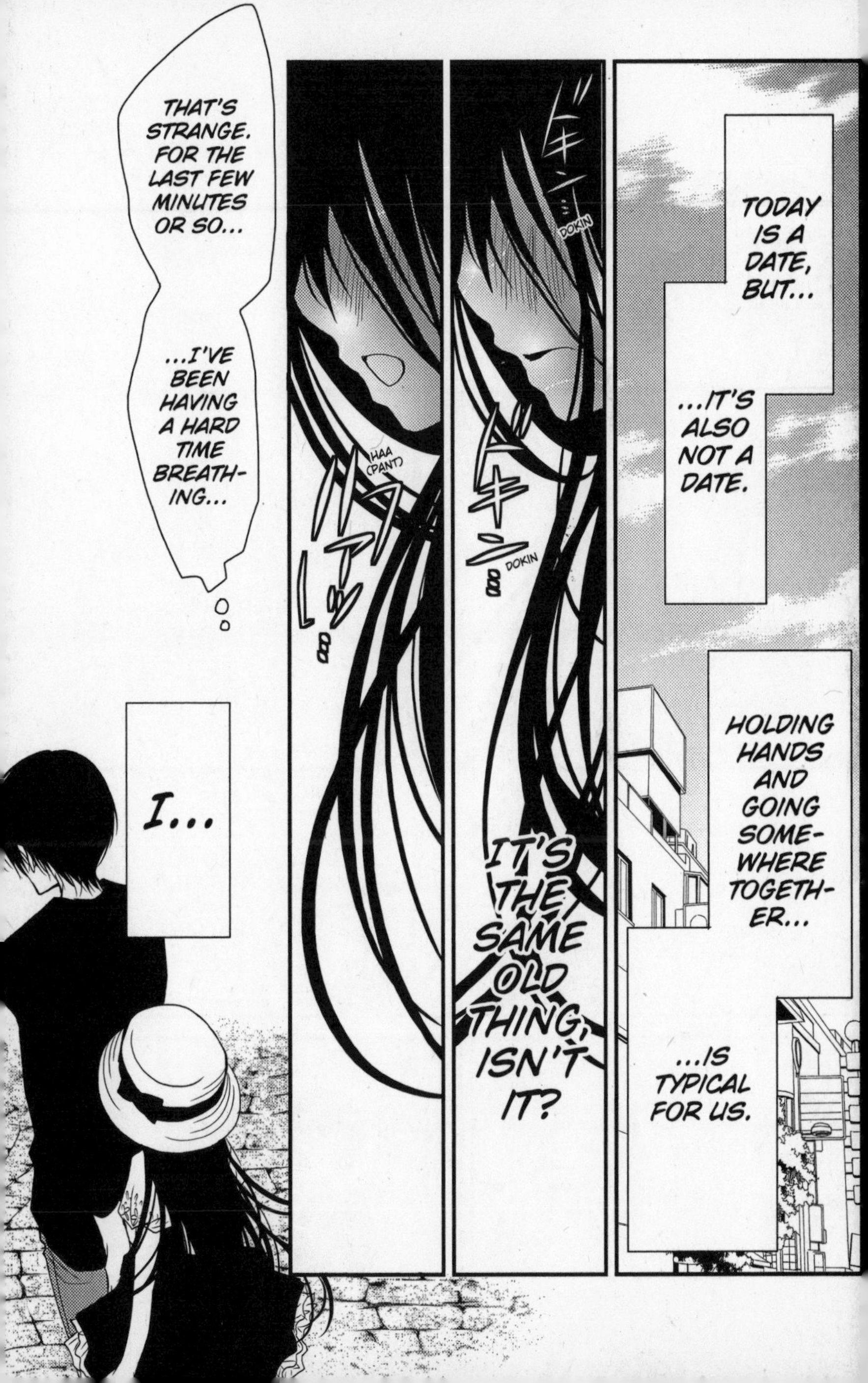
TODAY IS A DATE, BUT...
...IT'S ALSO NOT A DATE.
HOLDING HANDS AND GOING SOMEWHERE TOGETHER...
...IS TYPICAL FOR US.
DOKIN
DOKIN
IT'S THE SAME OLD THING, ISN'T IT?
HAA (PANT)
THAT'S STRANGE. FOR THE LAST FEW MINUTES OR SO...
...I'VE BEEN HAVING A HARD TIME BREATHING...
I...

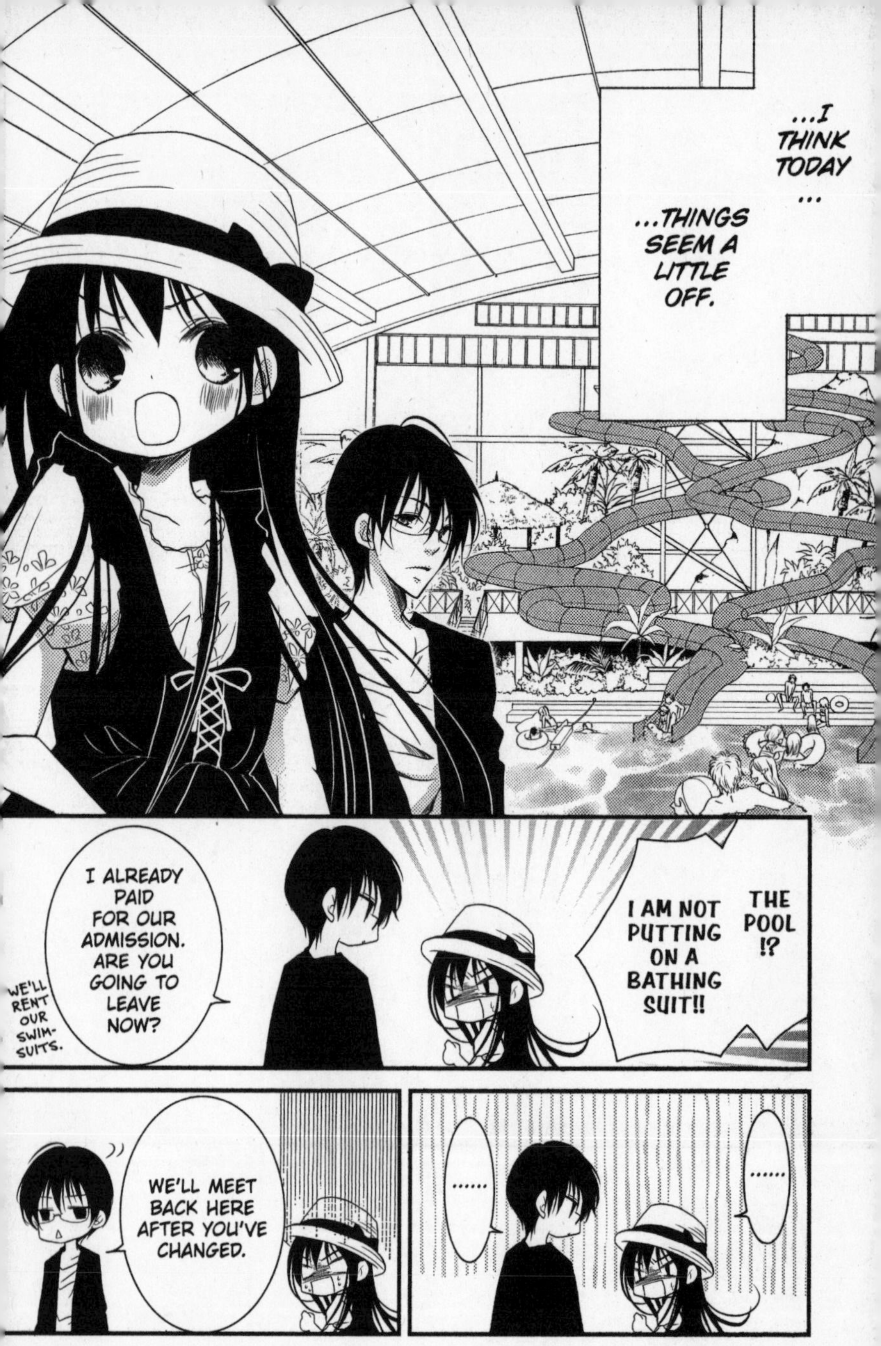
...I THINK TODAY ...
...THINGS SEEM A LITTLE OFF.
THE POOL !?
I AM NOT PUTTING ON A BATHING SUIT!!
I ALREADY PAID FOR OUR ADMISSION. ARE YOU GOING TO LEAVE NOW?
WE'LL RENT OUR SWIM-SUITS.
......
......
WE'LL MEET BACK HERE AFTER YOU'VE CHANGED.

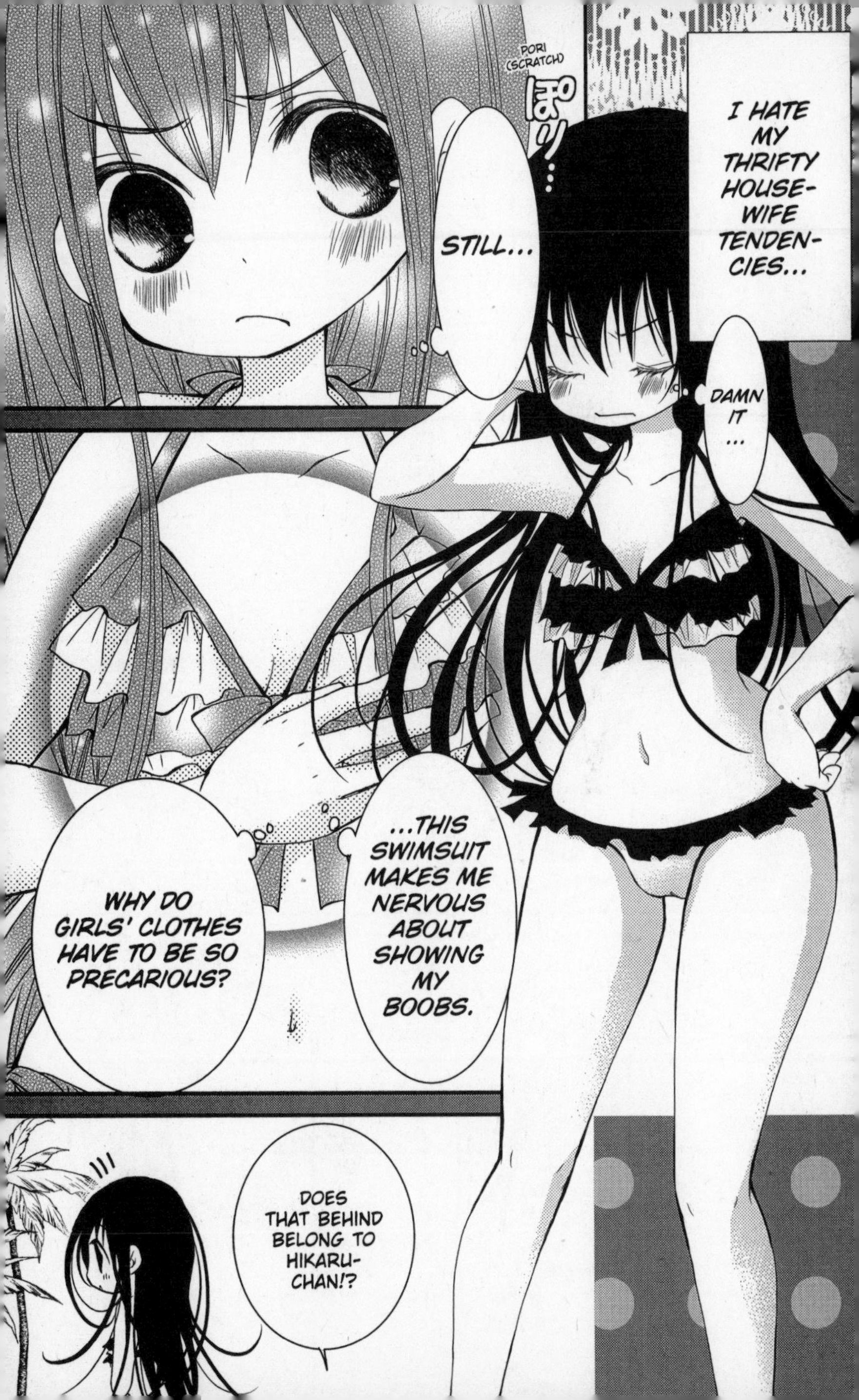

I HATE MY THRIFTY HOUSE-WIFE TENDEN-CIES...
DAMN IT ...
PORI (SCRATCH)
ぽり
STILL...
...THIS SWIMSUIT MAKES ME NERVOUS ABOUT SHOWING MY BOOBS.
WHY DO GIRLS' CLOTHES HAVE TO BE SO PRECARIOUS?
DOES THAT BEHIND BELONG TO HIKARU-CHAN!?

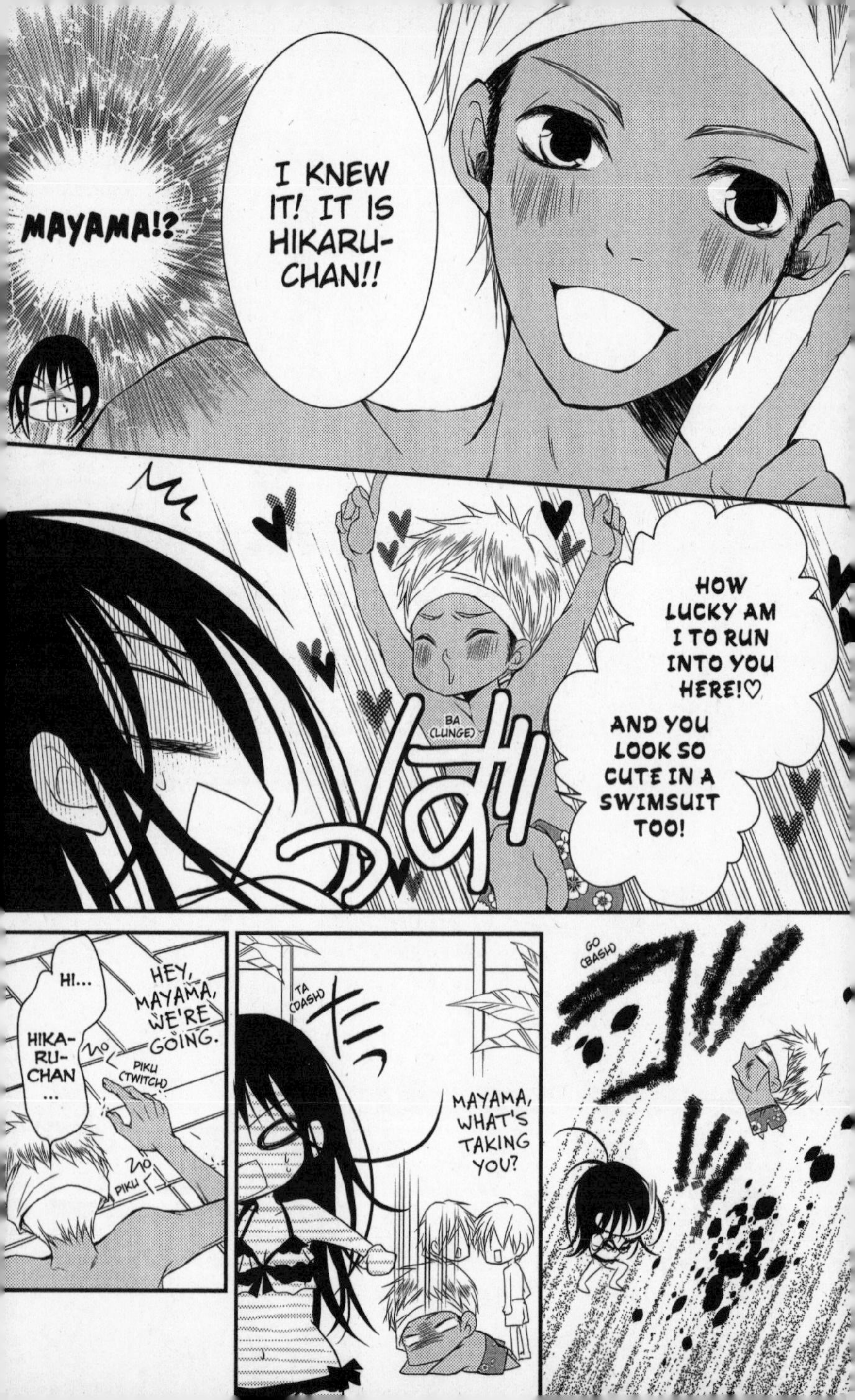
I KNEW IT! IT IS HIKARU-CHAN!!
MAYAMA!?
HOW LUCKY AM I TO RUN INTO YOU HERE!♡
AND YOU LOOK SO CUTE IN A SWIMSUIT TOO!
BA (LUNGE)
GO (BASH)
TA (DASH)
MAYAMA, WHAT'S TAKING YOU?
HEY, MAYAMA, WE'RE GOING.
HI... HIKARU-CHAN ...
PIKU (TWITCH)
PIKU

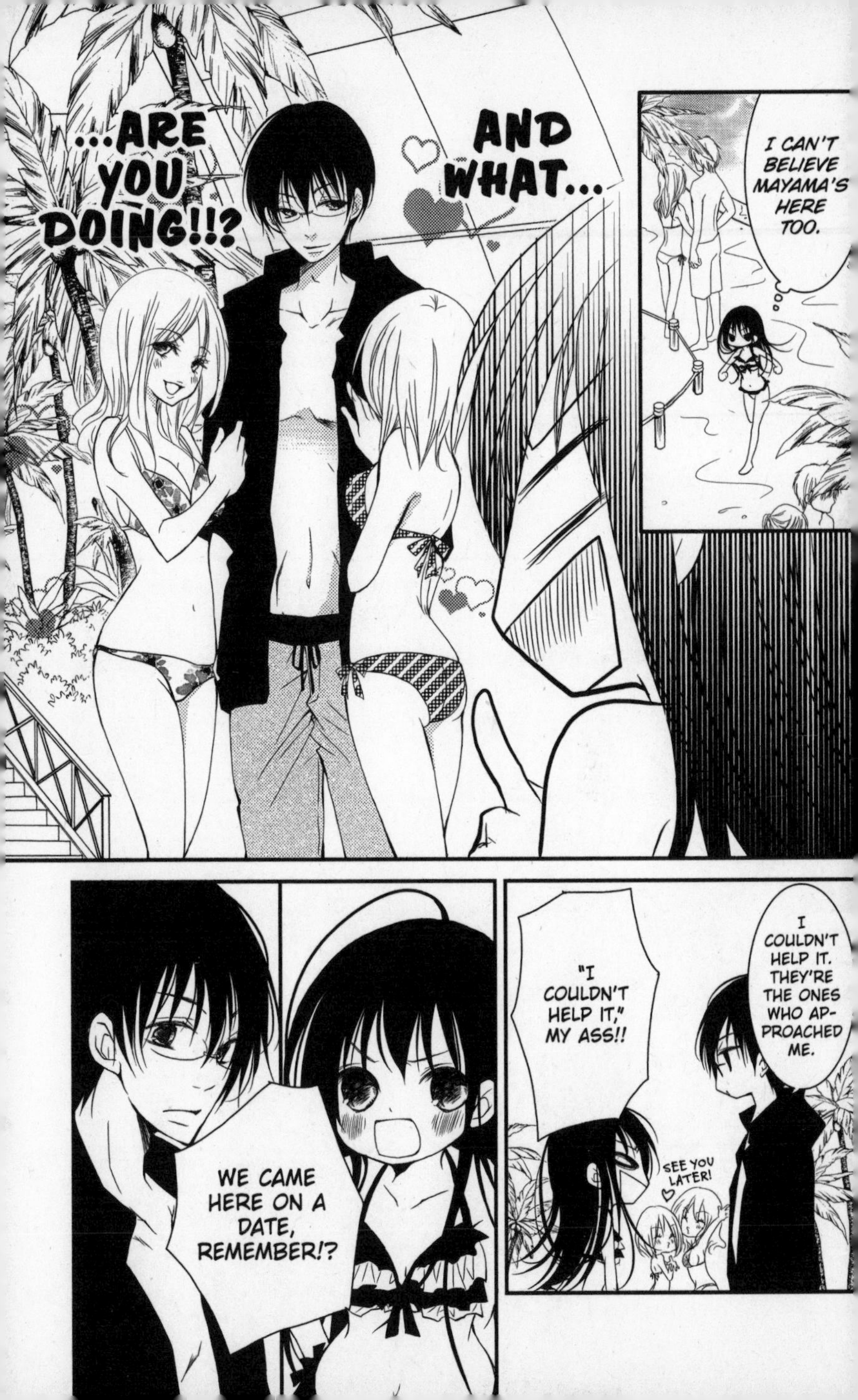
I CAN'T BELIEVE MAYAMA'S HERE TOO.
AND WHAT...
...ARE YOU DOING!!?
I COULDN'T HELP IT. THEY'RE THE ONES WHO APPROACHED ME.
SEE YOU LATER!
"I COULDN'T HELP IT," MY ASS!!
WE CAME HERE ON A DATE, REMEMBER!?

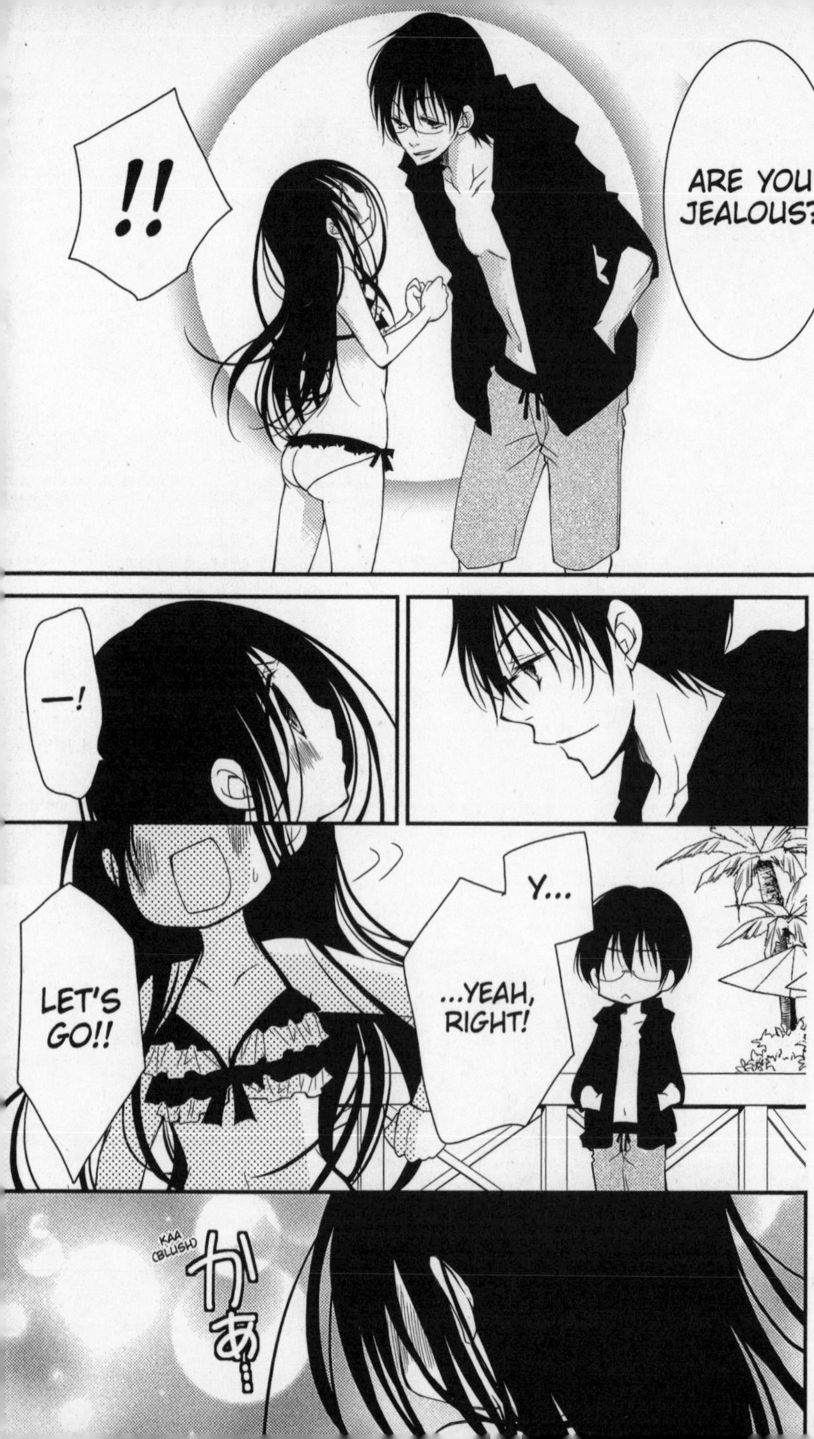
ARE YOU JEALOUS?
!!
—!
Y...
...YEAH, RIGHT!
LET'S GO!!
KAA (BLUSH)
かぁ…

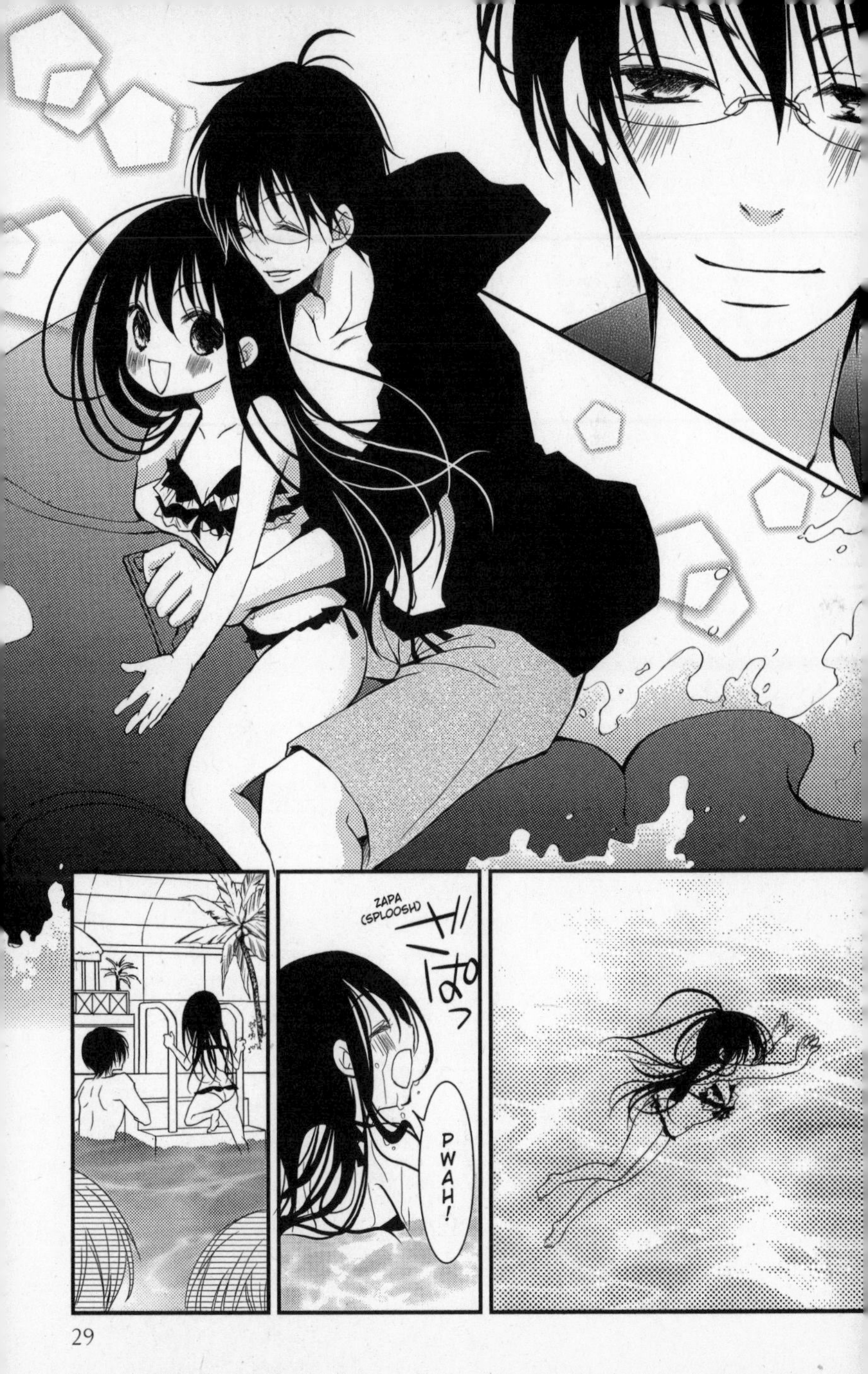
ZAPA (SPLOOSH)
PWAH!

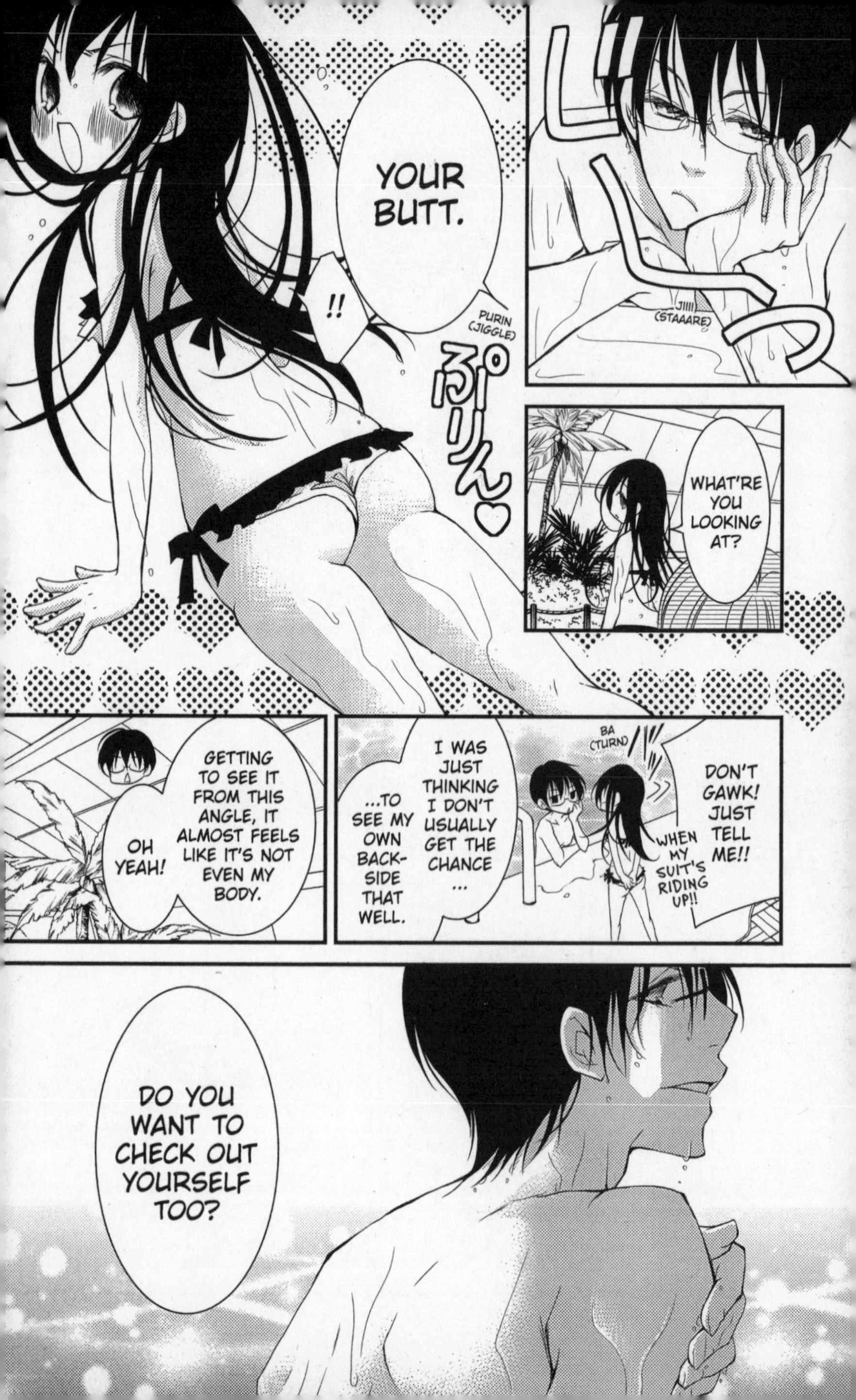
じーっ
JIIII (STAAARE)
WHAT'RE YOU LOOKING AT?
YOUR BUTT.
!!
PURIN (JIGGLE)
ぷりん♡
BA (TURN)
DON'T GAWK! JUST TELL ME!!
WHEN MY SUIT'S RIDING UP!!
I WAS JUST THINKING I DON'T USUALLY GET THE CHANCE ...
...TO SEE MY OWN BACK-SIDE THAT WELL.
GETTING TO SEE IT FROM THIS ANGLE, IT ALMOST FEELS LIKE IT'S NOT EVEN MY BODY.
OH YEAH!
DO YOU WANT TO CHECK OUT YOURSELF TOO?

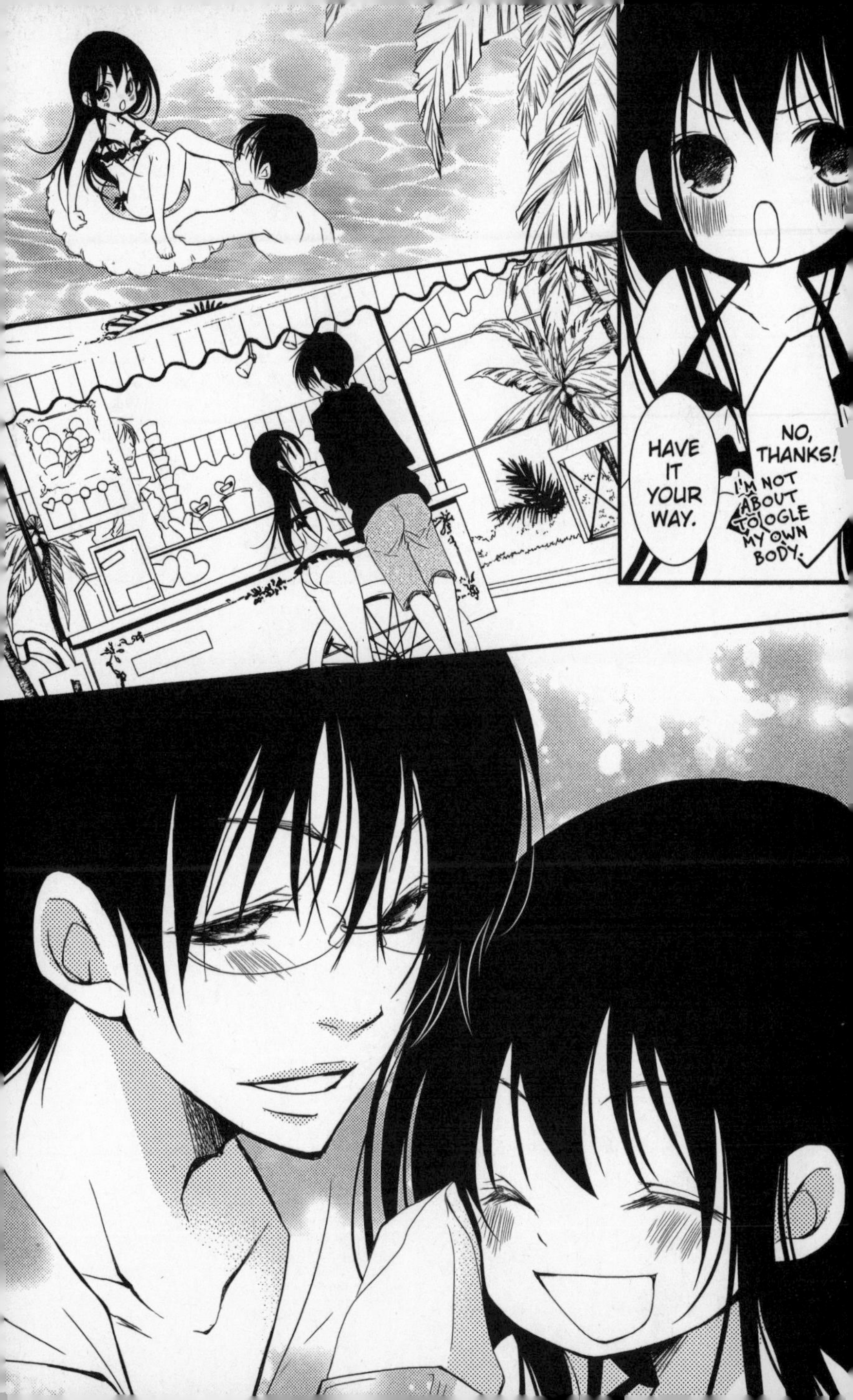
NO, THANKS!
I'M NOT ABOUT TO OGLE MY OWN BODY.
HAVE IT YOUR WAY.

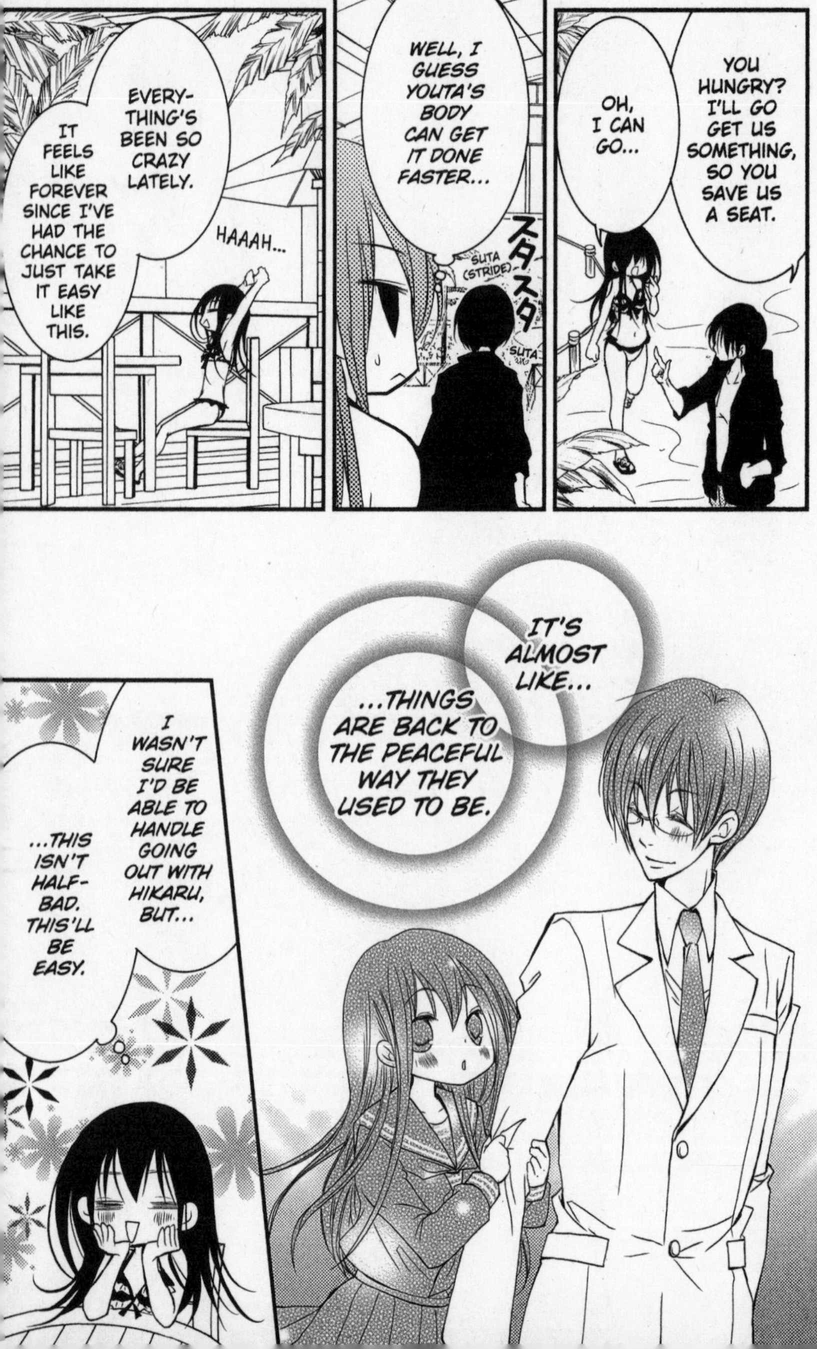
YOU HUNGRY? I'LL GO GET US SOMETHING, SO YOU SAVE US A SEAT.
OH, I CAN GO...
WELL, I GUESS YOUTA'S BODY CAN GET IT DONE FASTER...
スタスタ
SUTA (STRIDE)
SUTA
EVERY-THING'S BEEN SO CRAZY LATELY.
HAAAH...
IT FEELS LIKE FOREVER SINCE I'VE HAD THE CHANCE TO JUST TAKE IT EASY LIKE THIS.
IT'S ALMOST LIKE...
...THINGS ARE BACK TO THE PEACEFUL WAY THEY USED TO BE.
I WASN'T SURE I'D BE ABLE TO HANDLE GOING OUT WITH HIKARU, BUT...
...THIS ISN'T HALF-BAD. THIS'LL BE EASY.

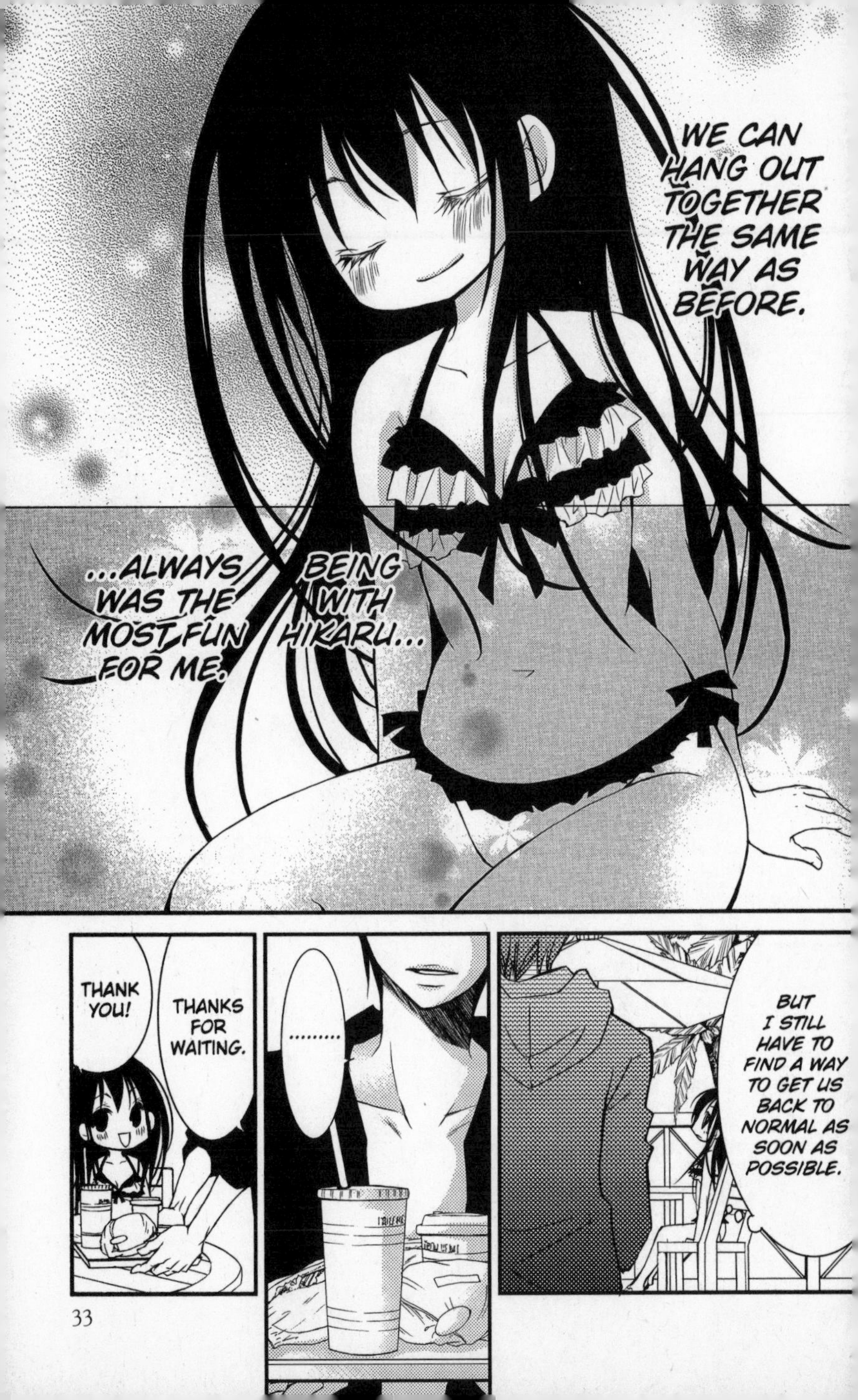
WE CAN HANG OUT TOGETHER THE SAME WAY AS BEFORE.
BEING WITH HIKARU...
...ALWAYS WAS THE MOST FUN FOR ME.
BUT I STILL HAVE TO FIND A WAY TO GET US BACK TO NORMAL AS SOON AS POSSIBLE.
....
THANKS FOR WAITING.
THANK YOU!

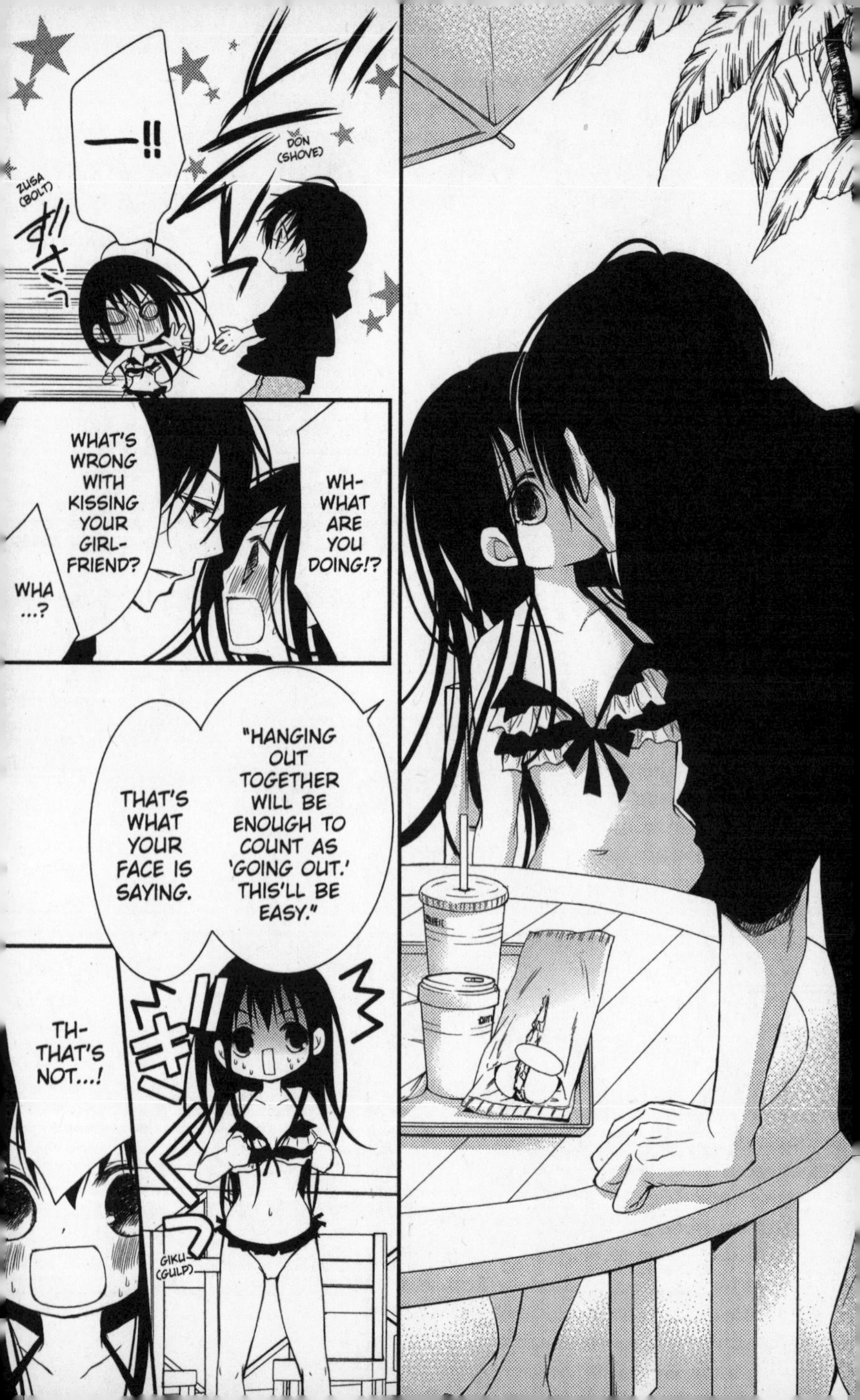
DON (SHOVE)
—!!
ZUSA (BOLT)
WH- WHAT ARE YOU DOING!?
WHAT'S WRONG WITH KISSING YOUR GIRL-FRIEND?
WHA ...?
"HANGING OUT TOGETHER WILL BE ENOUGH TO COUNT AS 'GOING OUT.' THIS'LL BE EASY."
THAT'S WHAT YOUR FACE IS SAYING.
GIKU (GULP)
TH- THAT'S NOT...!

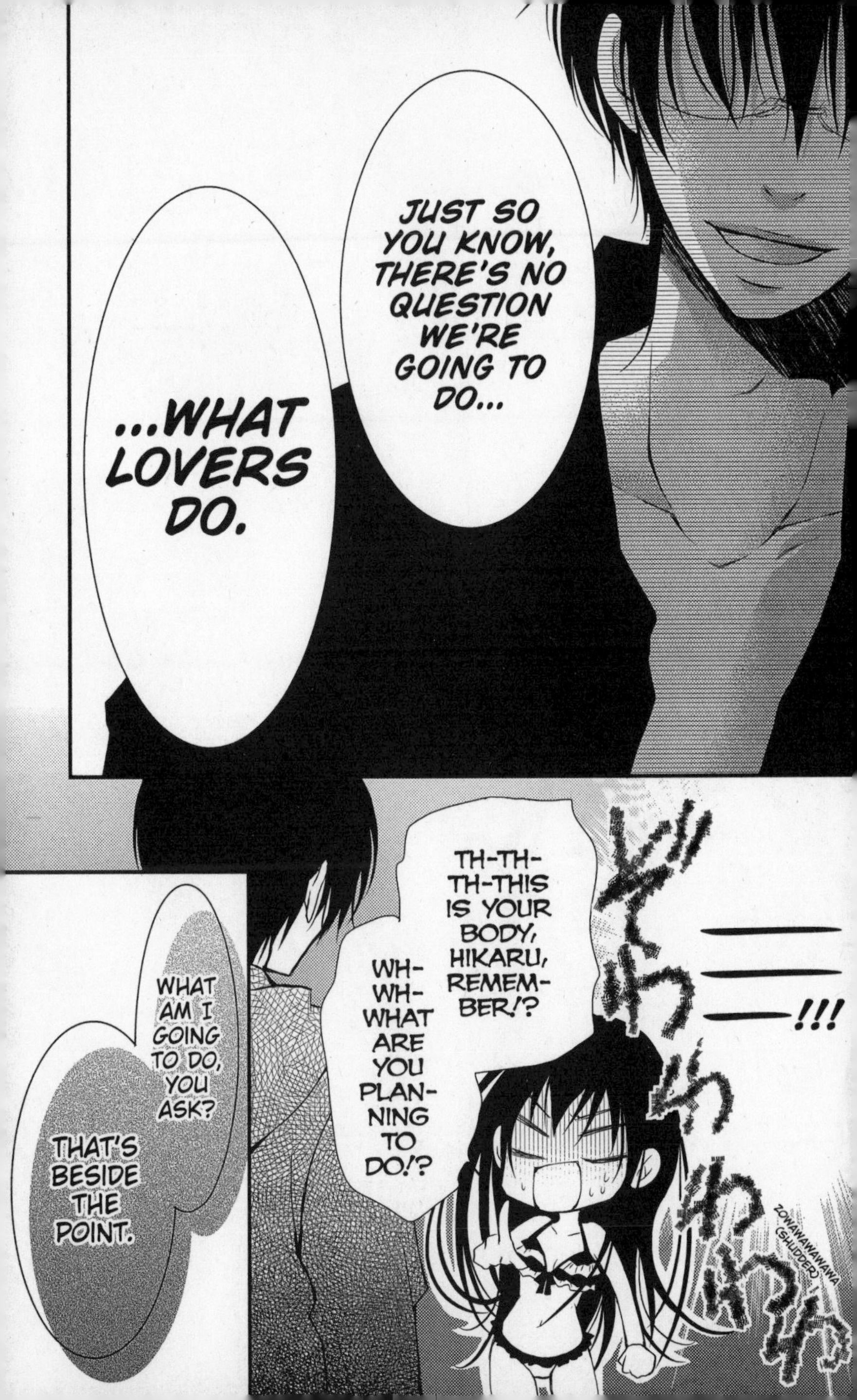
JUST SO YOU KNOW, THERE'S NO QUESTION WE'RE GOING TO DO...
...WHAT LOVERS DO.
ZOWAWAWAWA (SHUDDER)
———!!!
TH-TH-TH-THIS IS YOUR BODY, HIKARU, REMEMBER!?
WH-WH-WHAT ARE YOU PLAN-NING TO DO!?
WHAT AM I GOING TO DO, YOU ASK?
THAT'S BESIDE THE POINT.

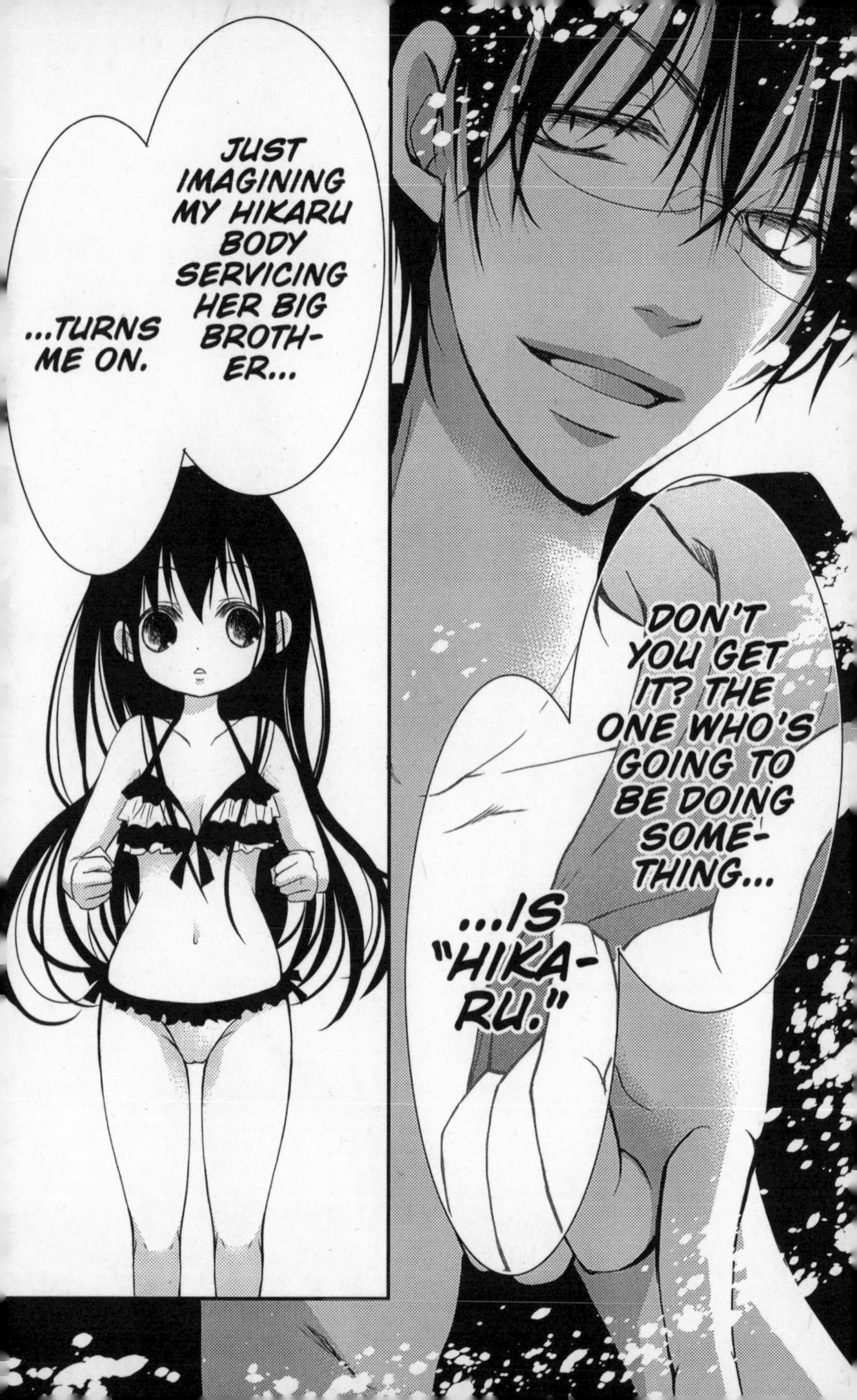
DON'T YOU GET IT? THE ONE WHO'S GOING TO BE DOING SOME-THING...
...IS "HIKA-RU."
JUST IMAGINING MY HIKARU BODY SERVICING HER BIG BROTH-ER...
...TURNS ME ON.

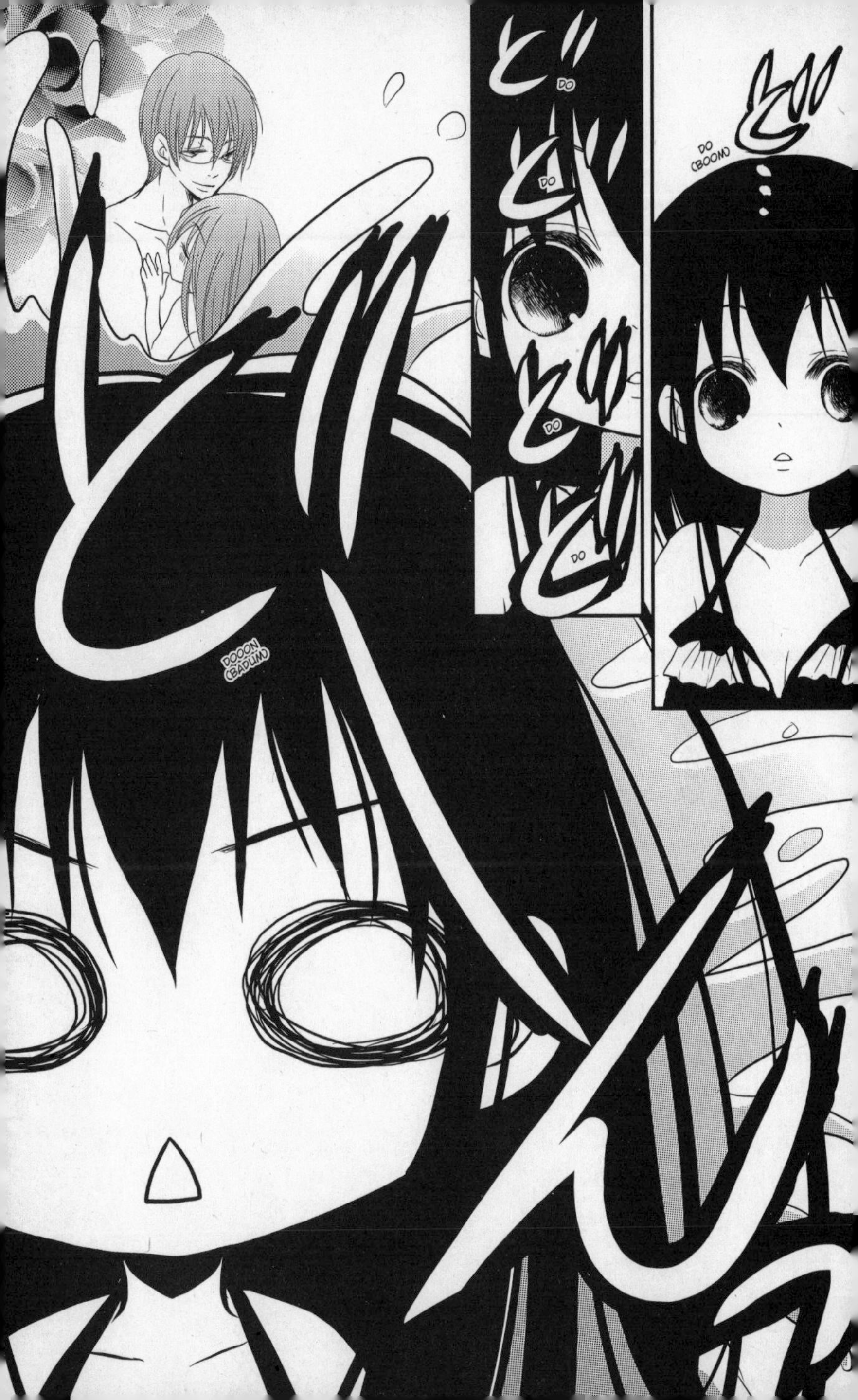
DO (BOOM)
DO
DO
DO
DO
DOOON (BADUM)

I HAVE
TO GET US
BACK TO
NORMAL...

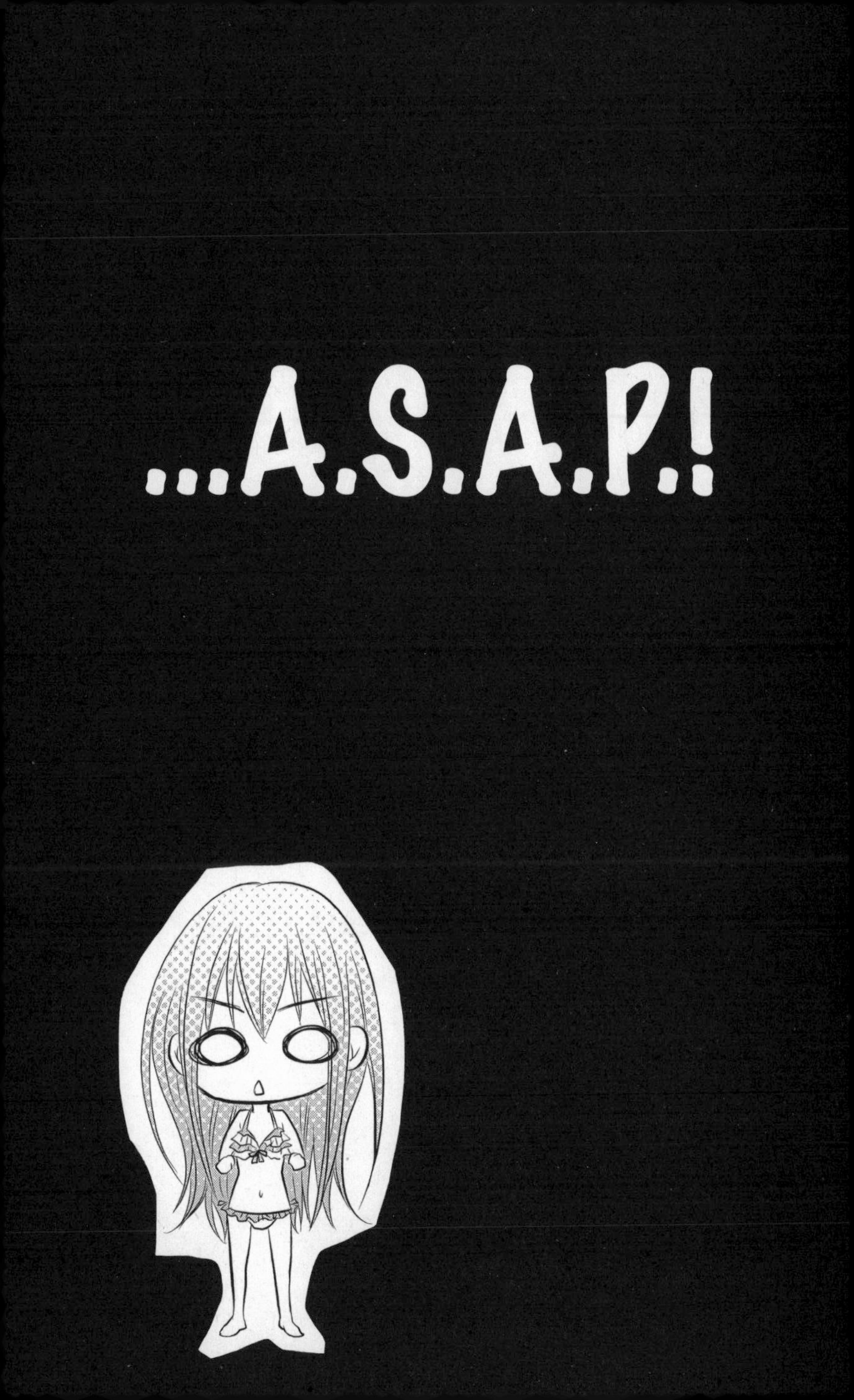
...A.S.A.P.!

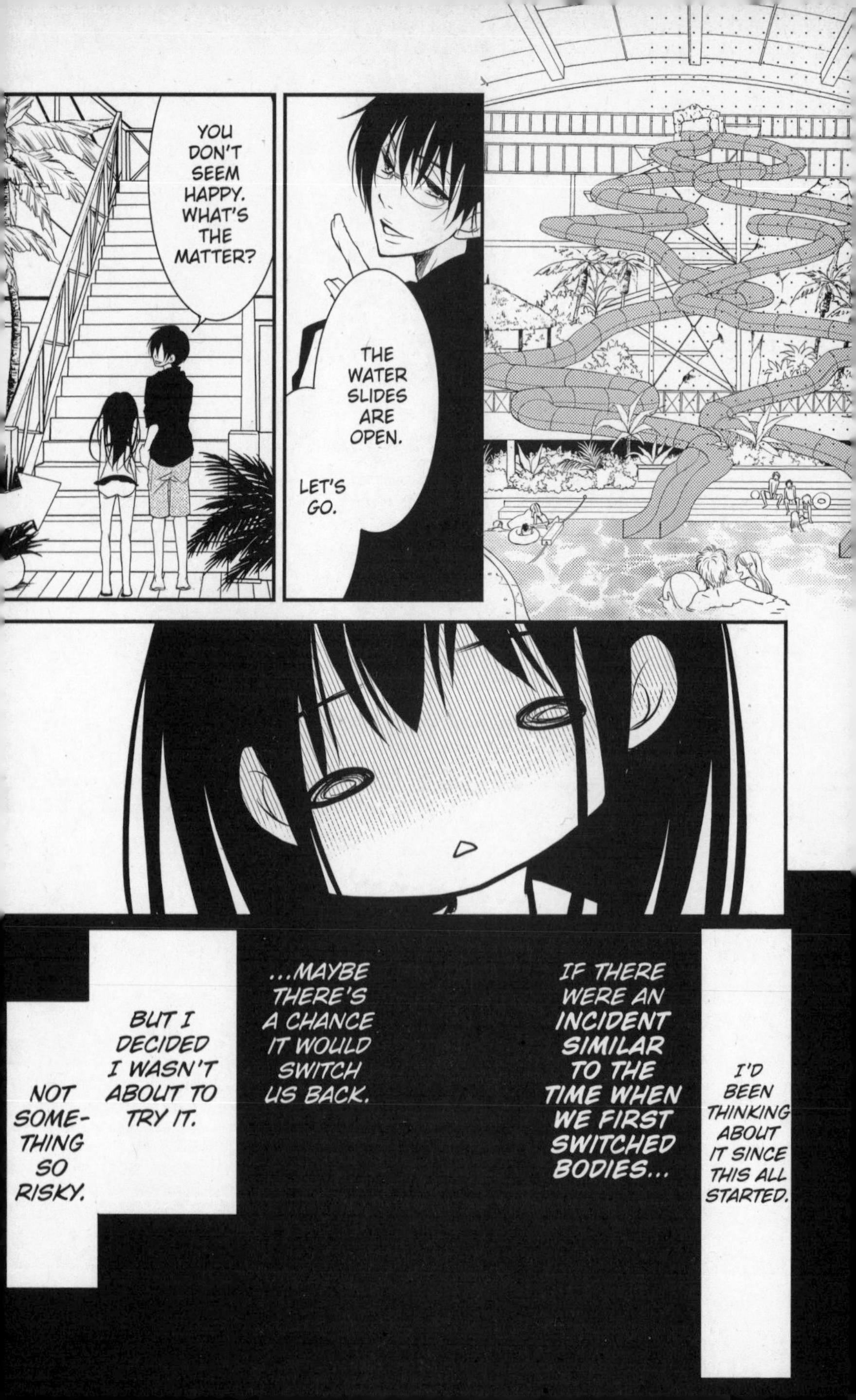
THE WATER SLIDES ARE OPEN.
LET'S GO.
YOU DON'T SEEM HAPPY. WHAT'S THE MATTER?
I'D BEEN THINKING ABOUT IT SINCE THIS ALL STARTED.
IF THERE WERE AN INCIDENT SIMILAR TO THE TIME WHEN WE FIRST SWITCHED BODIES...
...MAYBE THERE'S A CHANCE IT WOULD SWITCH US BACK.
BUT I DECIDED I WASN'T ABOUT TO TRY IT.
NOT SOMETHING SO RISKY.

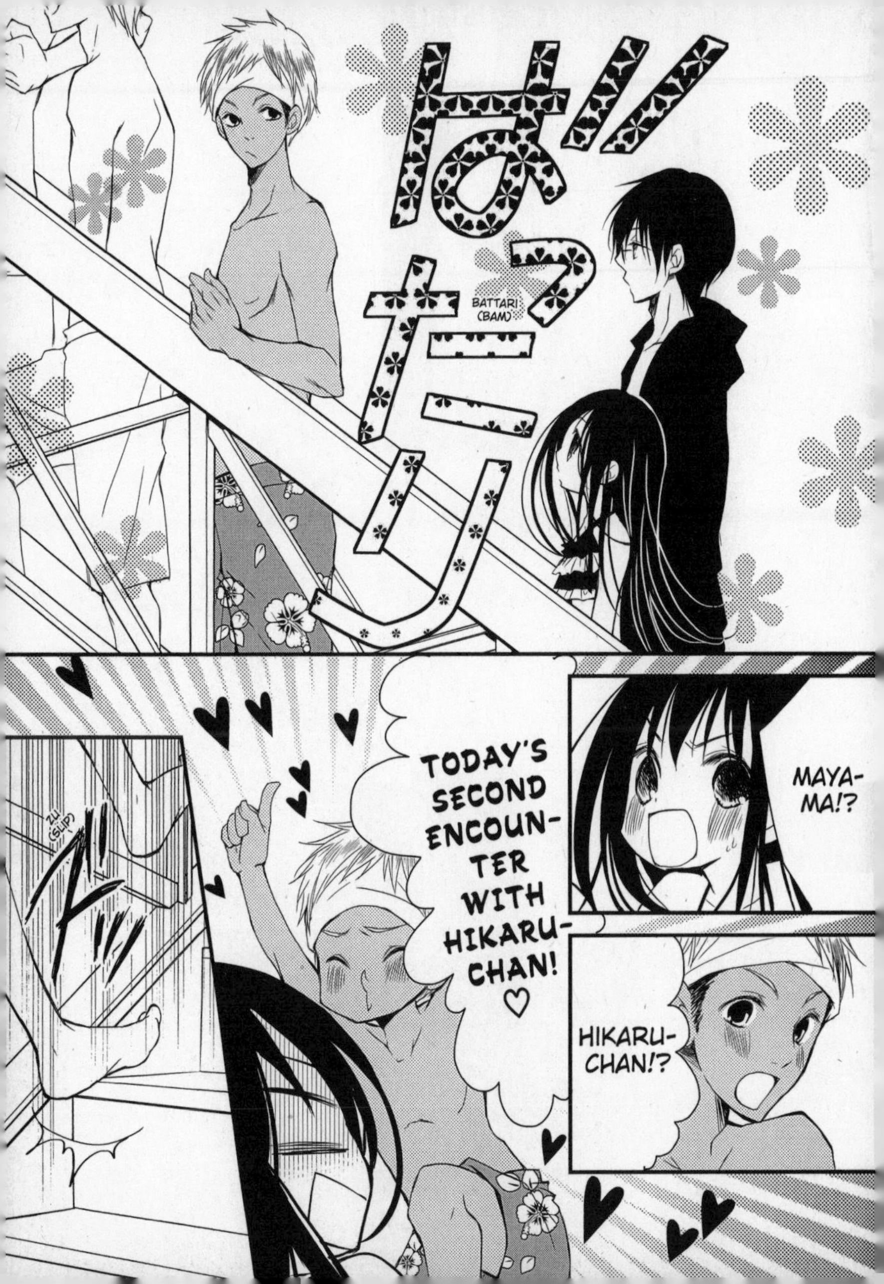
ばったーり
BATTARI (BAM)
MAYA-MA!?
HIKARU-CHAN!?
TODAY'S SECOND ENCOUNTER WITH HIKARU-CHAN! ♡
ZU (SLIP)

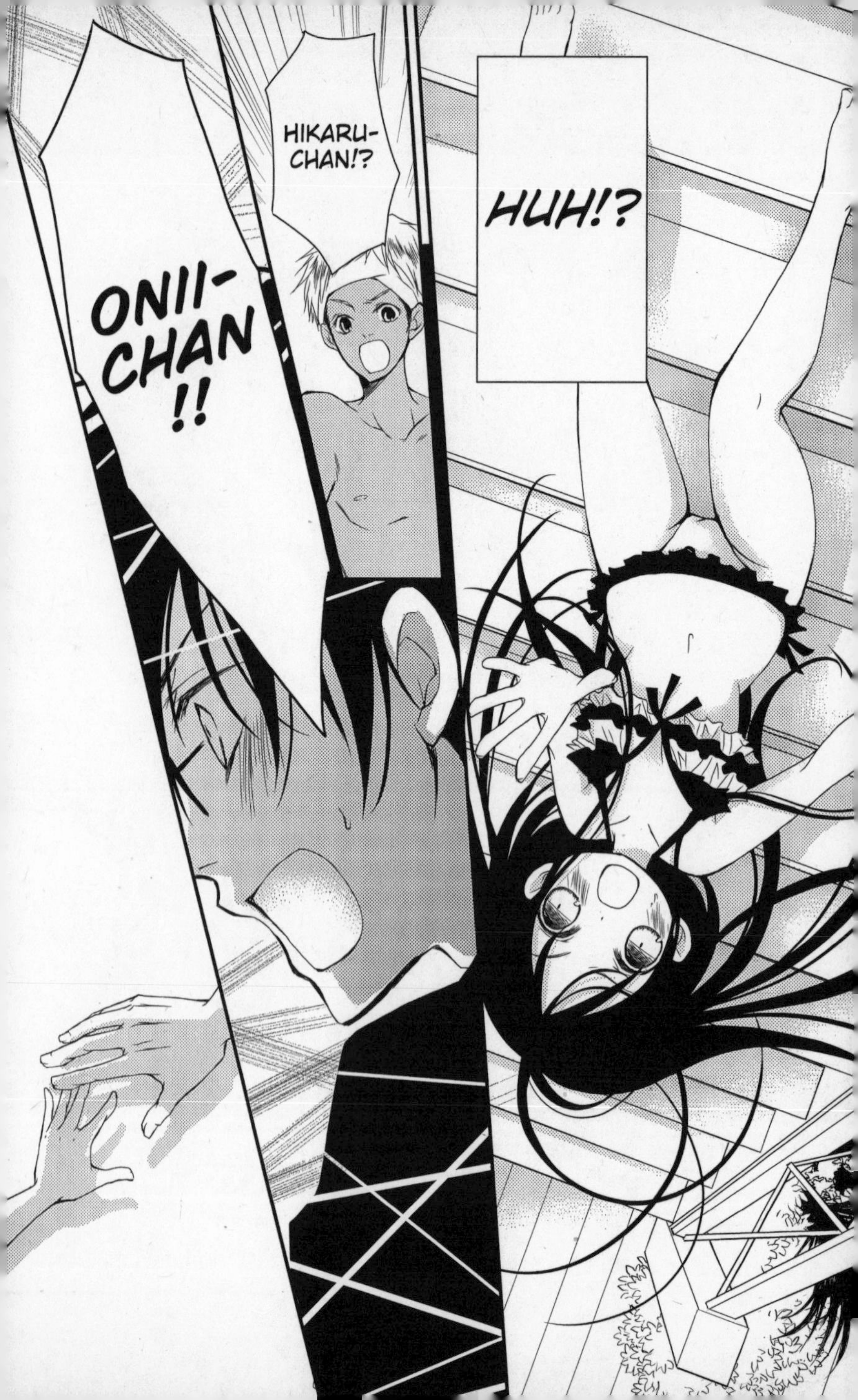
HUH!?
HIKARU-CHAN!?
ONII-CHAN!!

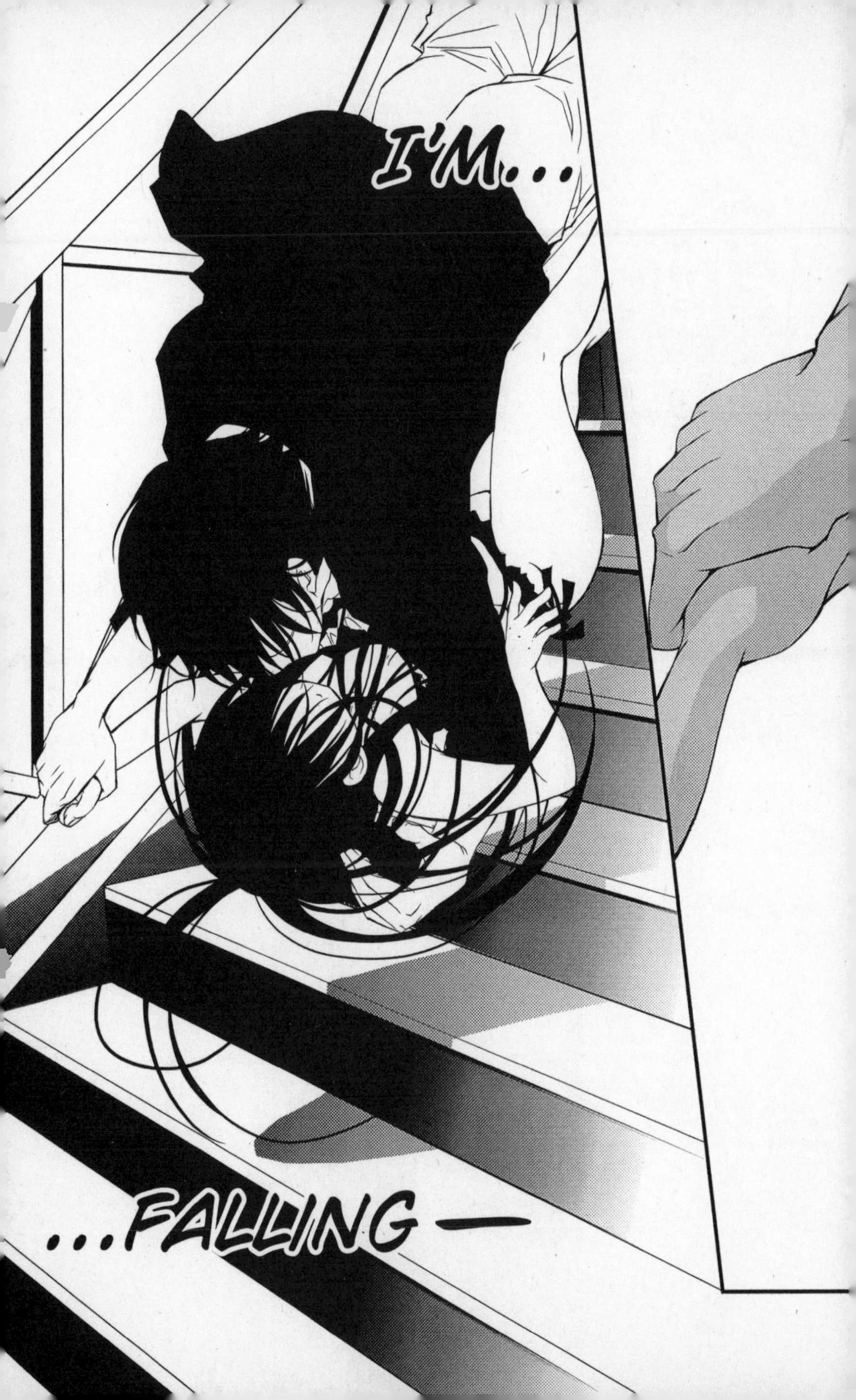
I'M...
...FALLING—

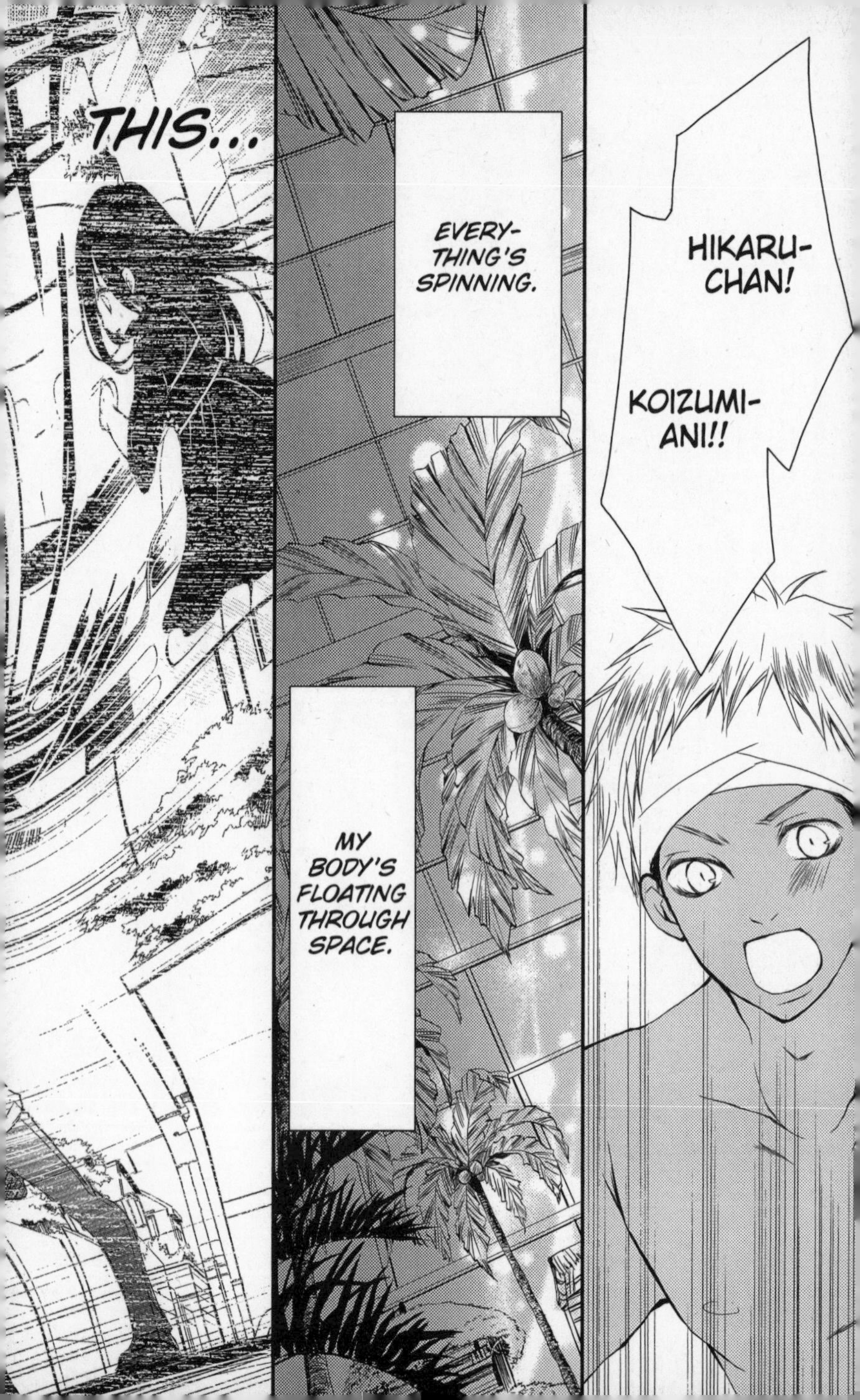
HIKARU-CHAN!
KOIZUMI-ANI!!
EVERY-THING'S SPINNING.
MY BODY'S FLOATING THROUGH SPACE.
THIS...

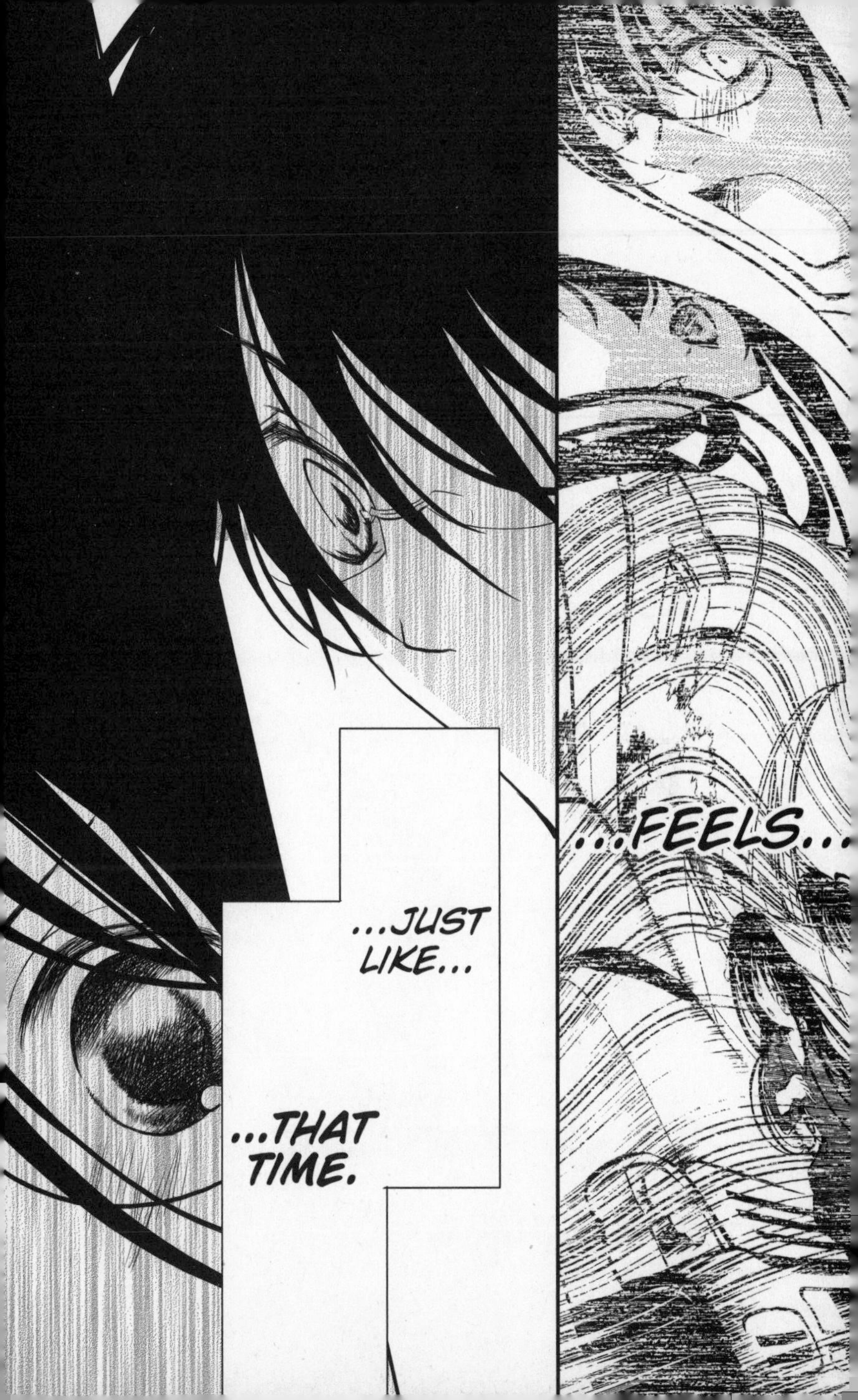
...FEELS...
...JUST LIKE...
...THAT TIME.

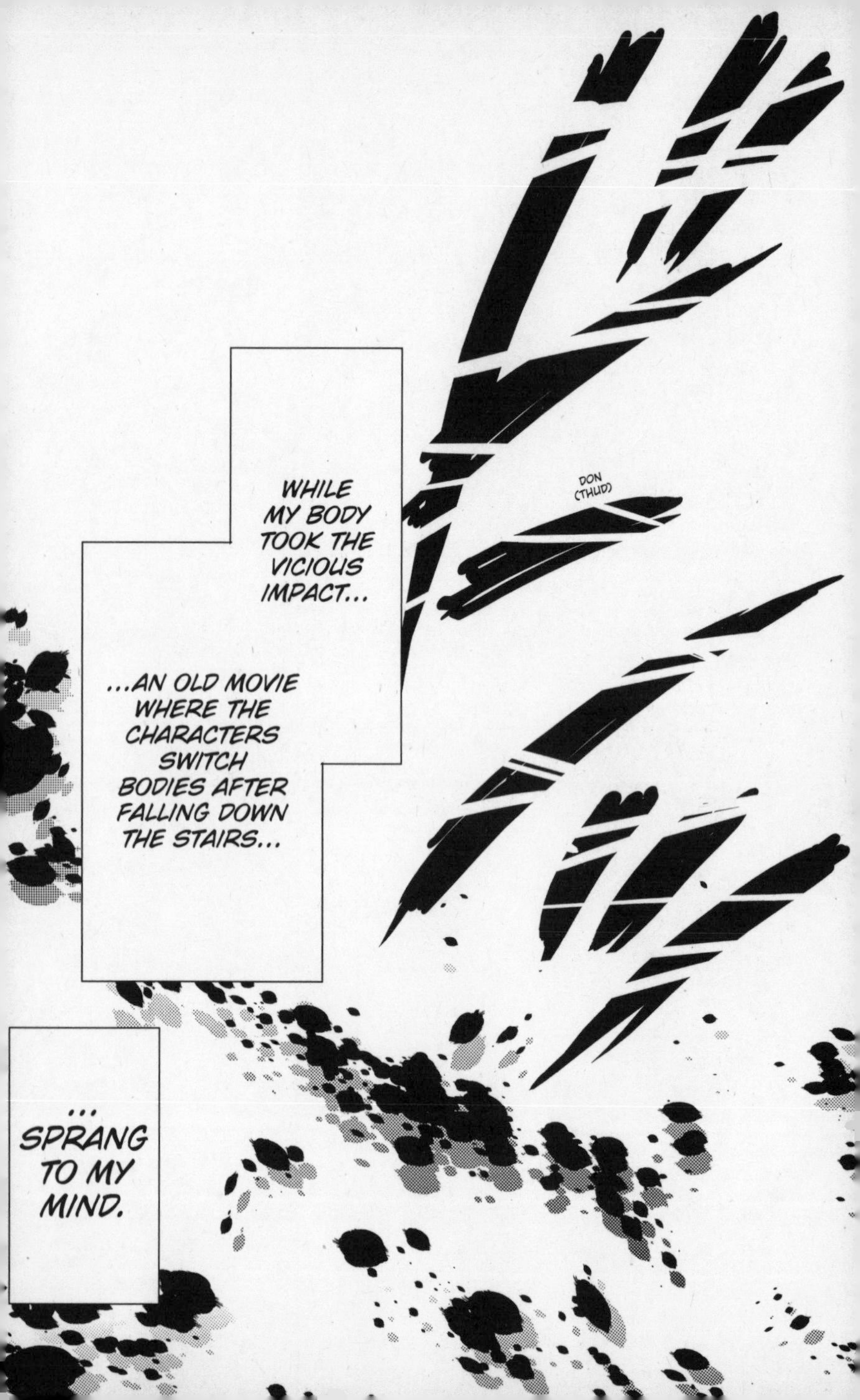
DON (THUD)
WHILE MY BODY TOOK THE VICIOUS IMPACT...
...AN OLD MOVIE WHERE THE CHARACTERS SWITCH BODIES AFTER FALLING DOWN THE STAIRS...
... SPRANG TO MY MIND.

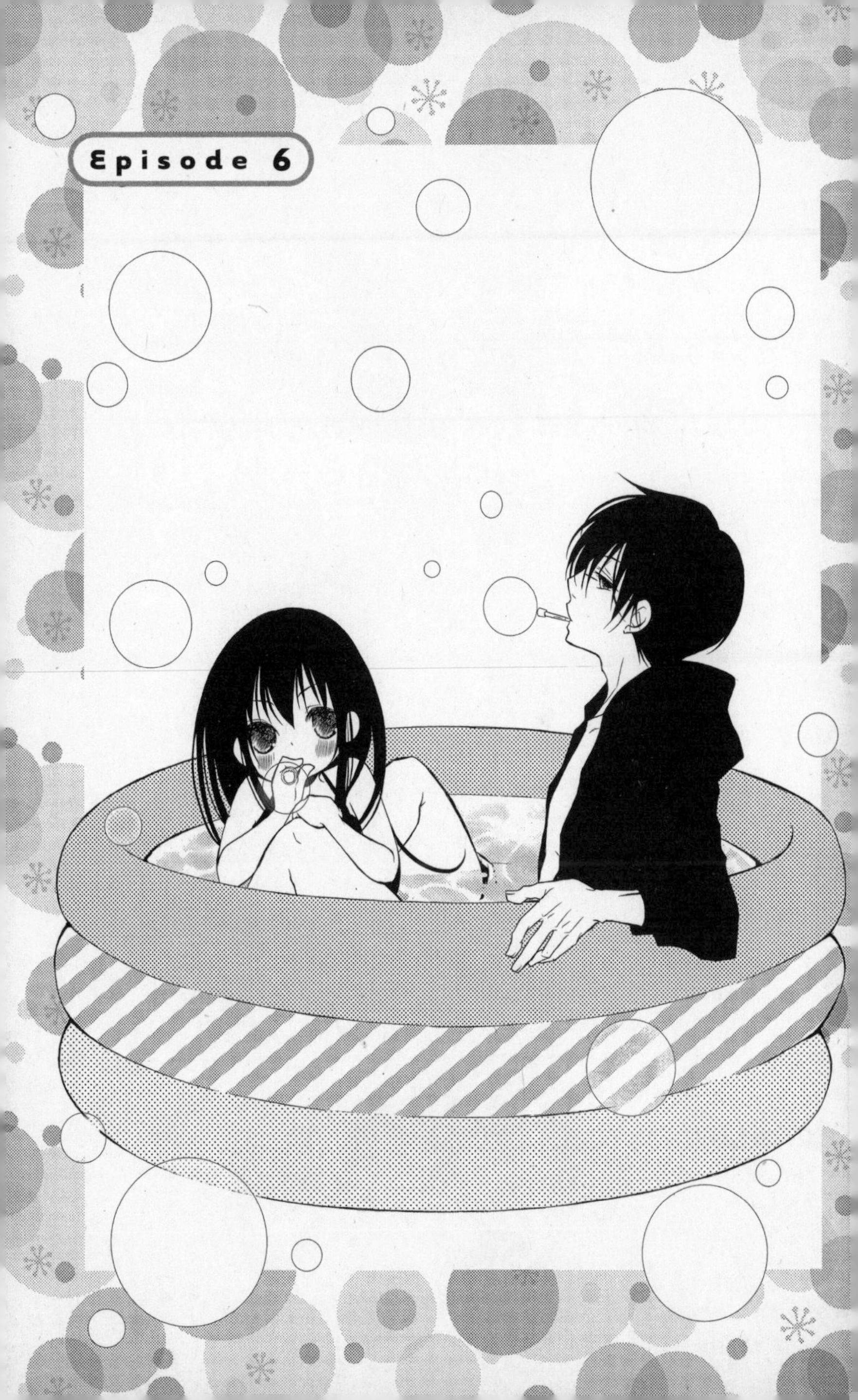
Episode 6

I THOUGHT THAT IF THE SAME THING HAPPENED TO US...

...LIKE IT DID WHEN WE FIRST SWITCHED BODIES...

...WE COULD GO BACK TO NORMAL.

I WAS AN IDIOT.

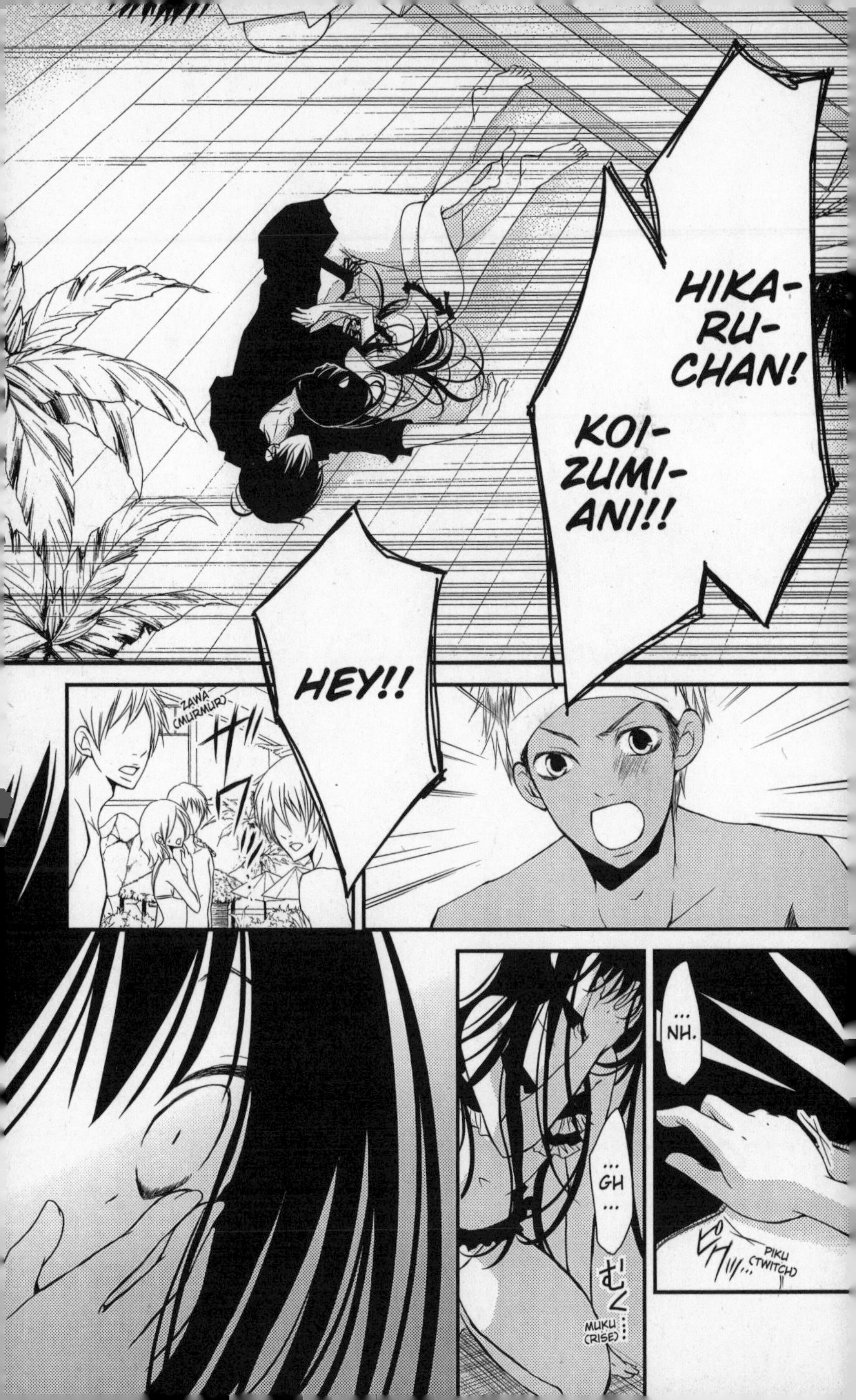
HIKA-
RU-
CHAN!
KOI-
ZUMI-
ANI!!
HEY!!
ZAWA
(MURMUR)
...
NH.
PIKU
(TWITCH)
...
GH
...
MUKU
(RISE)

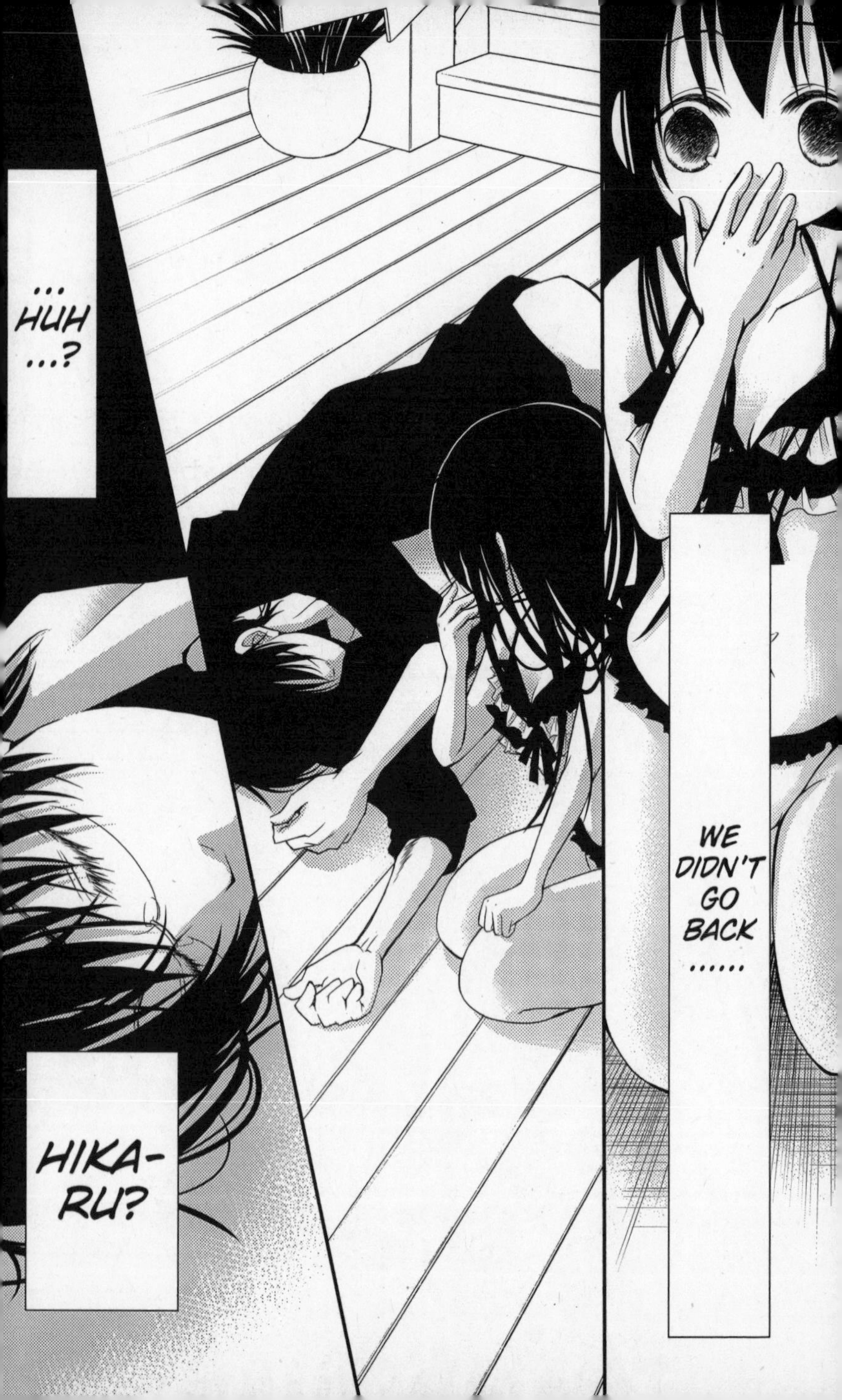
WE DIDN'T GO BACK ......
... HUH ...?
HIKA-RU?

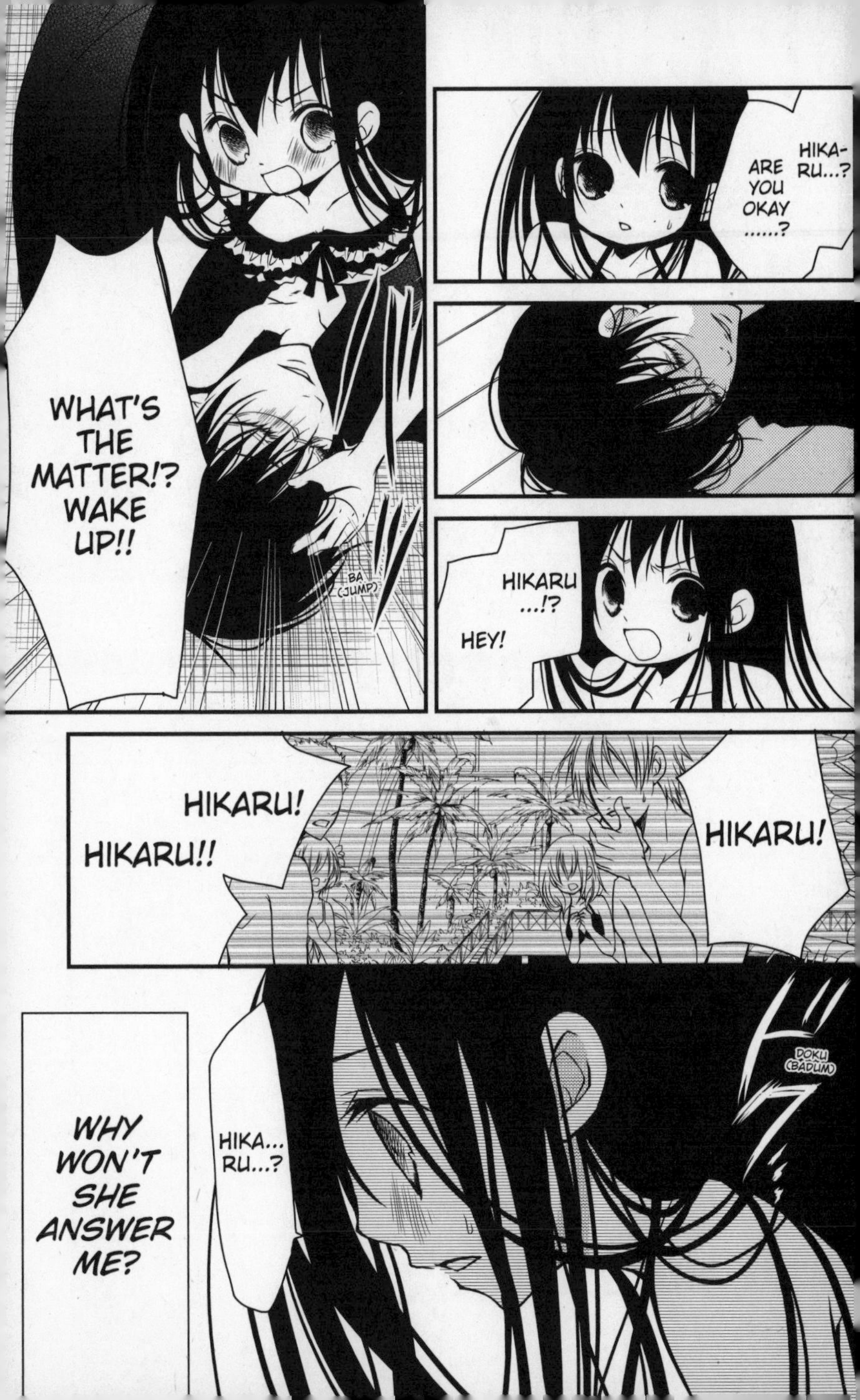
HIKA-RU...?
ARE YOU OKAY ......?
HIKARU ...!?
HEY!
WHAT'S THE MATTER!? WAKE UP!!
BA (JUMP)
HIKARU!
HIKARU!
HIKARU!!
DOKU (BADUM)
HIKA... RU...?
WHY WON'T SHE ANSWER ME?

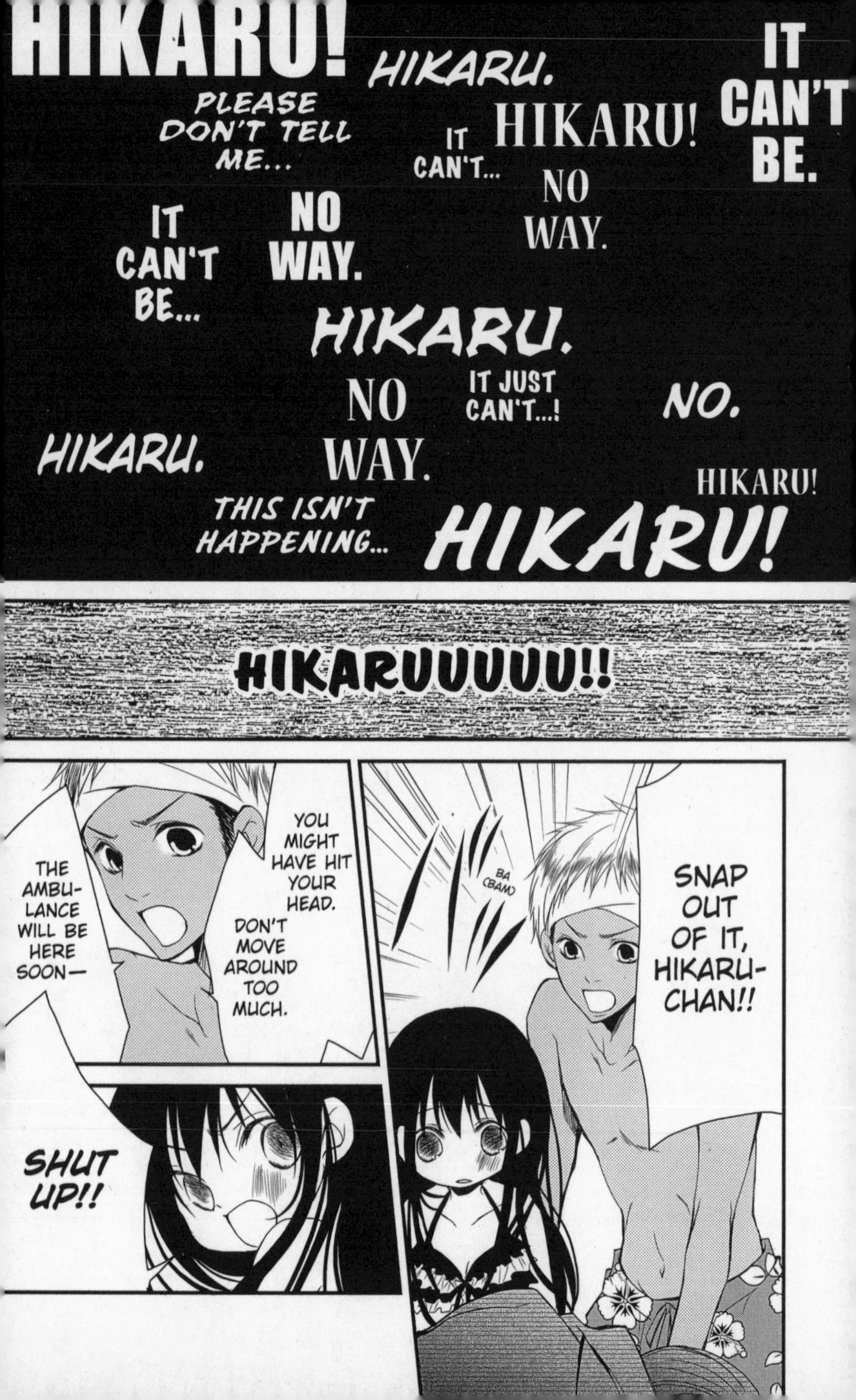
IT CAN'T BE.
HIKARU!
HIKARU.
IT CAN'T...
NO WAY.
HIKARU!
PLEASE DON'T TELL ME...
NO WAY.
IT CAN'T BE...
HIKARU.
NO.
IT JUST CAN'T...!
NO WAY.
HIKARU!
HIKARU.
HIKARU!
THIS ISN'T HAPPENING...
HIKARUUUUUU!!
SNAP OUT OF IT, HIKARU-CHAN!!
BA (BAM)
YOU MIGHT HAVE HIT YOUR HEAD.
DON'T MOVE AROUND TOO MUCH.
THE AMBULANCE WILL BE HERE SOON—
SHUT UP!!

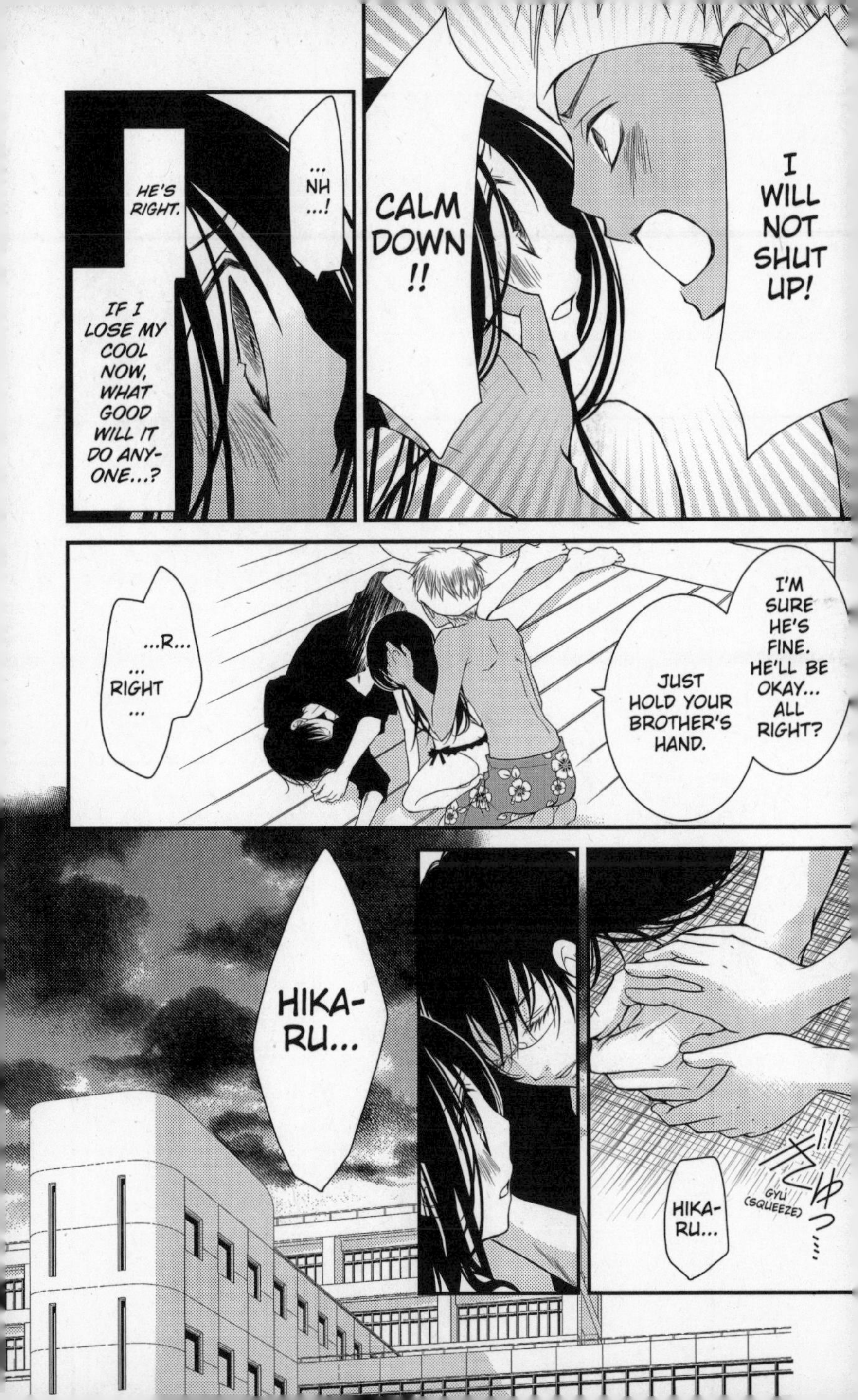
I WILL NOT SHUT UP!
CALM DOWN!!
...NH ...!
HE'S RIGHT.
IF I LOSE MY COOL NOW, WHAT GOOD WILL IT DO ANY-ONE...?
I'M SURE HE'S FINE. HE'LL BE OKAY... ALL RIGHT?
JUST HOLD YOUR BROTHER'S HAND.
...R... ... RIGHT ...
GYU (SQUEEZE)
HIKA-RU...
HIKA-RU...

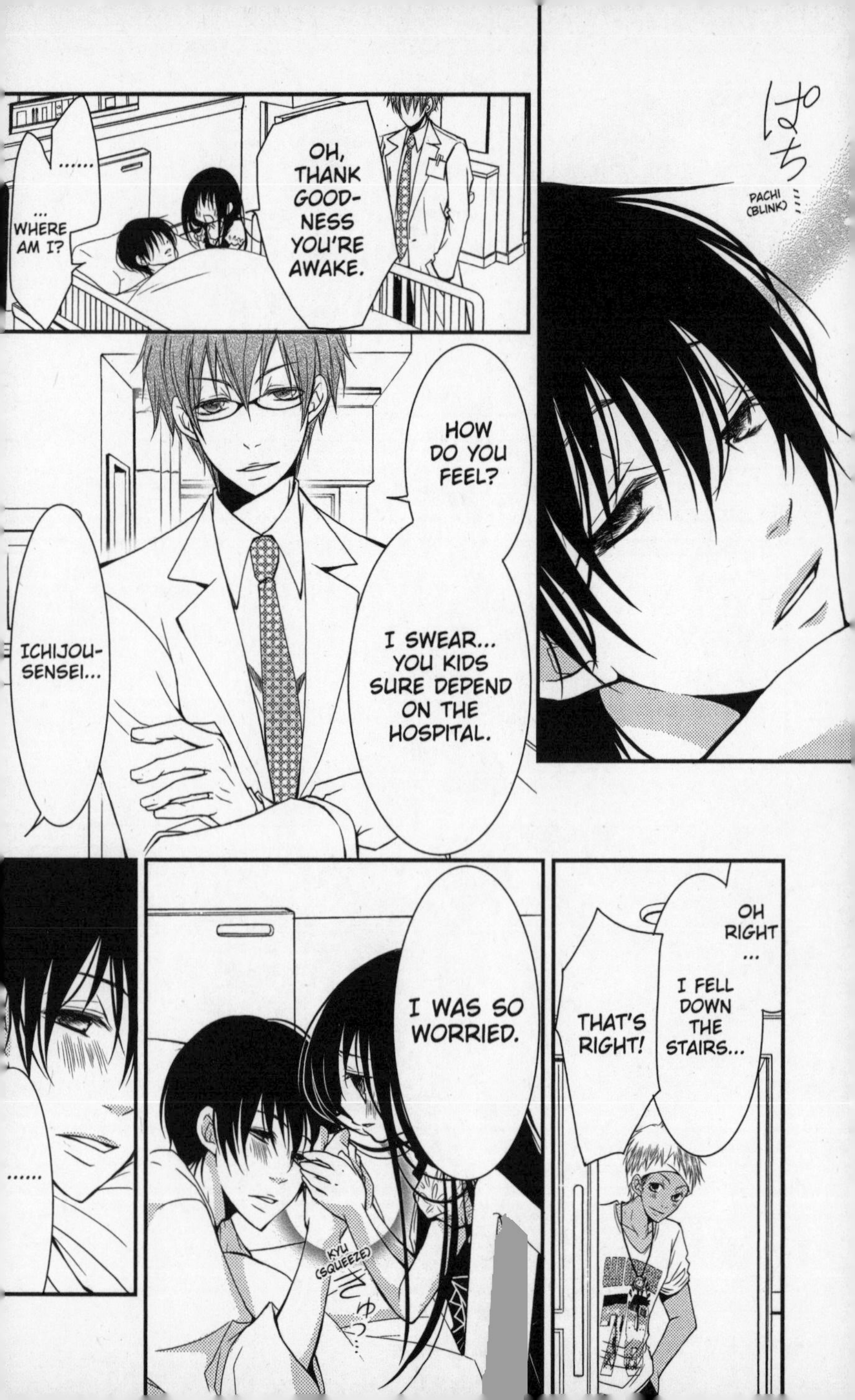
ぱち
PACHI (BLINK)
OH, THANK GOODNESS YOU'RE AWAKE.
......
... WHERE AM I?
HOW DO YOU FEEL?
I SWEAR... YOU KIDS SURE DEPEND ON THE HOSPITAL.
ICHIJOU-SENSEI...
OH RIGHT... I FELL DOWN THE STAIRS...
THAT'S RIGHT!
I WAS SO WORRIED.
KYU (SQUEEZE)
きゅっ...
......

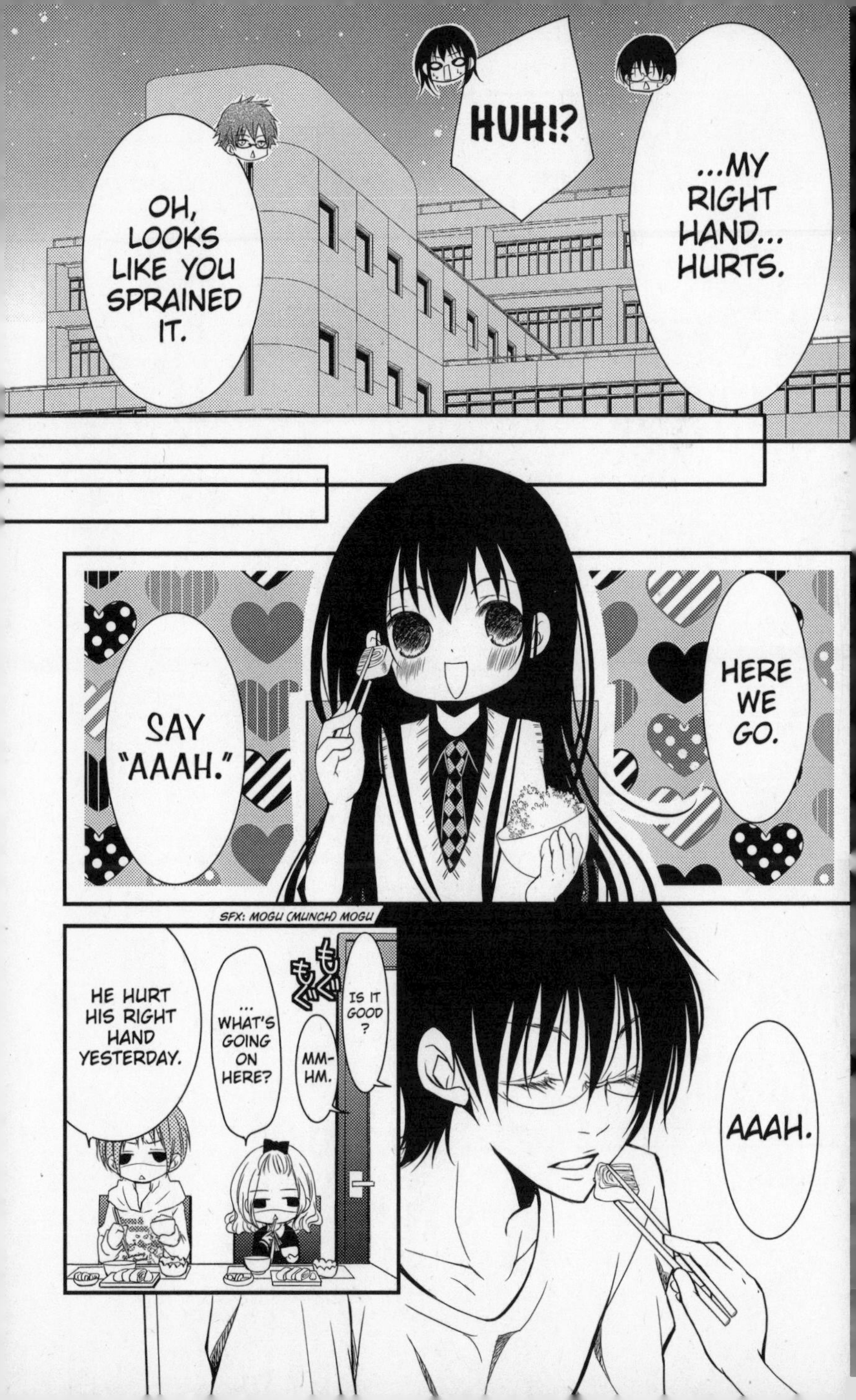
...MY RIGHT HAND... HURTS.
HUH!?
OH, LOOKS LIKE YOU SPRAINED IT.
HERE WE GO.
SAY "AAAH."
SFX: MOGU (MUNCH) MOGU
AAAH.
IS IT GOOD?
MM-HM.
もぐもぐ
...WHAT'S GOING ON HERE?
HE HURT HIS RIGHT HAND YESTERDAY.

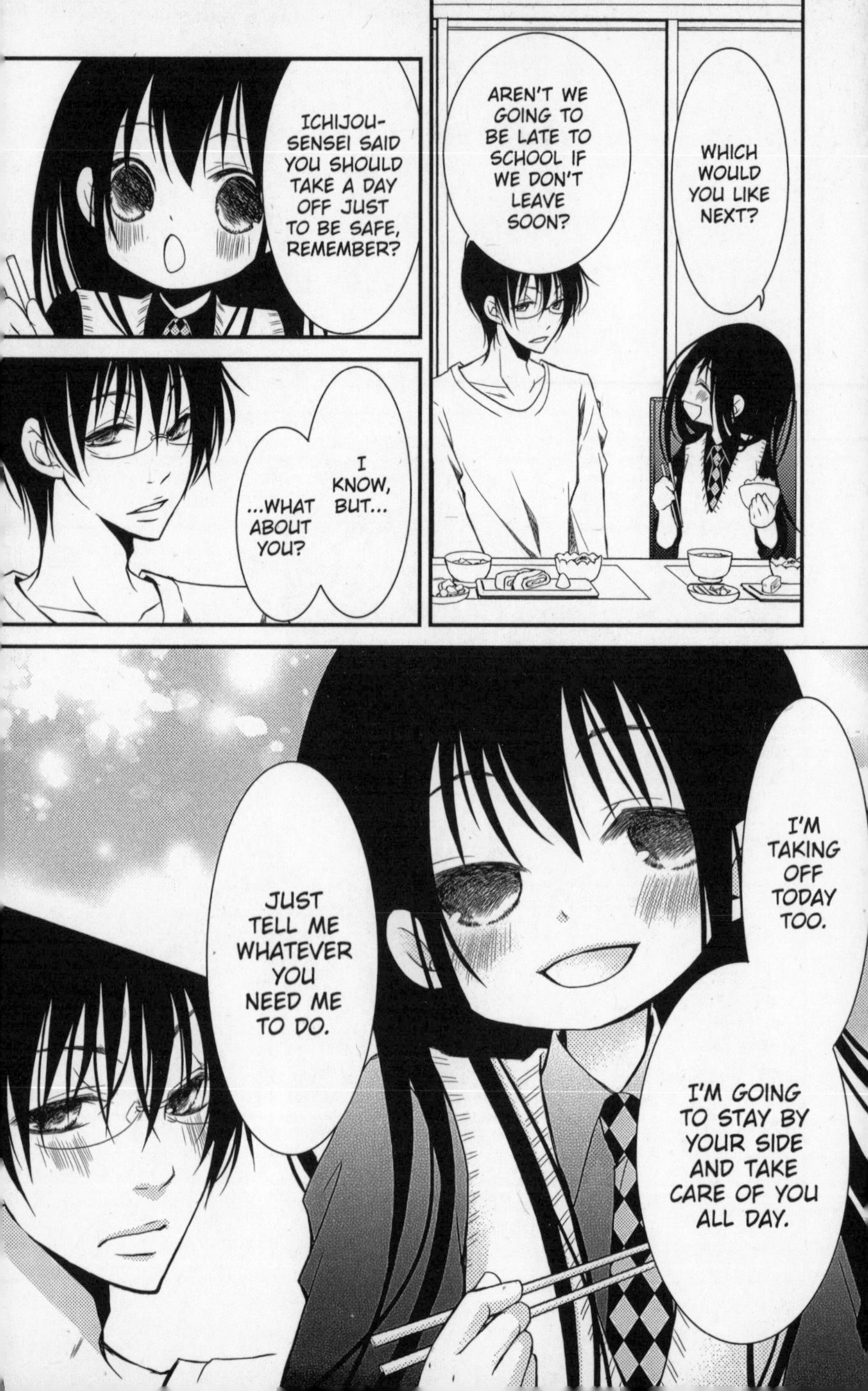
WHICH WOULD YOU LIKE NEXT?
AREN'T WE GOING TO BE LATE TO SCHOOL IF WE DON'T LEAVE SOON?
ICHIJOU-SENSEI SAID YOU SHOULD TAKE A DAY OFF JUST TO BE SAFE, REMEMBER?
I KNOW, BUT...
...WHAT ABOUT YOU?
I'M TAKING OFF TODAY TOO.
I'M GOING TO STAY BY YOUR SIDE AND TAKE CARE OF YOU ALL DAY.
JUST TELL ME WHATEVER YOU NEED ME TO DO.

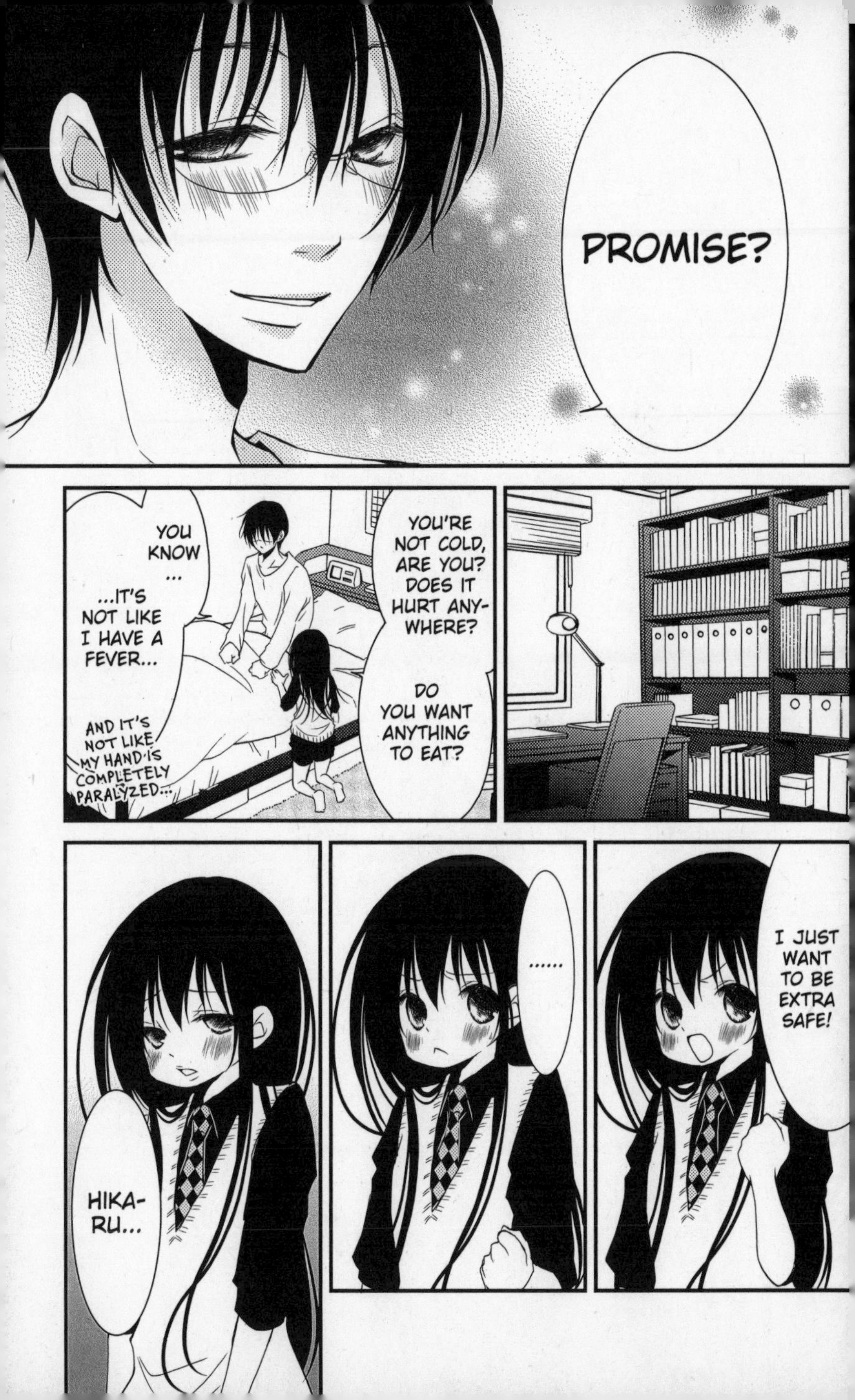
PROMISE?
YOU'RE NOT COLD, ARE YOU? DOES IT HURT ANY-WHERE?
DO YOU WANT ANYTHING TO EAT?
YOU KNOW...
...IT'S NOT LIKE I HAVE A FEVER...
AND IT'S NOT LIKE MY HAND IS COMPLETELY PARALYZED...
I JUST WANT TO BE EXTRA SAFE!
......
HIKA-RU...

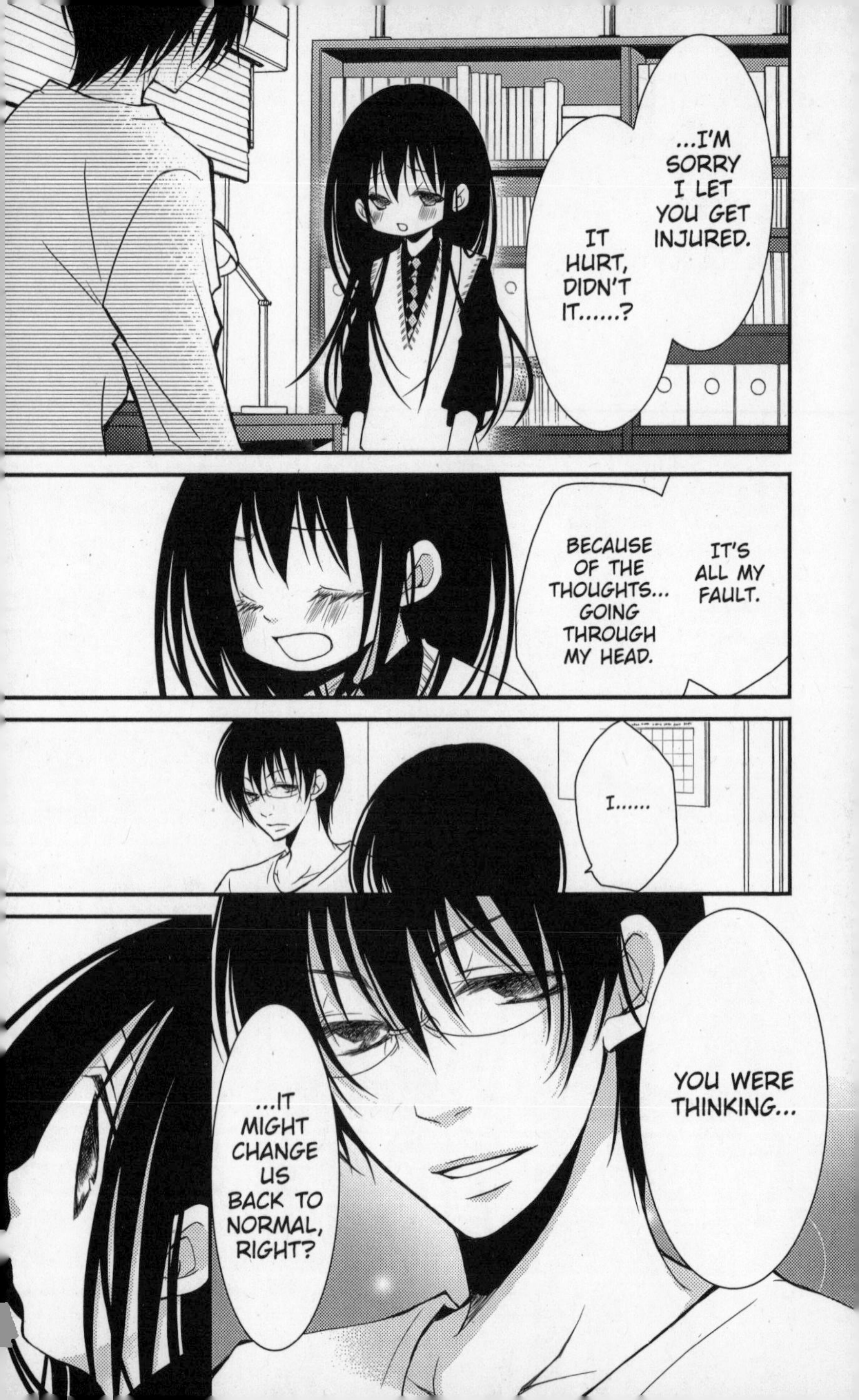
...I'M SORRY I LET YOU GET INJURED.
IT HURT, DIDN'T IT......?
IT'S ALL MY FAULT.
BECAUSE OF THE THOUGHTS... GOING THROUGH MY HEAD.
I......
YOU WERE THINKING...
...IT MIGHT CHANGE US BACK TO NORMAL, RIGHT?

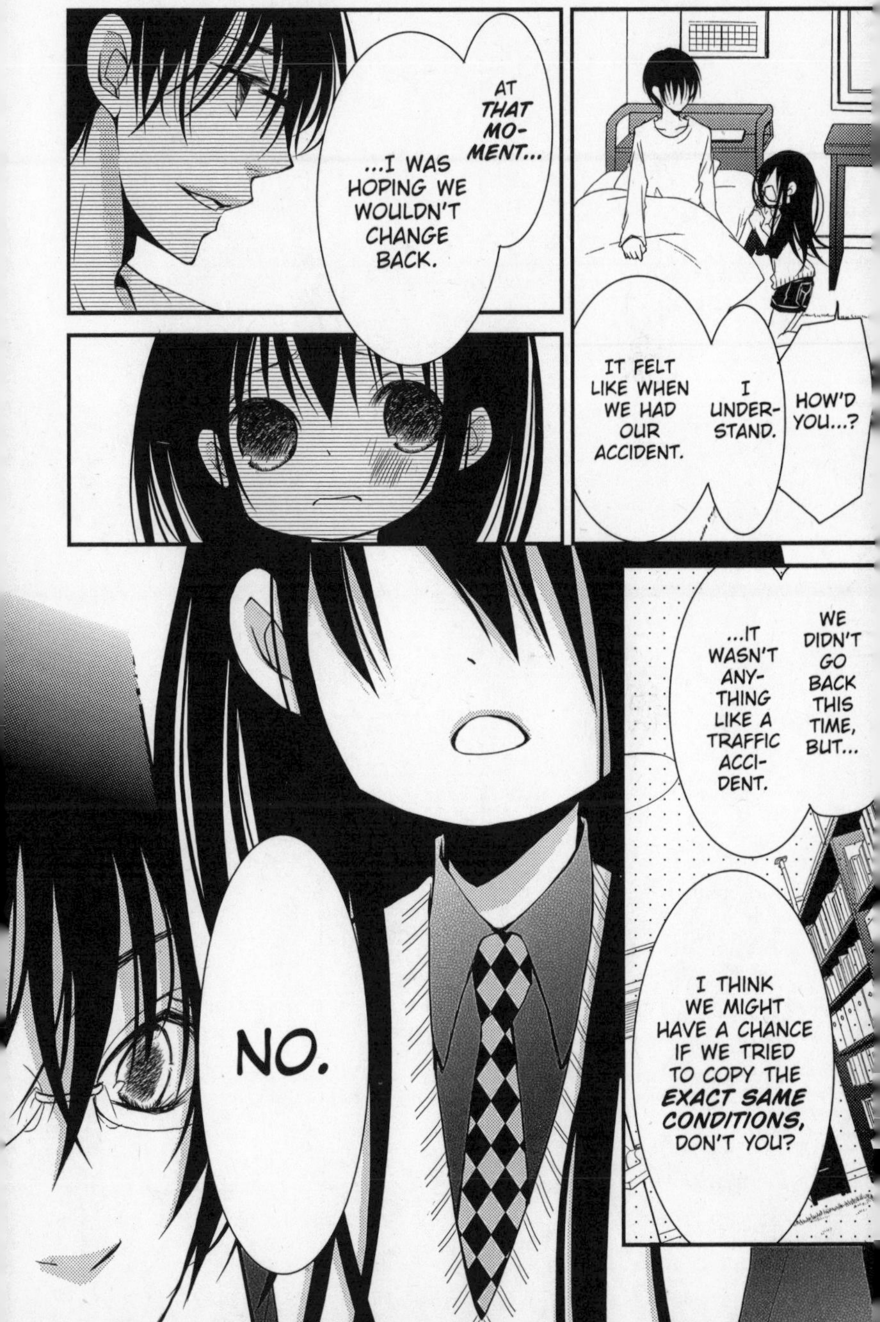
HOW'D YOU...?
I UNDERSTAND.
IT FELT LIKE WHEN WE HAD OUR ACCIDENT.
AT *THAT* MOMENT... ...I WAS HOPING WE WOULDN'T CHANGE BACK.
WE DIDN'T GO BACK THIS TIME, BUT...
...IT WASN'T ANYTHING LIKE A TRAFFIC ACCIDENT.
I THINK WE MIGHT HAVE A CHANCE IF WE TRIED TO COPY THE ***EXACT SAME CONDITIONS,*** DON'T YOU?
NO.

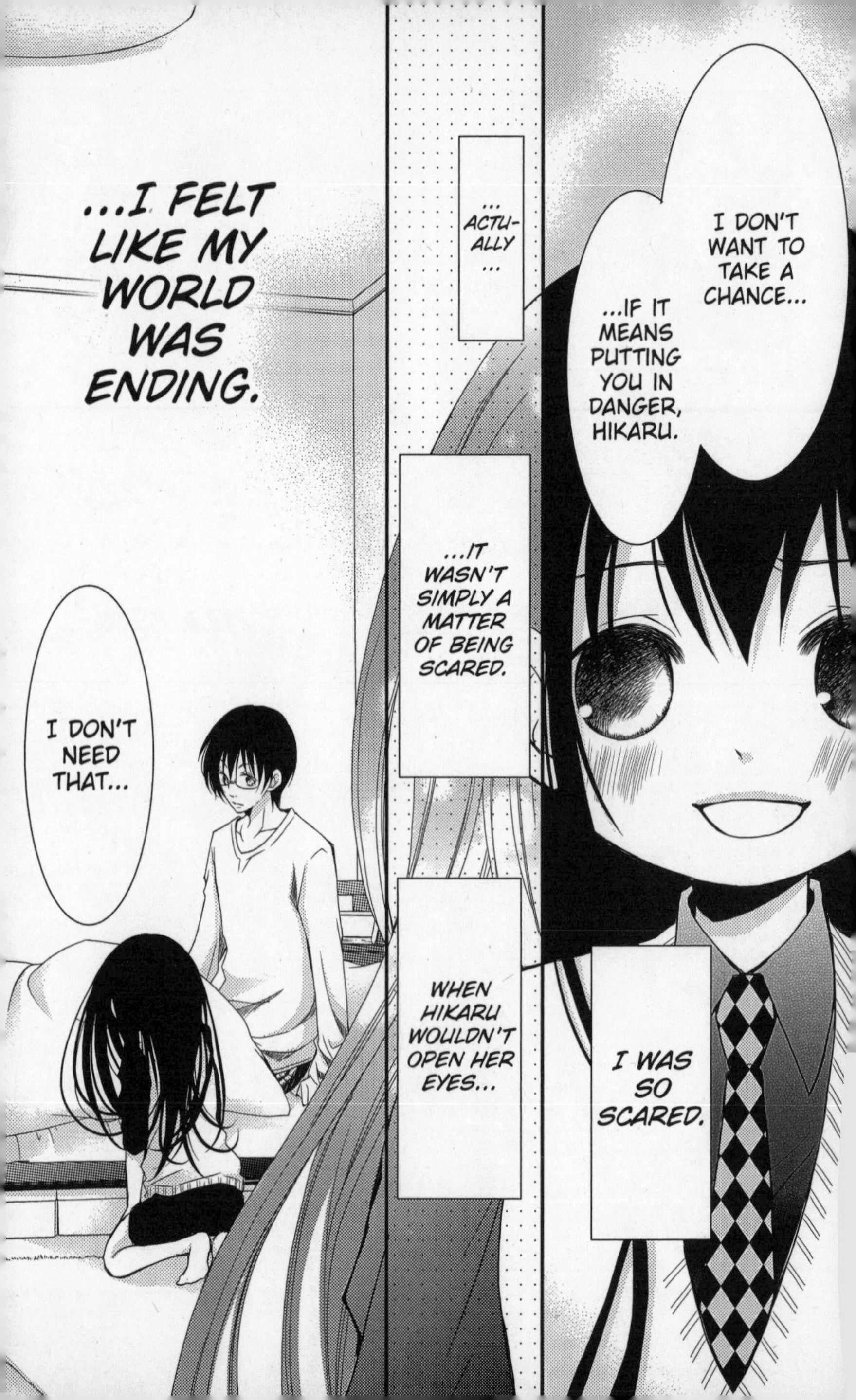
I DON'T WANT TO TAKE A CHANCE...
...IF IT MEANS PUTTING YOU IN DANGER, HIKARU.
I WAS SO SCARED.
...ACTUALLY...
...IT WASN'T SIMPLY A MATTER OF BEING SCARED.
WHEN HIKARU WOULDN'T OPEN HER EYES...
...I FELT LIKE MY WORLD WAS ENDING.
I DON'T NEED THAT...

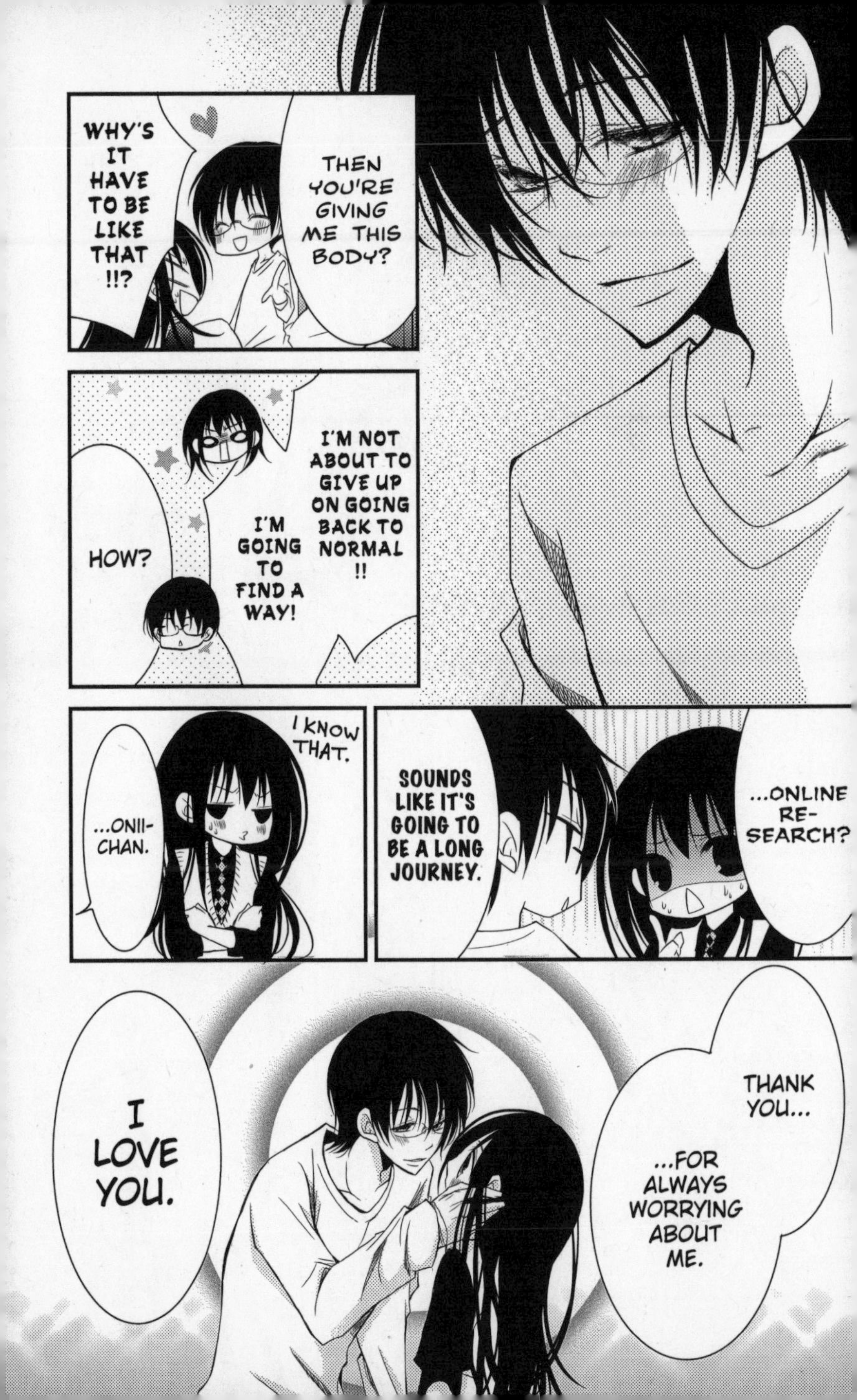
THEN YOU'RE GIVING ME THIS BODY?
WHY'S IT HAVE TO BE LIKE THAT!!?
I'M NOT ABOUT TO GIVE UP ON GOING BACK TO NORMAL!!
I'M GOING TO FIND A WAY!
HOW?
...ONLINE RE-SEARCH?
SOUNDS LIKE IT'S GOING TO BE A LONG JOURNEY.
I KNOW THAT.
...ONII-CHAN.
THANK YOU...
...FOR ALWAYS WORRYING ABOUT ME.
I LOVE YOU.

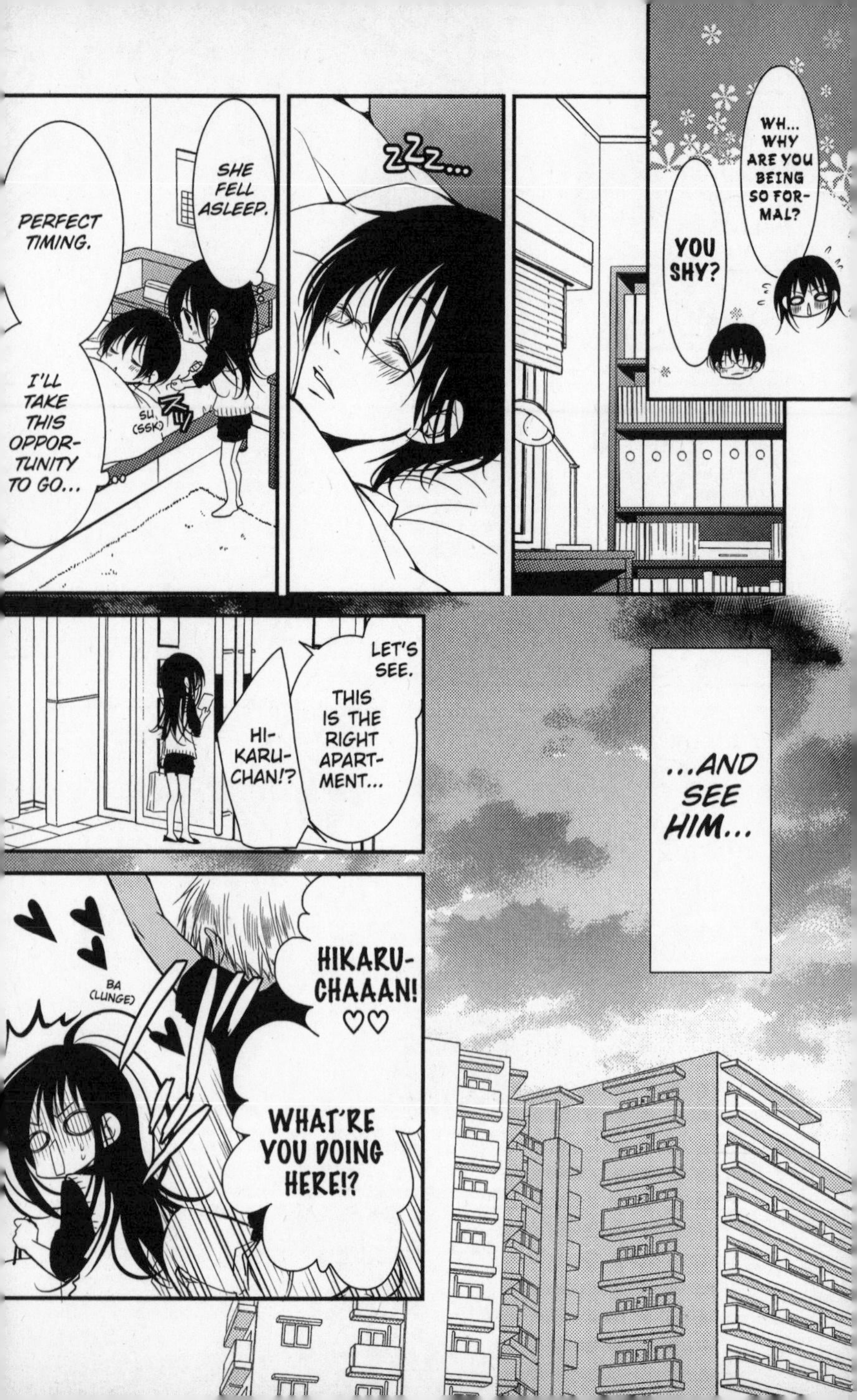
WH... WHY ARE YOU BEING SO FOR-MAL?
YOU SHY?
Zzz...
SHE FELL ASLEEP.
SU (SSK)
PERFECT TIMING.
I'LL TAKE THIS OPPORTUNITY TO GO...
...AND SEE HIM...
LET'S SEE.
THIS IS THE RIGHT APARTMENT...
HI-KARU-CHAN!?
HIKARU-CHAAAN! ♡♡
BA (LUNGE)
WHAT'RE YOU DOING HERE!?

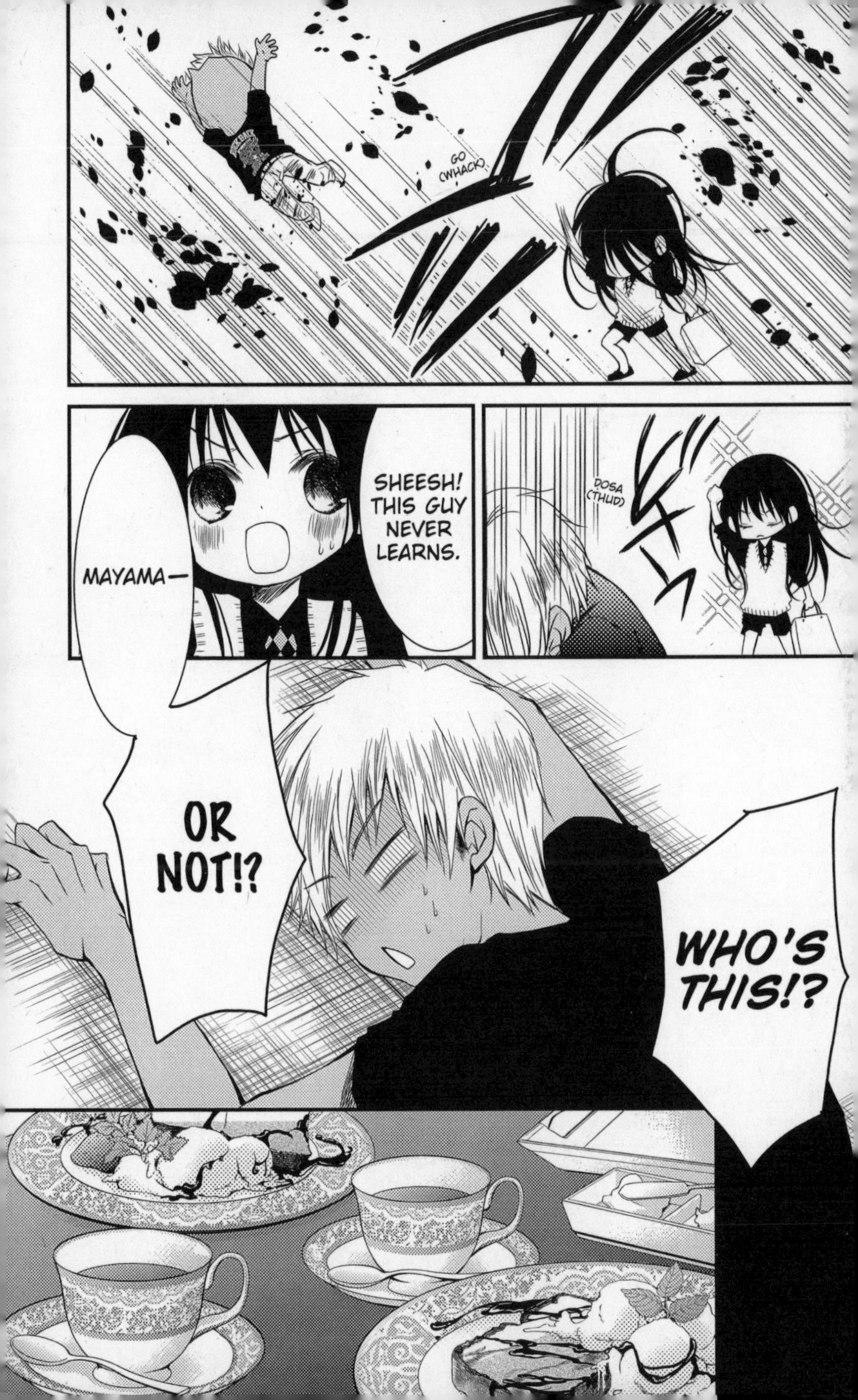
GO
(WHACK)
DOSA
(THUD)
SHEESH! THIS GUY NEVER LEARNS.
MAYAMA—
OR NOT!?
WHO'S THIS!?

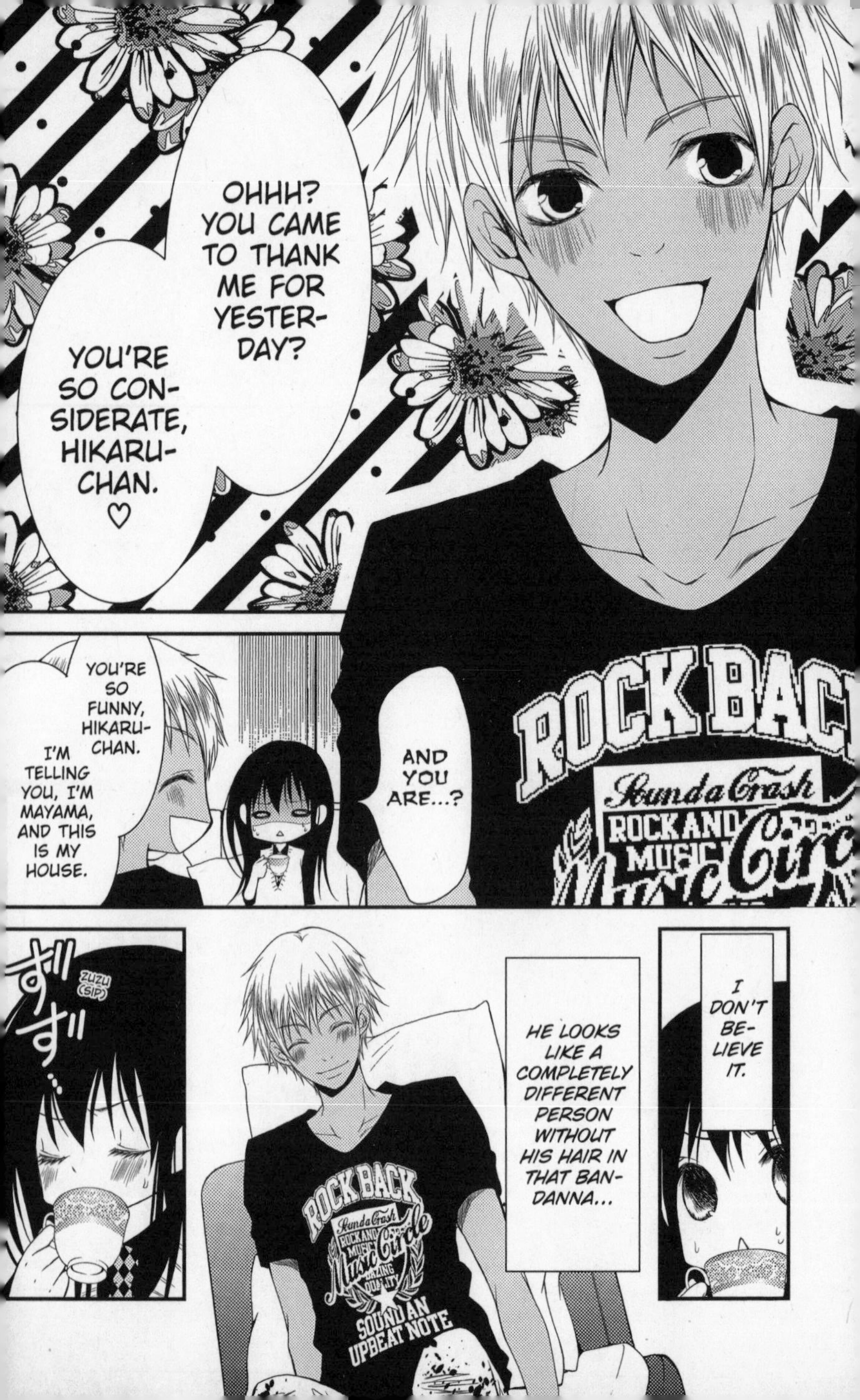
OHHH? YOU CAME TO THANK ME FOR YESTER-DAY?
YOU'RE SO CON-SIDERATE, HIKARU-CHAN. ♡
AND YOU ARE...?
YOU'RE SO FUNNY, HIKARU-CHAN.
I'M TELLING YOU, I'M MAYAMA, AND THIS IS MY HOUSE.
I DON'T BE-LIEVE IT.
HE LOOKS LIKE A COMPLETELY DIFFERENT PERSON WITHOUT HIS HAIR IN THAT BAN-DANNA...
ZUZU (SIP)

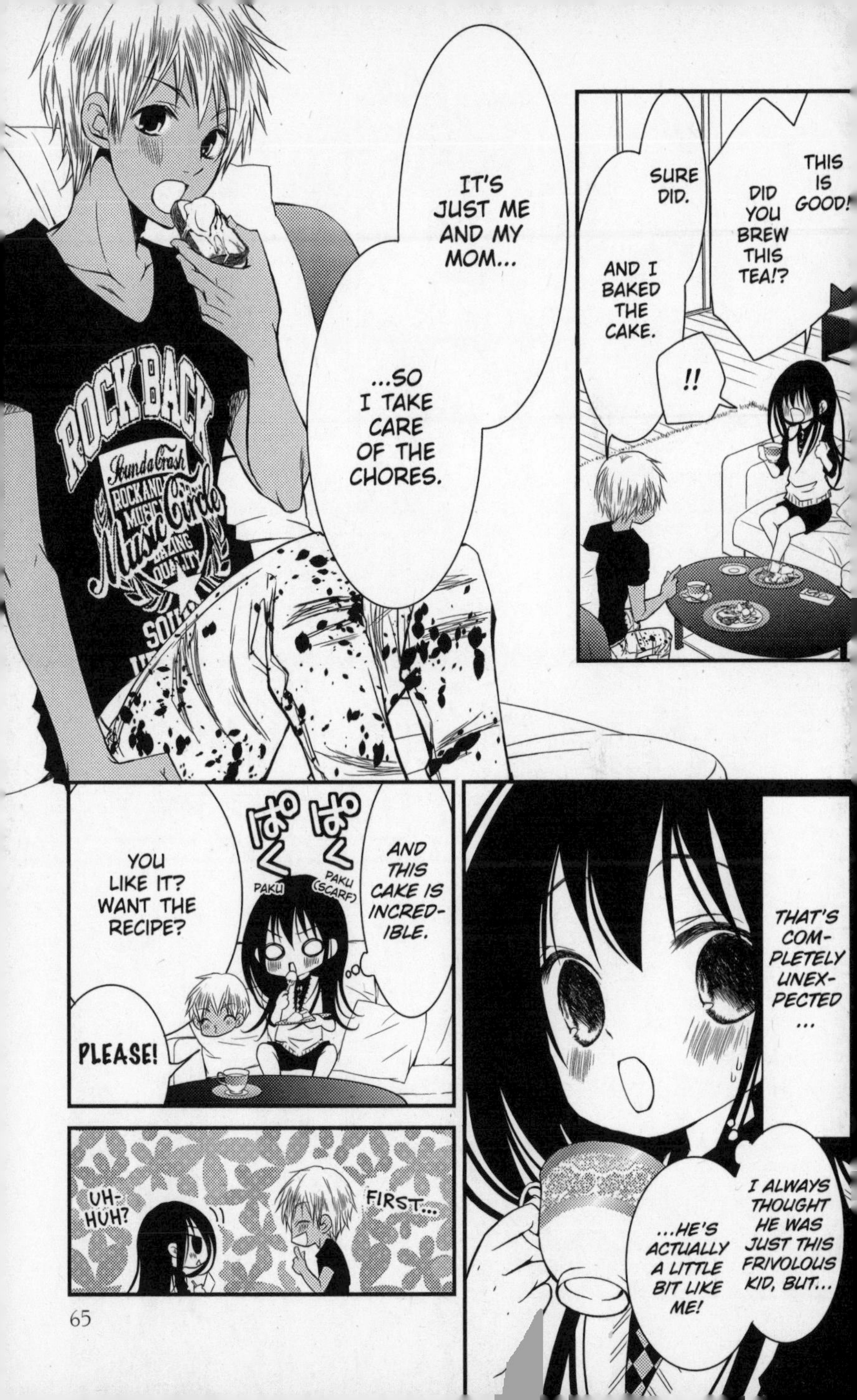
THIS IS GOOD!
DID YOU BREW THIS TEA!?
SURE DID.
AND I BAKED THE CAKE.
!!
IT'S JUST ME AND MY MOM...
...SO I TAKE CARE OF THE CHORES.
THAT'S COMPLETELY UNEXPECTED...
I ALWAYS THOUGHT HE WAS JUST THIS FRIVOLOUS KID, BUT...
...HE'S ACTUALLY A LITTLE BIT LIKE ME!
ぱく
PAKU (SCARF)
ぱく
PAKU
AND THIS CAKE IS INCREDIBLE.
YOU LIKE IT? WANT THE RECIPE?
PLEASE!
FIRST...
UH-HUH?

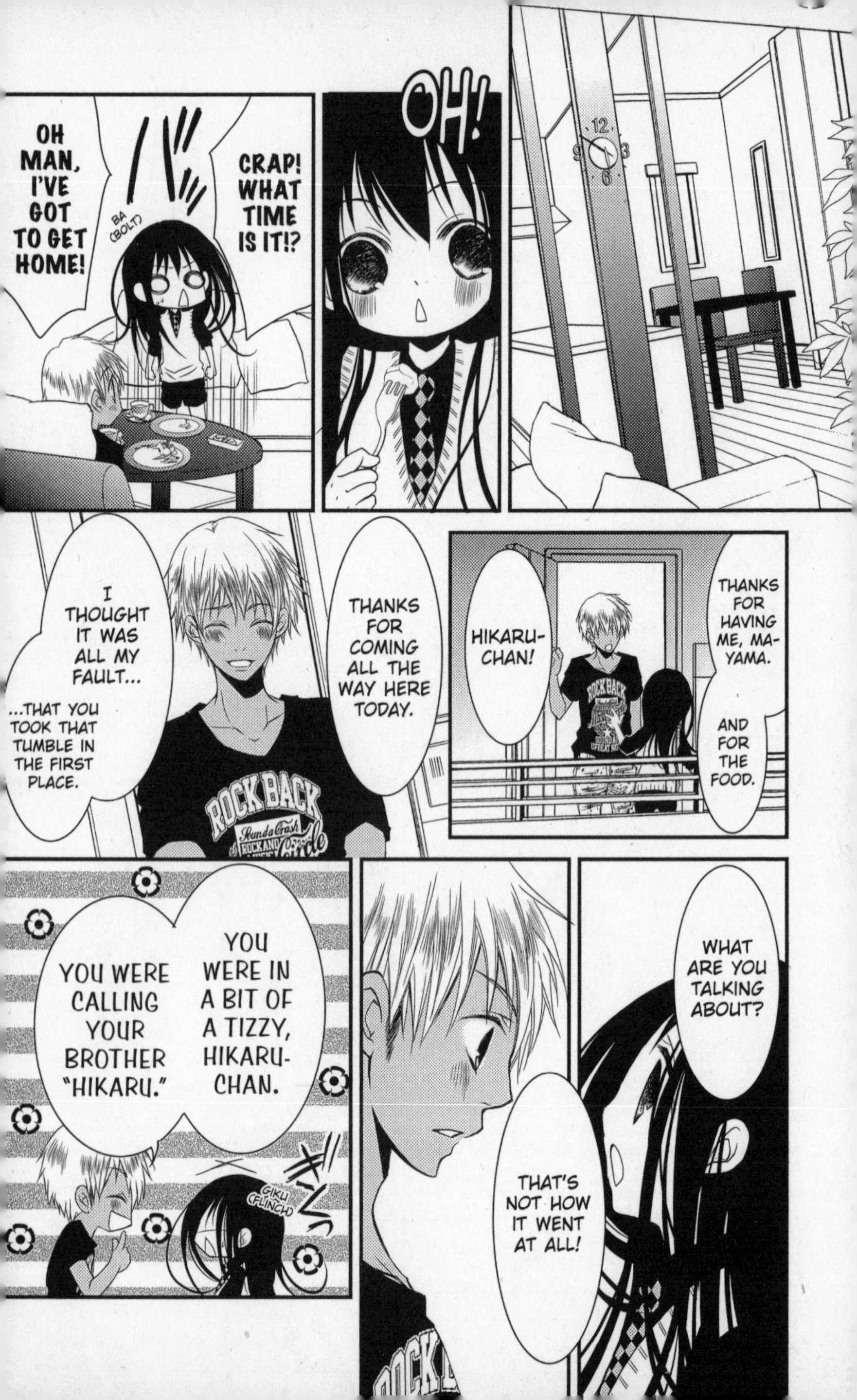
OH!
CRAP! WHAT TIME IS IT!?
BA (BOLT)
OH MAN, I'VE GOT TO GET HOME!
THANKS FOR HAVING ME, MA-YAMA.
AND FOR THE FOOD.
HIKARU-CHAN!
THANKS FOR COMING ALL THE WAY HERE TODAY.
I THOUGHT IT WAS ALL MY FAULT...
...THAT YOU TOOK THAT TUMBLE IN THE FIRST PLACE.
WHAT ARE YOU TALKING ABOUT?
THAT'S NOT HOW IT WENT AT ALL!
YOU WERE IN A BIT OF A TIZZY, HIKARU-CHAN.
YOU WERE CALLING YOUR BROTHER "HIKARU."
GIKU (FLINCH)

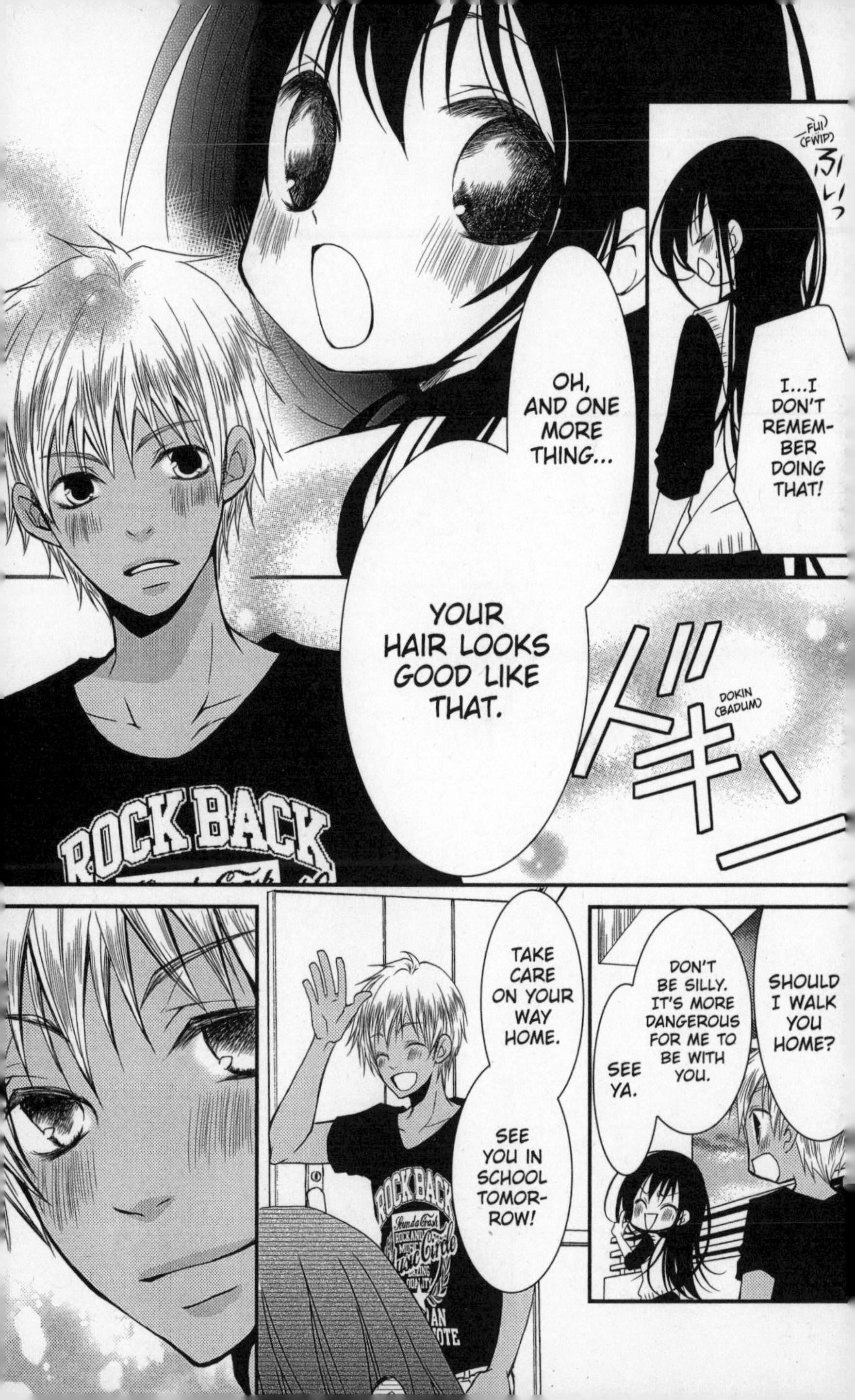
FUI (FWIP)
I...I DON'T REMEMBER DOING THAT!
OH, AND ONE MORE THING...
YOUR HAIR LOOKS GOOD LIKE THAT.
DOKIN (BADUM)
ROCK BACK
SHOULD I WALK YOU HOME?
DON'T BE SILLY. IT'S MORE DANGEROUS FOR ME TO BE WITH YOU.
SEE YA.
TAKE CARE ON YOUR WAY HOME.
SEE YOU IN SCHOOL TOMORROW!
ROCK BACK

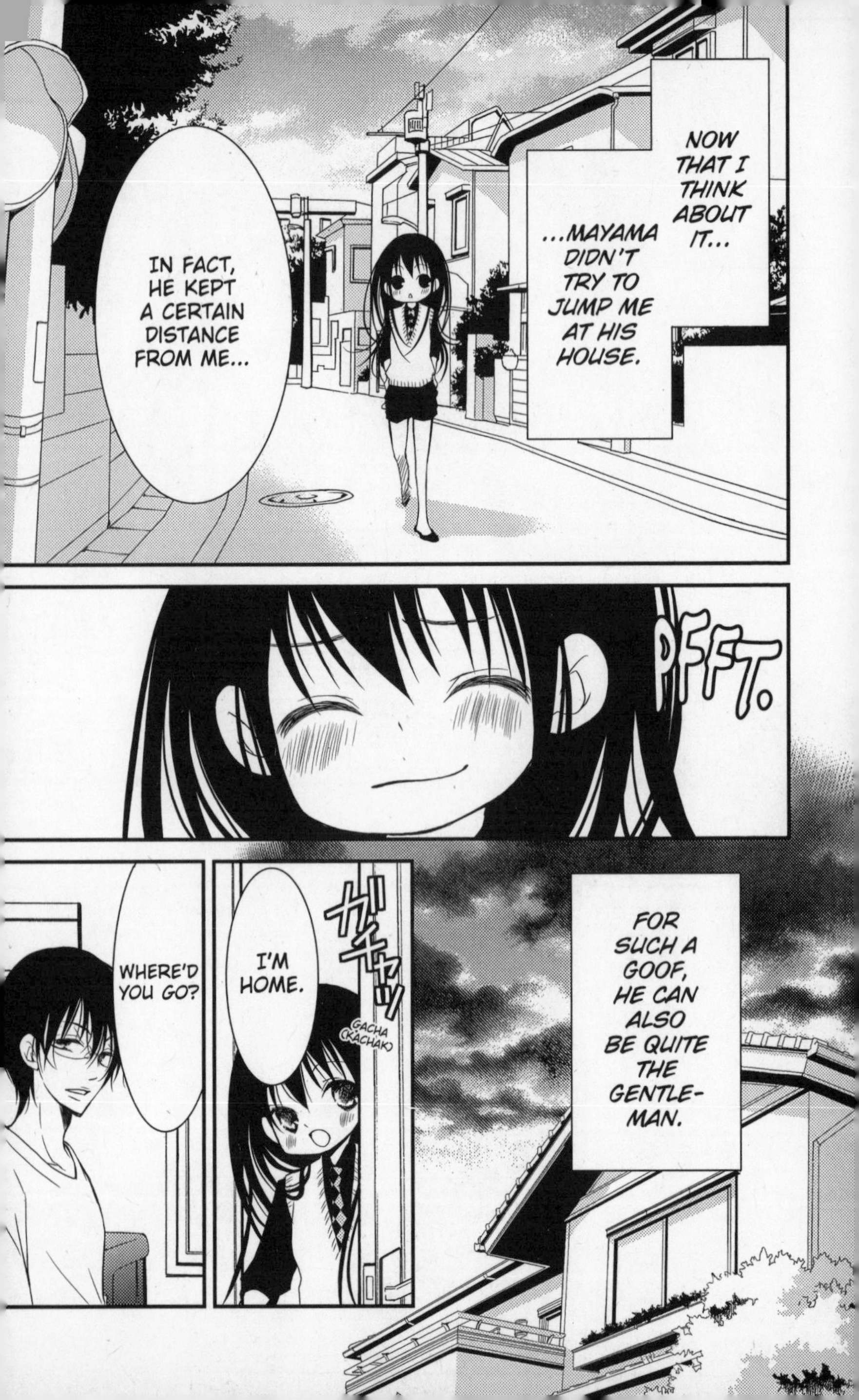
NOW THAT I THINK ABOUT IT...
...MAYAMA DIDN'T TRY TO JUMP ME AT HIS HOUSE.
IN FACT, HE KEPT A CERTAIN DISTANCE FROM ME...
PFFT.
FOR SUCH A GOOF, HE CAN ALSO BE QUITE THE GENTLE-MAN.
GACHA (KACHAK)
I'M HOME.
WHERE'D YOU GO?

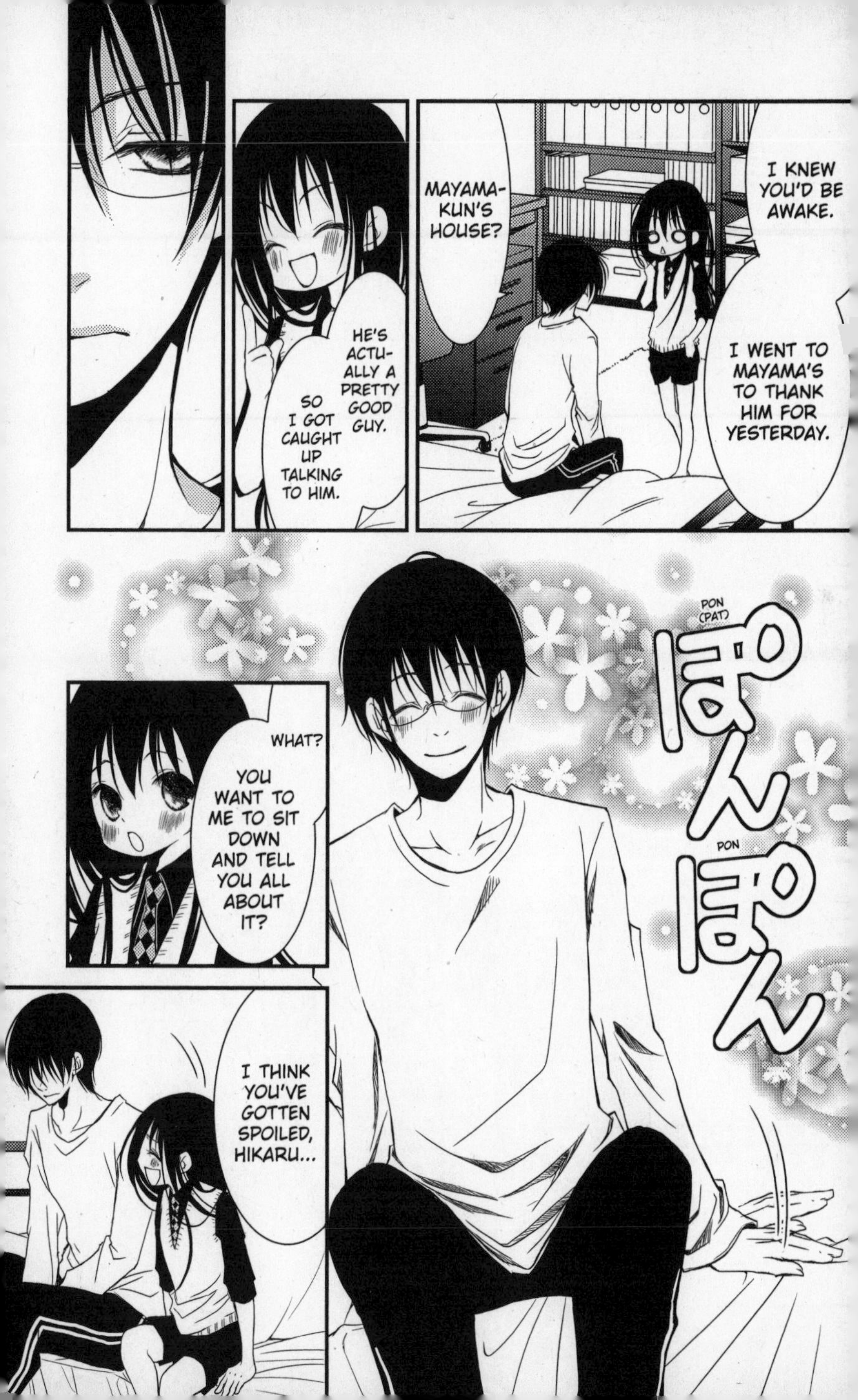

I KNEW YOU'D BE AWAKE.
I WENT TO MAYAMA'S TO THANK HIM FOR YESTERDAY.
MAYAMA-KUN'S HOUSE?
HE'S ACTUALLY A PRETTY GOOD GUY.
SO I GOT CAUGHT UP TALKING TO HIM.
PON (PAT)
ぽん
PON
ぽん
WHAT?
YOU WANT TO ME TO SIT DOWN AND TELL YOU ALL ABOUT IT?
I THINK YOU'VE GOTTEN SPOILED, HIKARU...

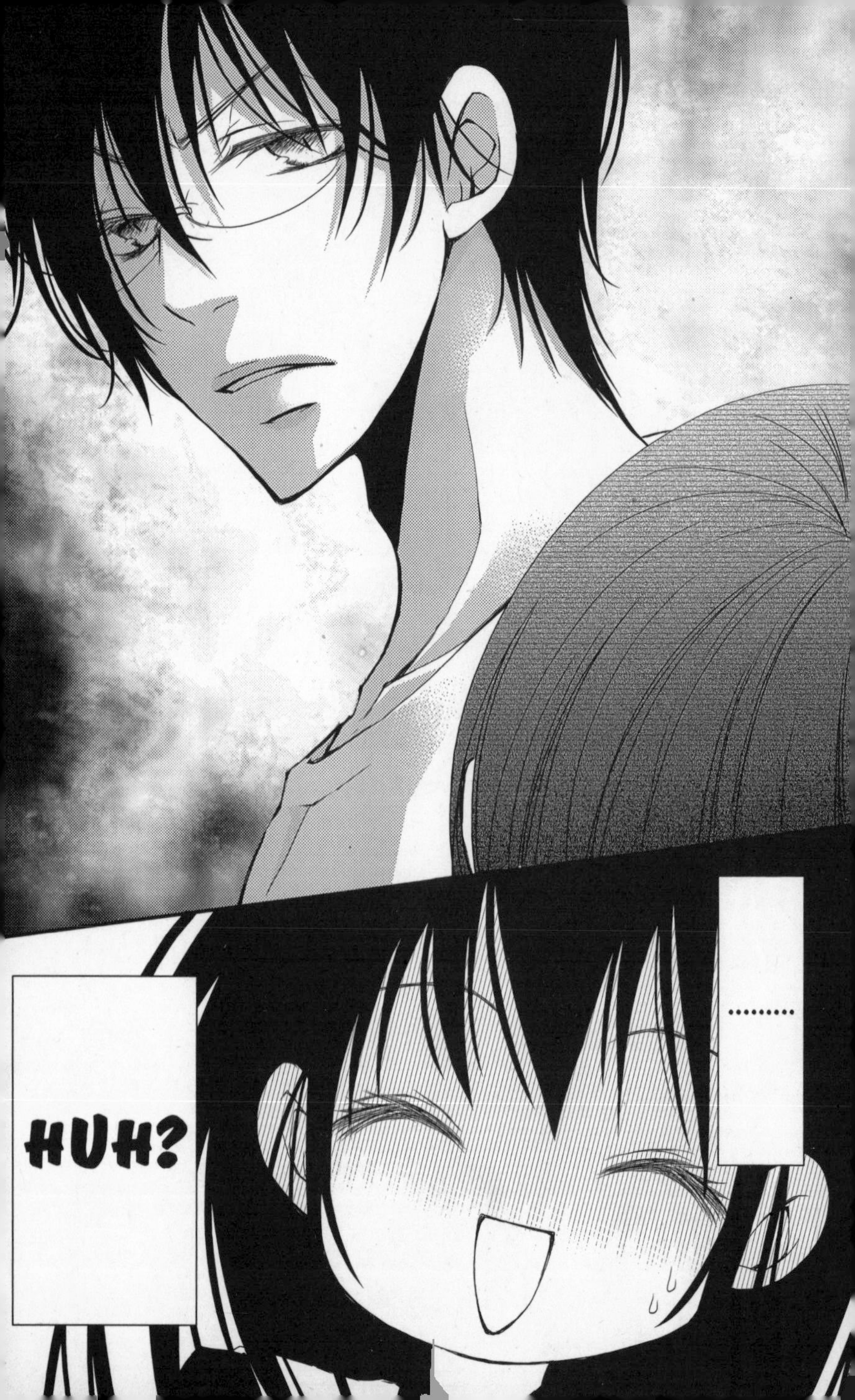
....
HUH?

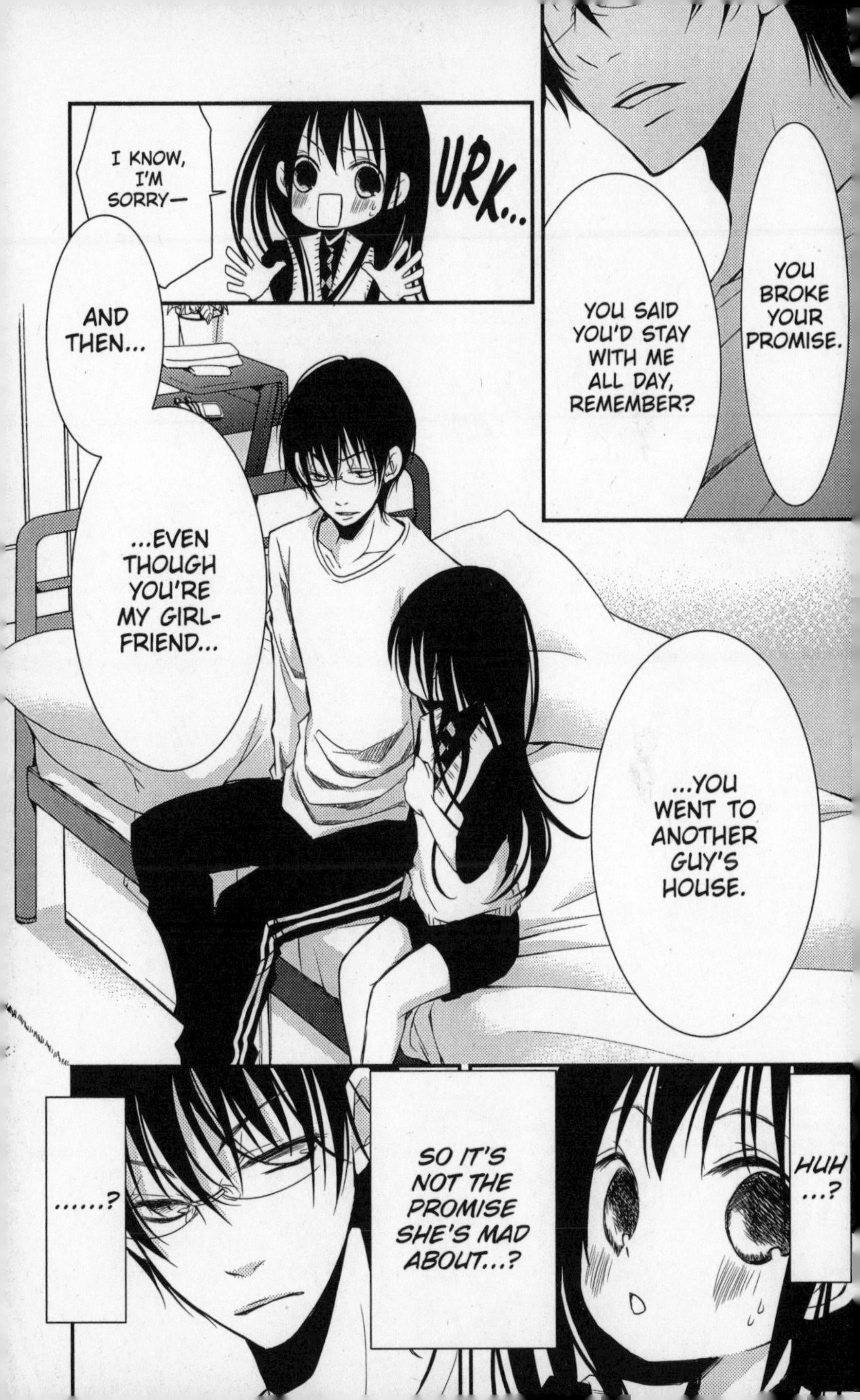
YOU BROKE YOUR PROMISE.
YOU SAID YOU'D STAY WITH ME ALL DAY, REMEMBER?
URK...
I KNOW, I'M SORRY—
AND THEN...
...EVEN THOUGH YOU'RE MY GIRL-FRIEND...
...YOU WENT TO ANOTHER GUY'S HOUSE.
HUH ...?
SO IT'S NOT THE PROMISE SHE'S MAD ABOUT...?
......?

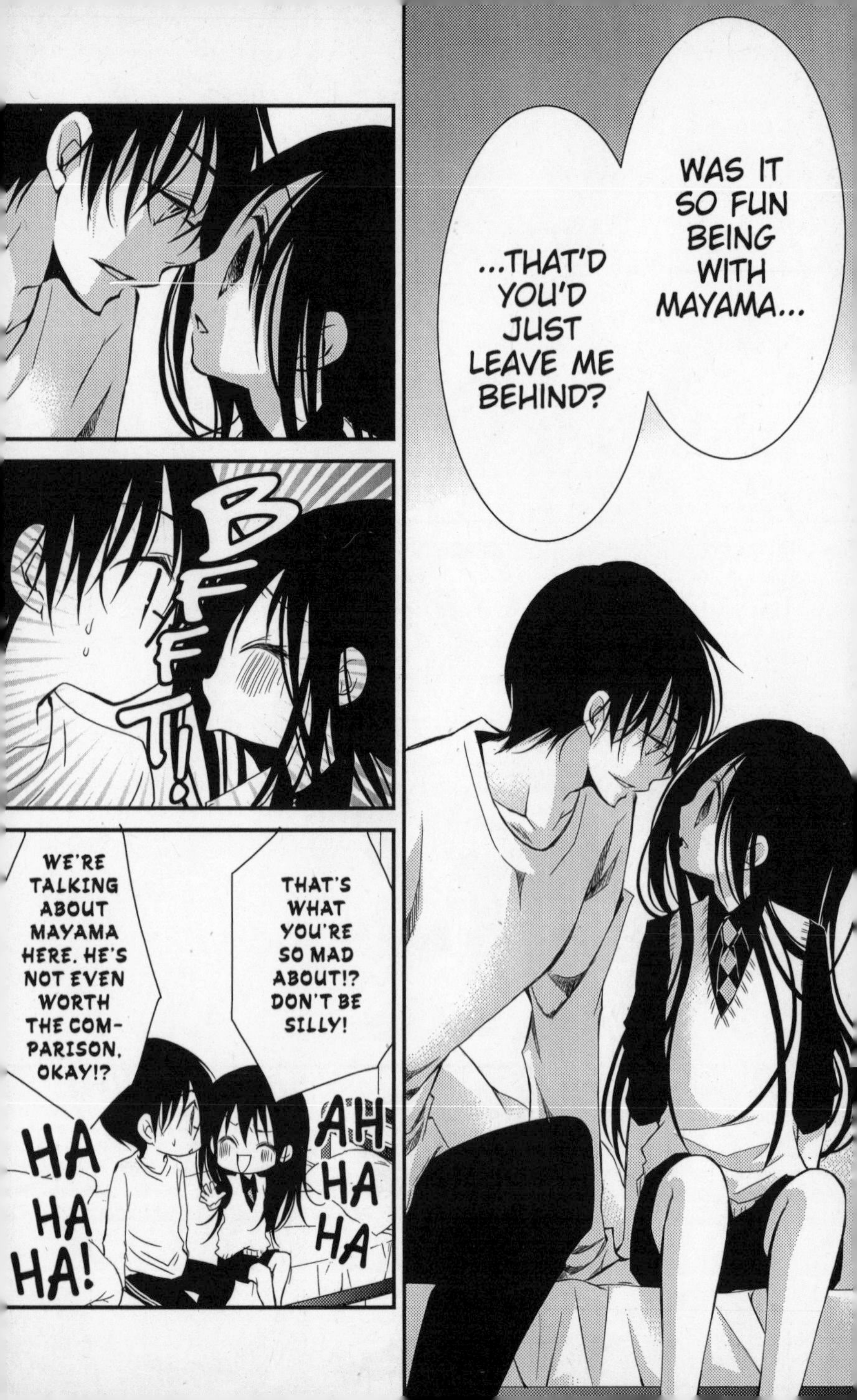
WAS IT SO FUN BEING WITH MAYAMA... ...THAT'D YOU'D JUST LEAVE ME BEHIND?
BFFT!
THAT'S WHAT YOU'RE SO MAD ABOUT!? DON'T BE SILLY!
WE'RE TALKING ABOUT MAYAMA HERE. HE'S NOT EVEN WORTH THE COM-PARISON, OKAY!?
AH HA HA
HA HA HA!

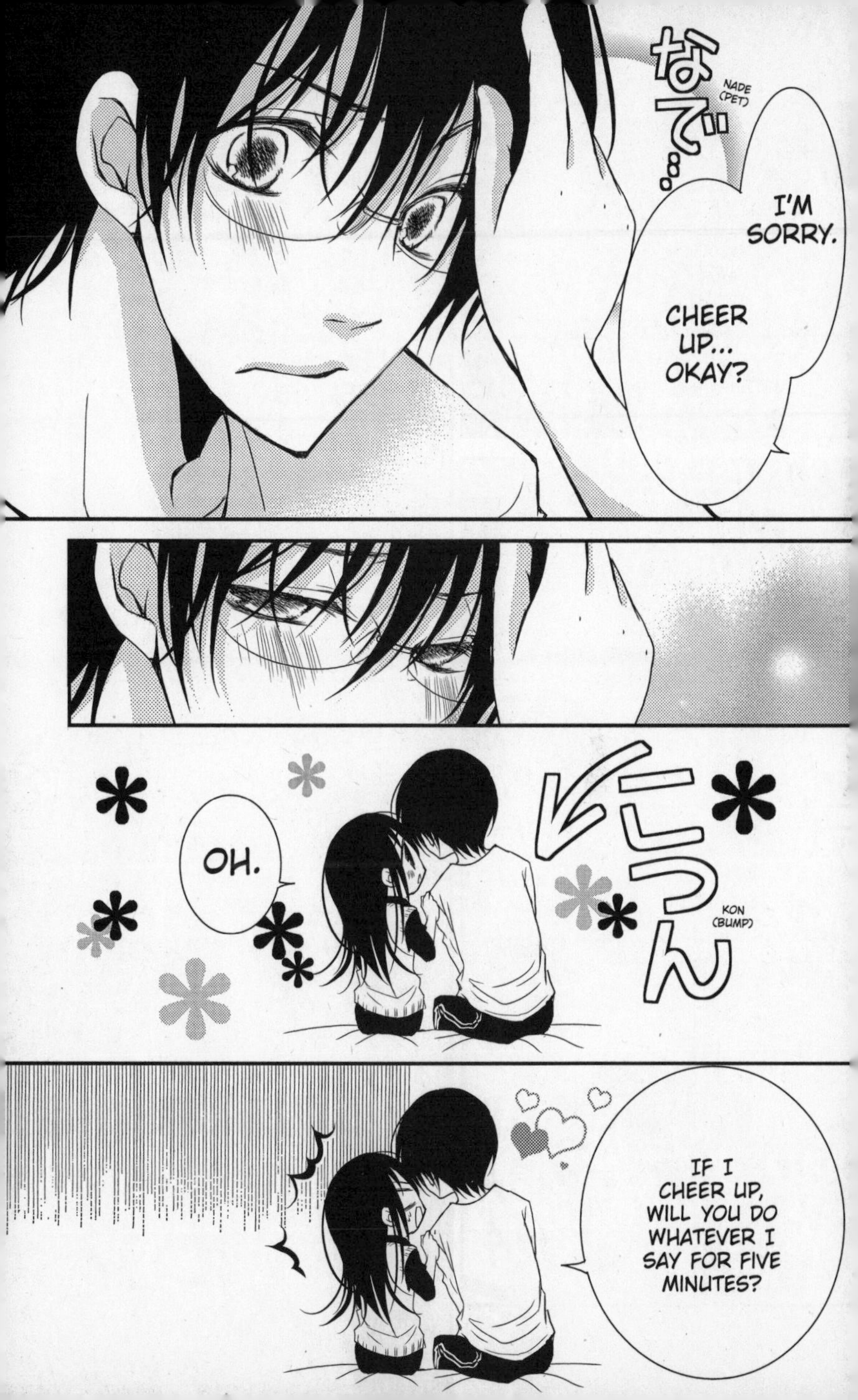
なで…
NADE (PET)
I'M SORRY.
CHEER UP... OKAY?
こつん
KON (BUMP)
OH.
IF I CHEER UP, WILL YOU DO WHATEVER I SAY FOR FIVE MINUTES?

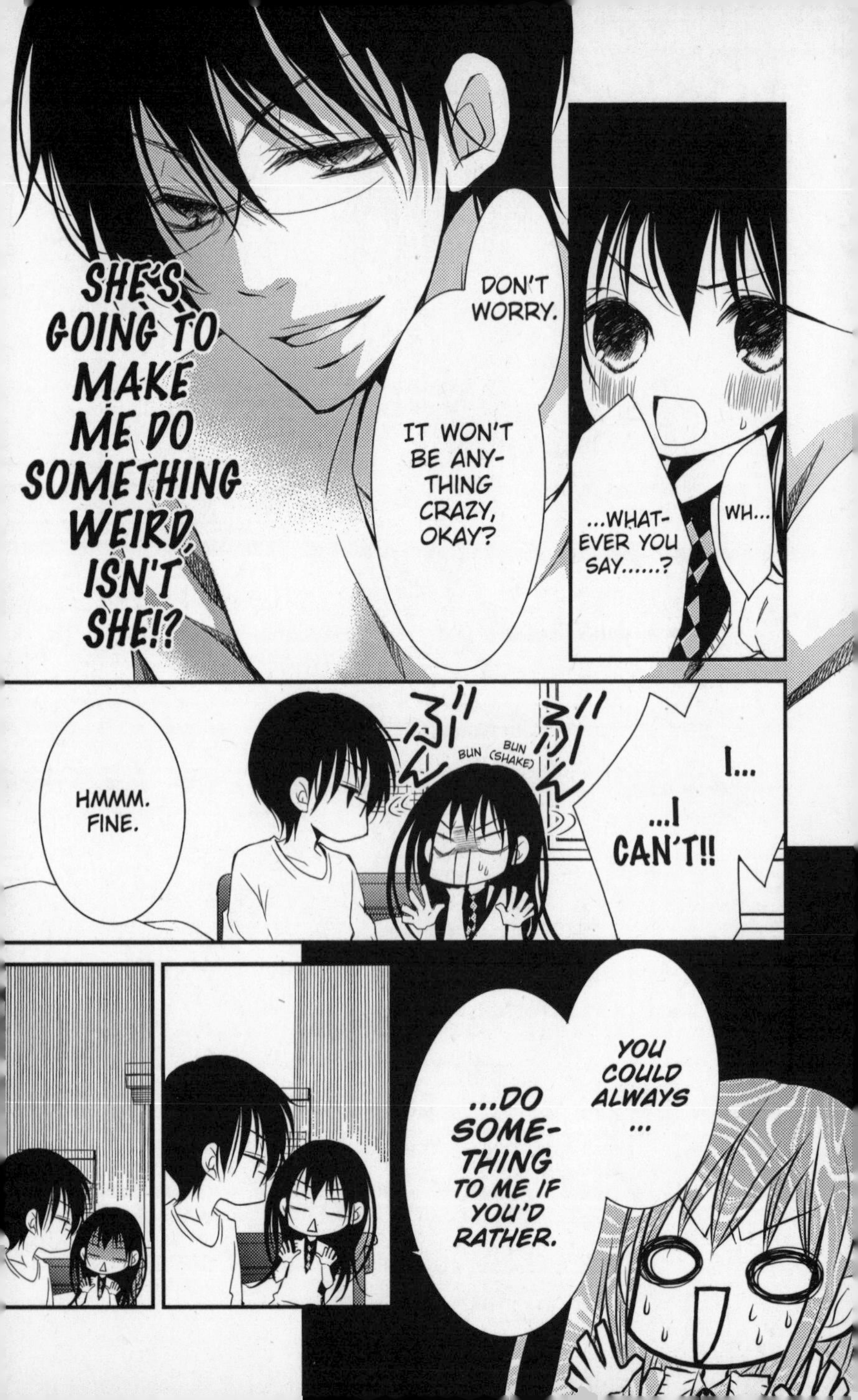
WH...
...WHAT-EVER YOU SAY......?
DON'T WORRY.
IT WON'T BE ANY-THING CRAZY, OKAY?
SHE'S GOING TO MAKE ME DO SOMETHING WEIRD, ISN'T SHE!?
I...
...I CAN'T!!
ぶん
BUN (SHAKE)
ぶん
BUN
HMMM. FINE.
YOU COULD ALWAYS ...
...DO SOME-THING TO ME IF YOU'D RATHER.

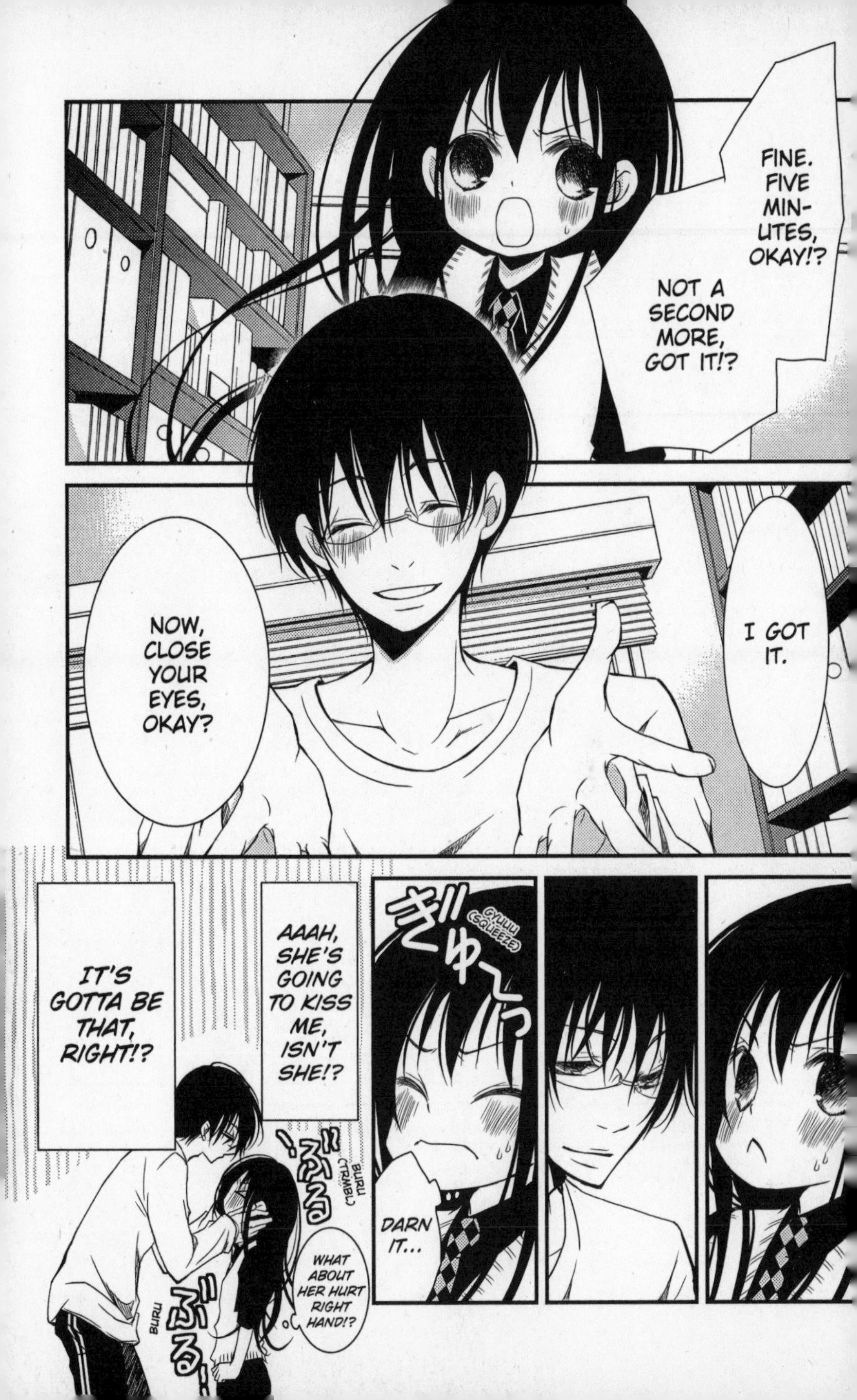
FINE. FIVE MIN-UTES, OKAY!?
NOT A SECOND MORE, GOT IT!?
I GOT IT.
NOW, CLOSE YOUR EYES, OKAY?
ぎゅーっ
GYUUU (SQUEEZE)
DARN IT...
AAAH, SHE'S GOING TO KISS ME, ISN'T SHE!?
IT'S GOTTA BE THAT, RIGHT!?
ぶるっ
BURU (TRMBL)
WHAT ABOUT HER HURT RIGHT HAND!?
ぶるっ
BURU

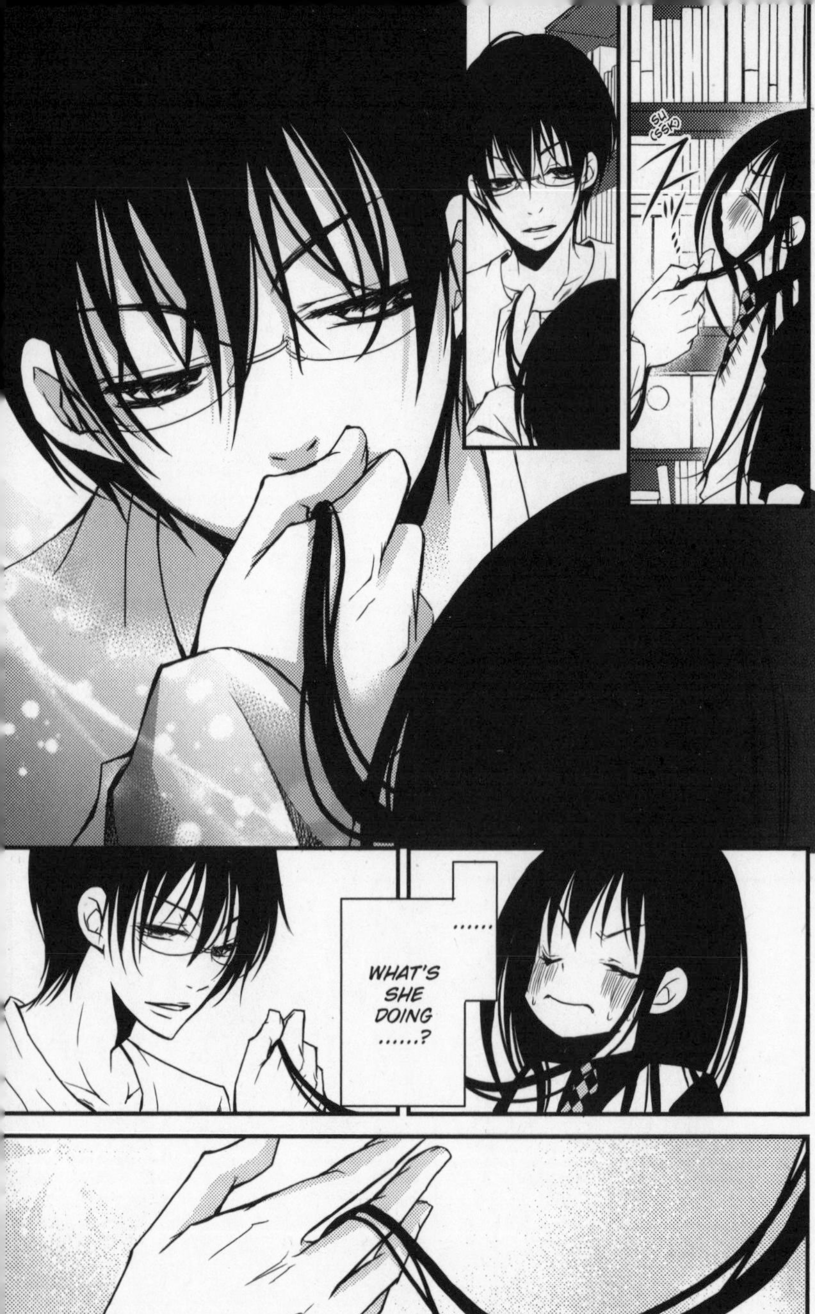
SU (SSK)
......
WHAT'S SHE DOING ......?

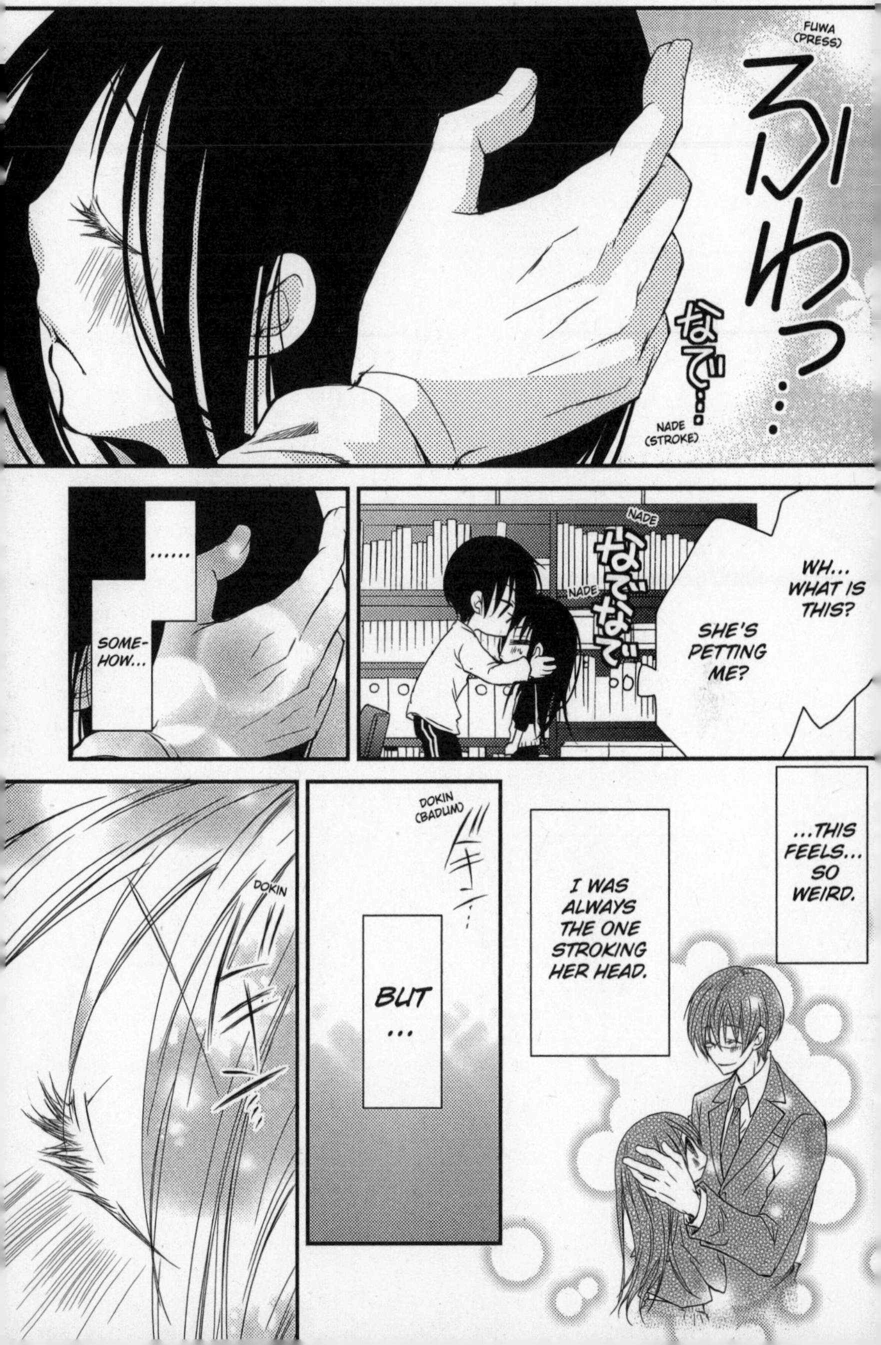
ふわっ…
FUWA (PRESS)
なで…
NADE (STROKE)
WH... WHAT IS THIS?
SHE'S PETTING ME?
なでなで
NADE
NADE
......
SOME-HOW...
...THIS FEELS... SO WEIRD.
I WAS ALWAYS THE ONE STROKING HER HEAD.
DOKIN (BADUM)
BUT ...
DOKIN

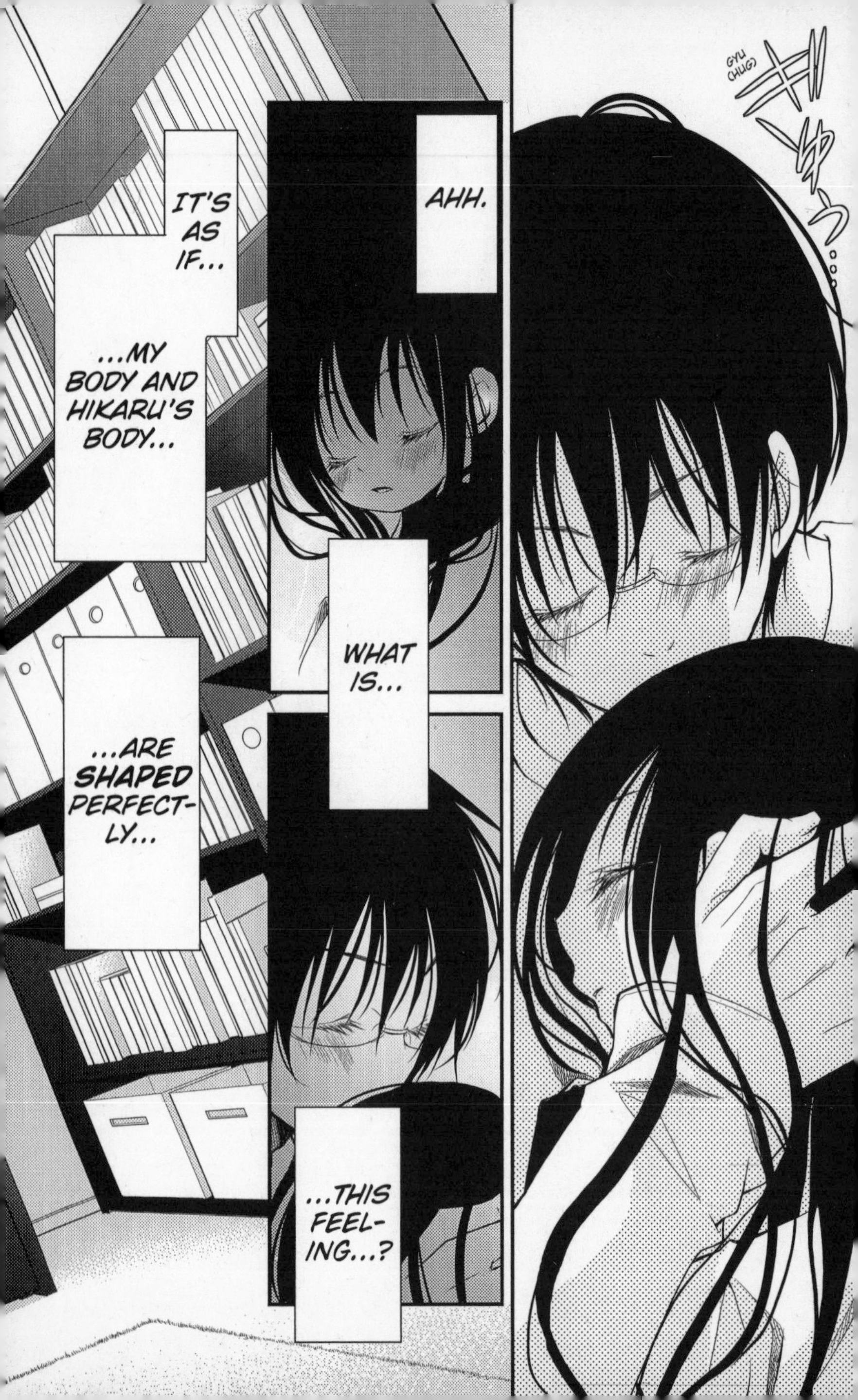
GYU (HUG)
AHH.
WHAT IS...
...THIS FEEL-ING...?
IT'S AS IF...
...MY BODY AND HIKARU'S BODY...
...ARE SHAPED PERFECT-LY...

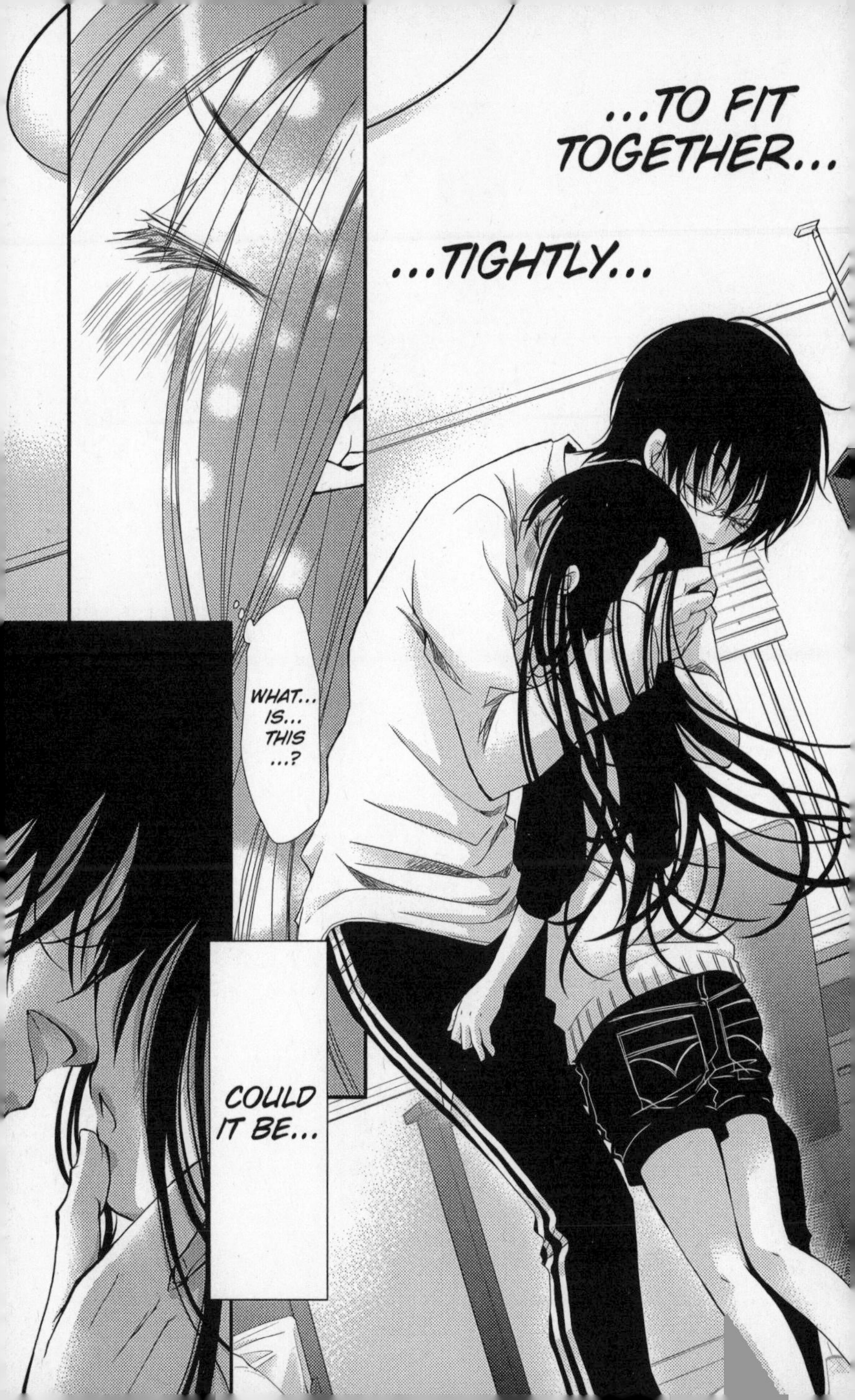
...TO FIT TOGETHER...
...TIGHTLY...
WHAT... IS... THIS ...?
COULD IT BE...

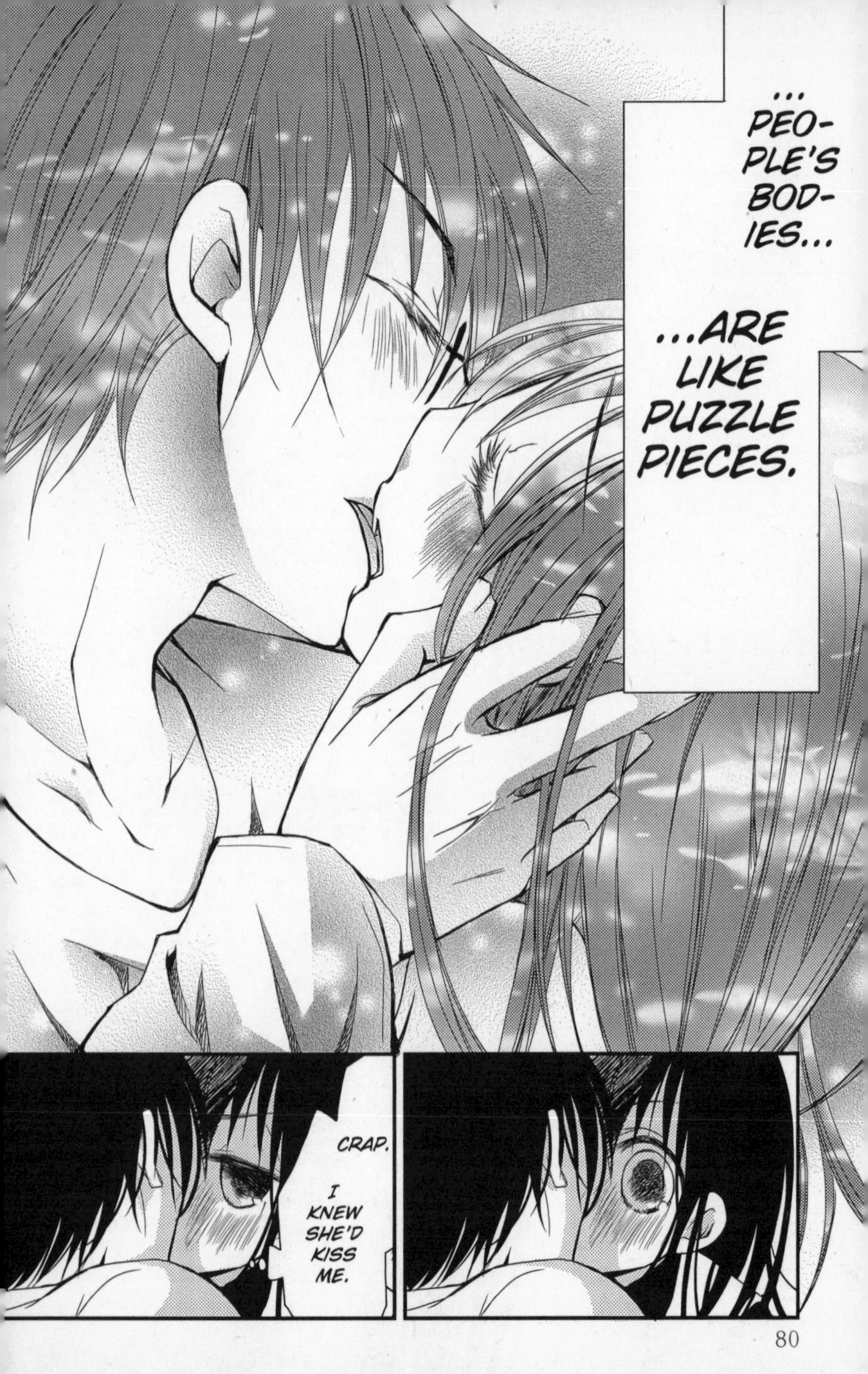
...PEOPLE'S BODIES...
...ARE LIKE PUZZLE PIECES.
CRAP.
I KNEW SHE'D KISS ME.

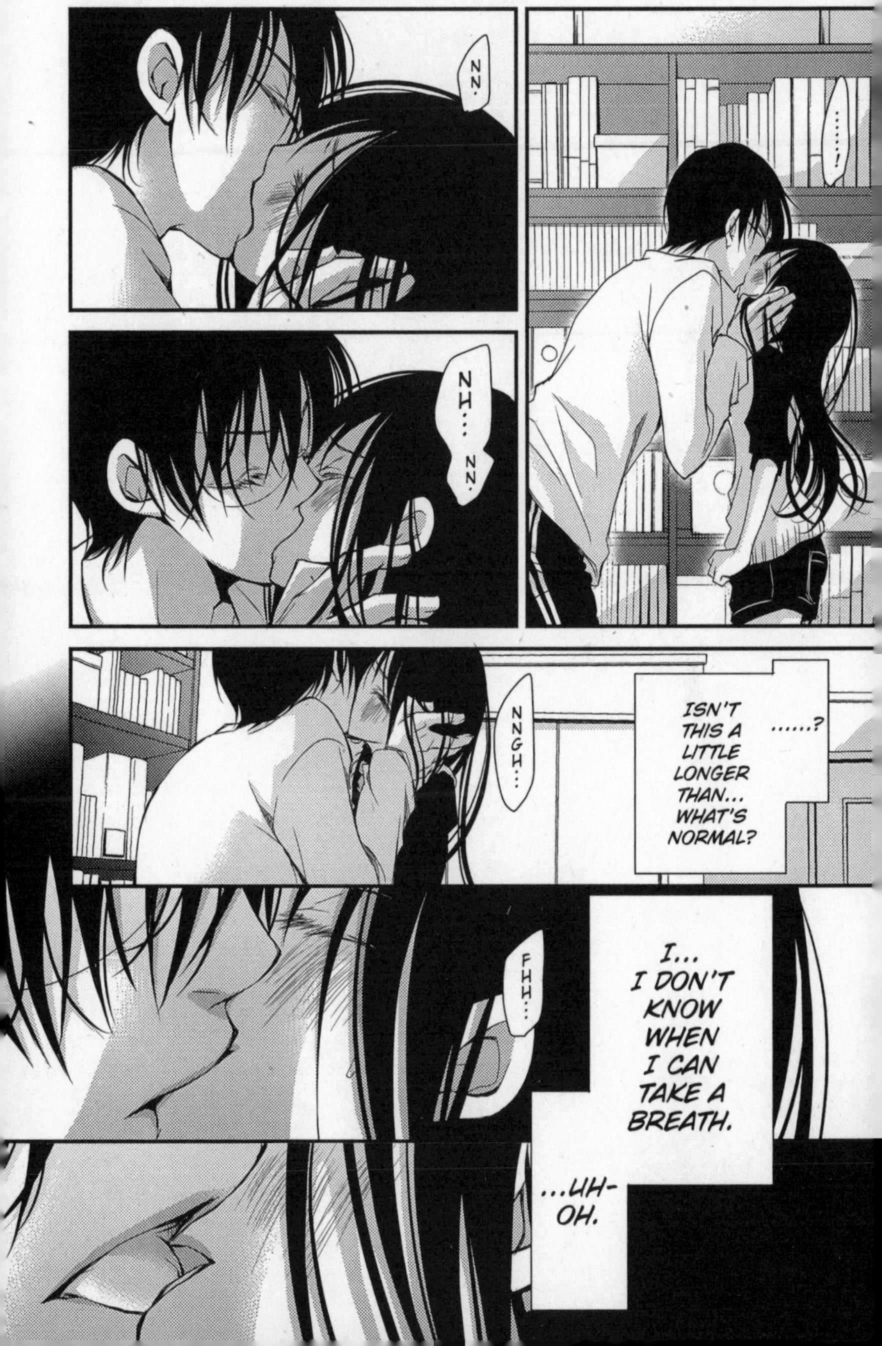
......!
NN.
NH... NN.
......?
ISN'T THIS A LITTLE LONGER THAN... WHAT'S NORMAL?
NNGH...
I... I DON'T KNOW WHEN I CAN TAKE A BREATH.
FHH...
...UH-OH.

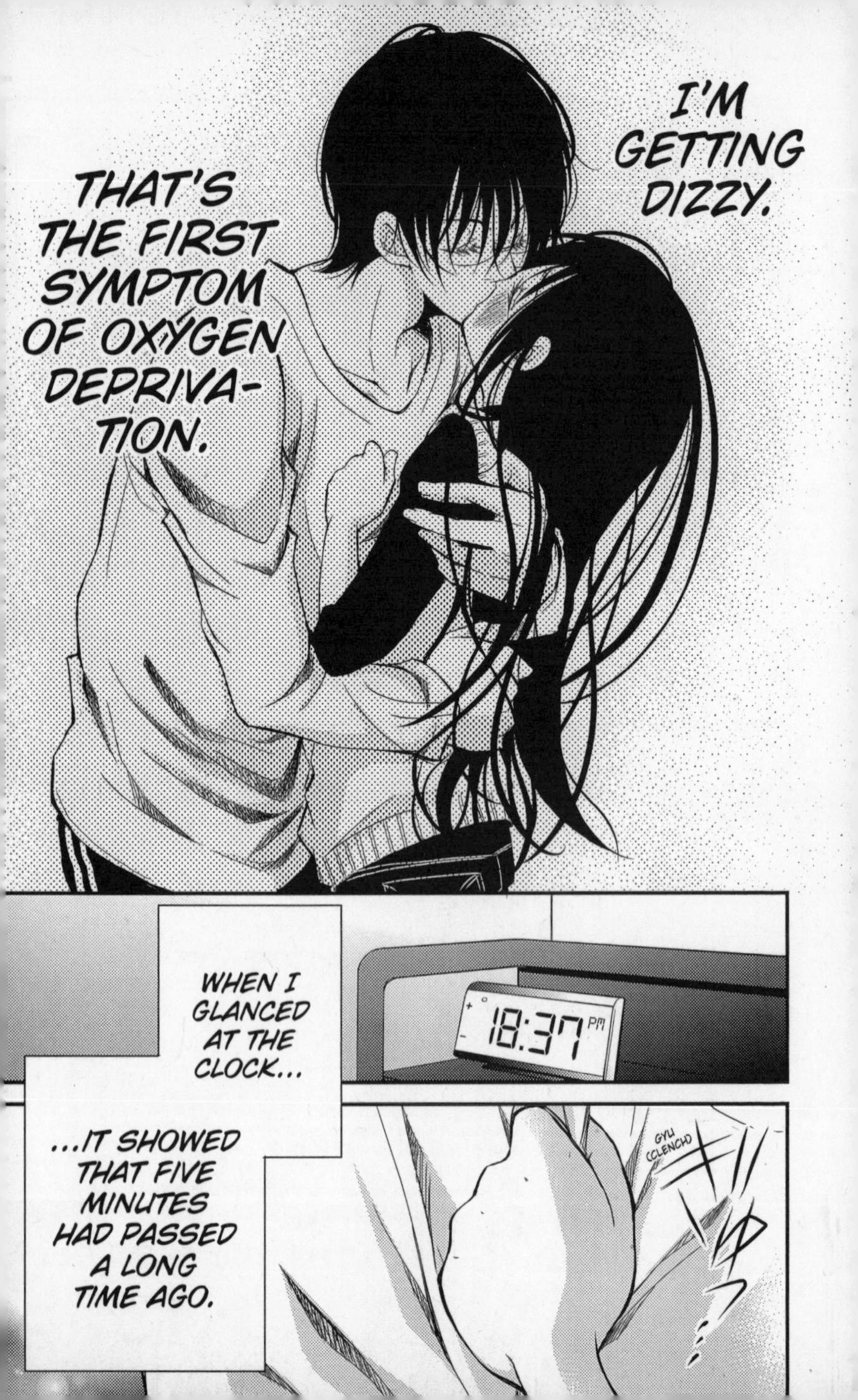
I'M GETTING DIZZY.
THAT'S THE FIRST SYMPTOM OF OXYGEN DEPRIVA-TION.
18:37 PM
WHEN I GLANCED AT THE CLOCK...
GYU (CLENCH)
...IT SHOWED THAT FIVE MINUTES HAD PASSED A LONG TIME AGO.

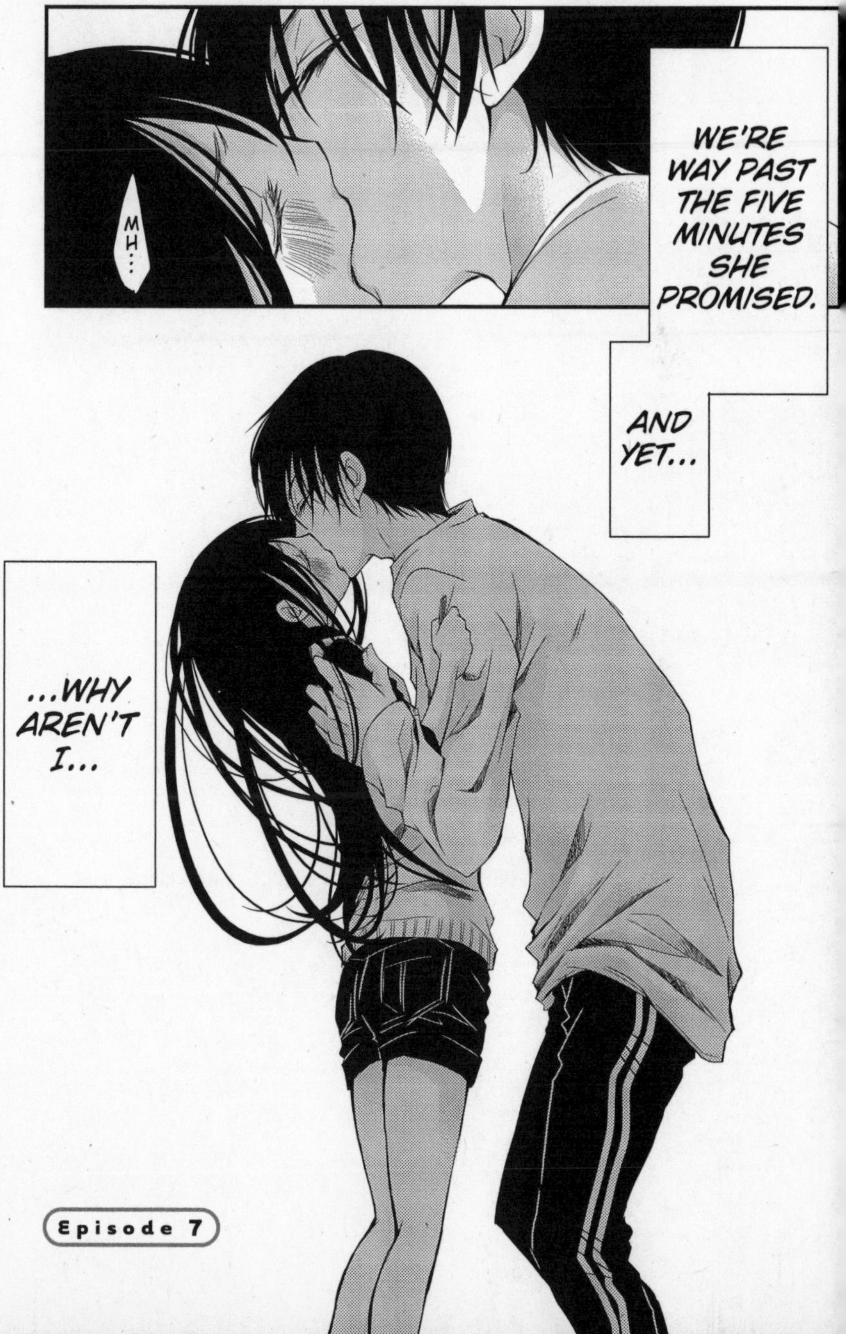
WE'RE WAY PAST THE FIVE MINUTES SHE PROMISED.
MH...
AND YET...
...WHY AREN'T I...
Episode 7

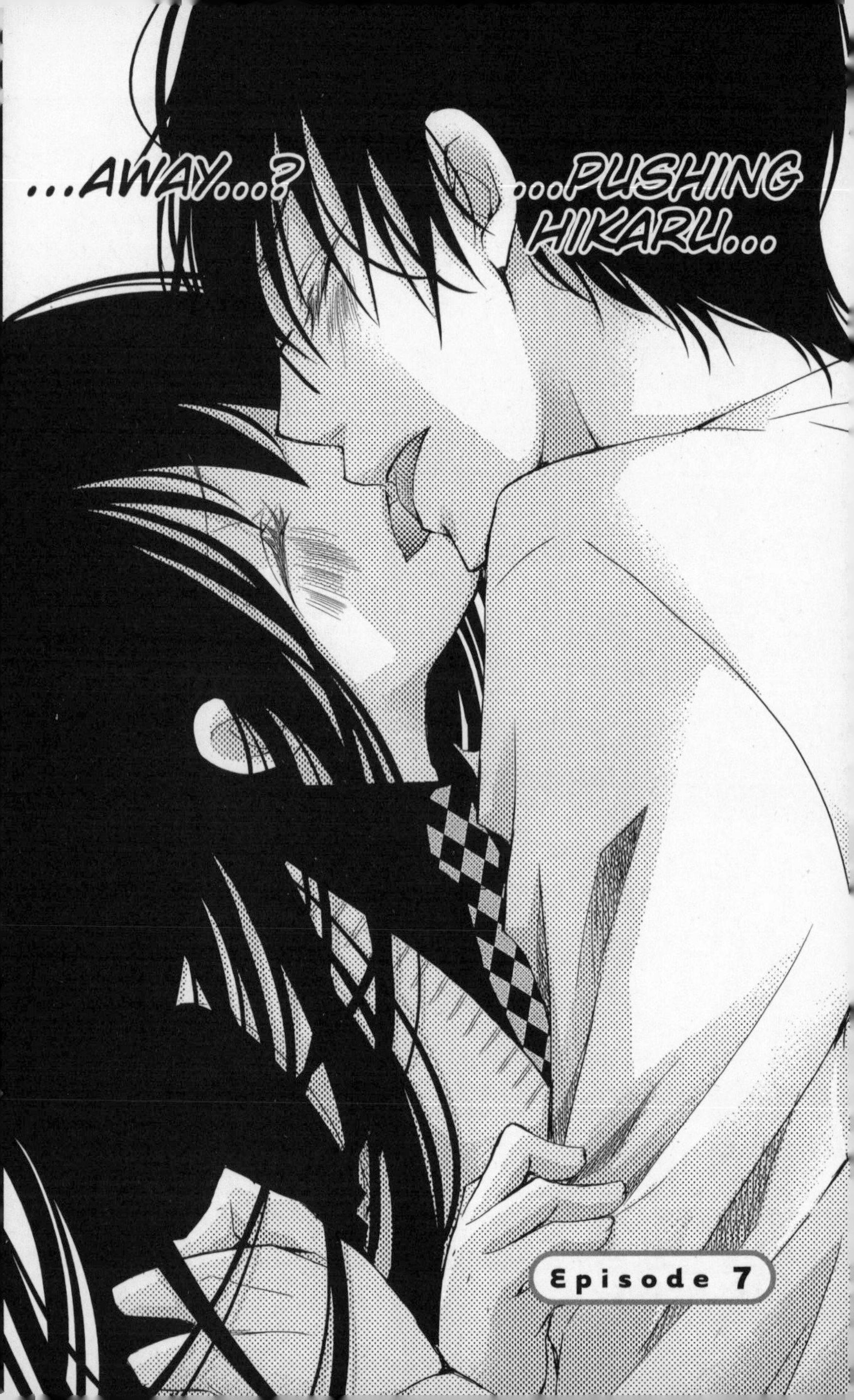
...PUSHING HIKARU...
...AWAY...?
Episode 7

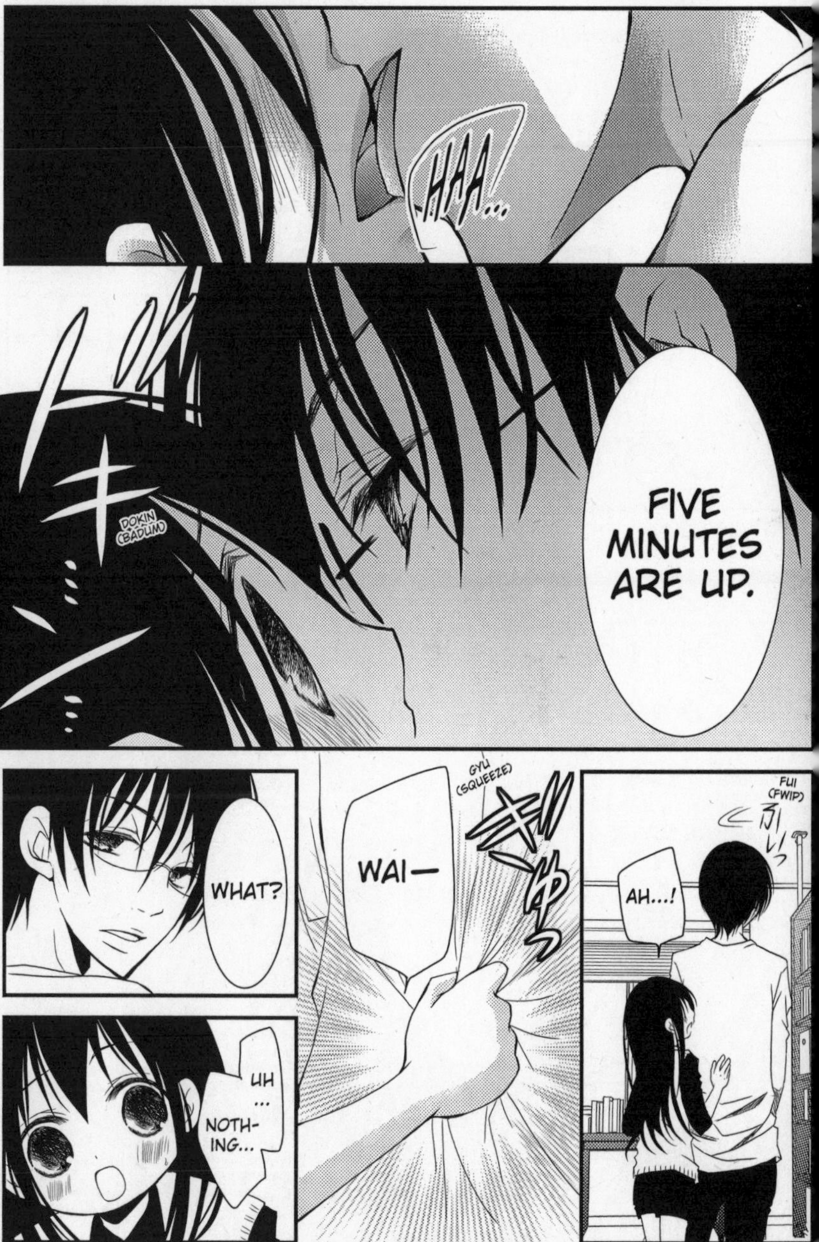
HAA...
FIVE MINUTES ARE UP.
DOKIN (BADUM)
FUI (FWIP)
AH...!
GYU (SQUEEZE)
WAI—
WHAT?
UH ... NOTHING...

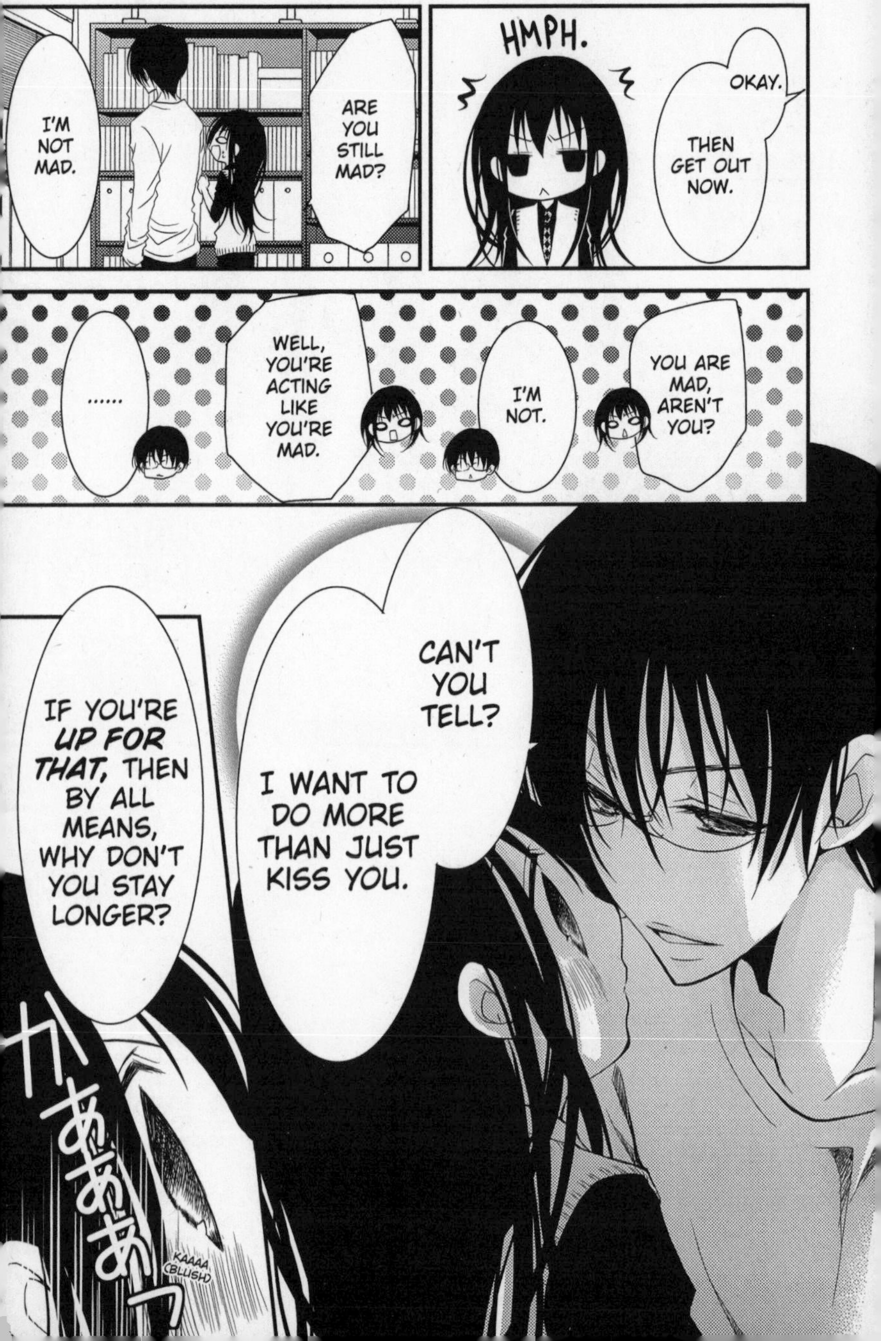
HMPH.
OKAY.
THEN GET OUT NOW.
ARE YOU STILL MAD?
I'M NOT MAD.
YOU ARE MAD, AREN'T YOU?
I'M NOT.
WELL, YOU'RE ACTING LIKE YOU'RE MAD.
......
CAN'T YOU TELL?
I WANT TO DO MORE THAN JUST KISS YOU.
IF YOU'RE *UP FOR THAT,* THEN BY ALL MEANS, WHY DON'T YOU STAY LONGER?
かあああっ
KAAAA (BLUSH)

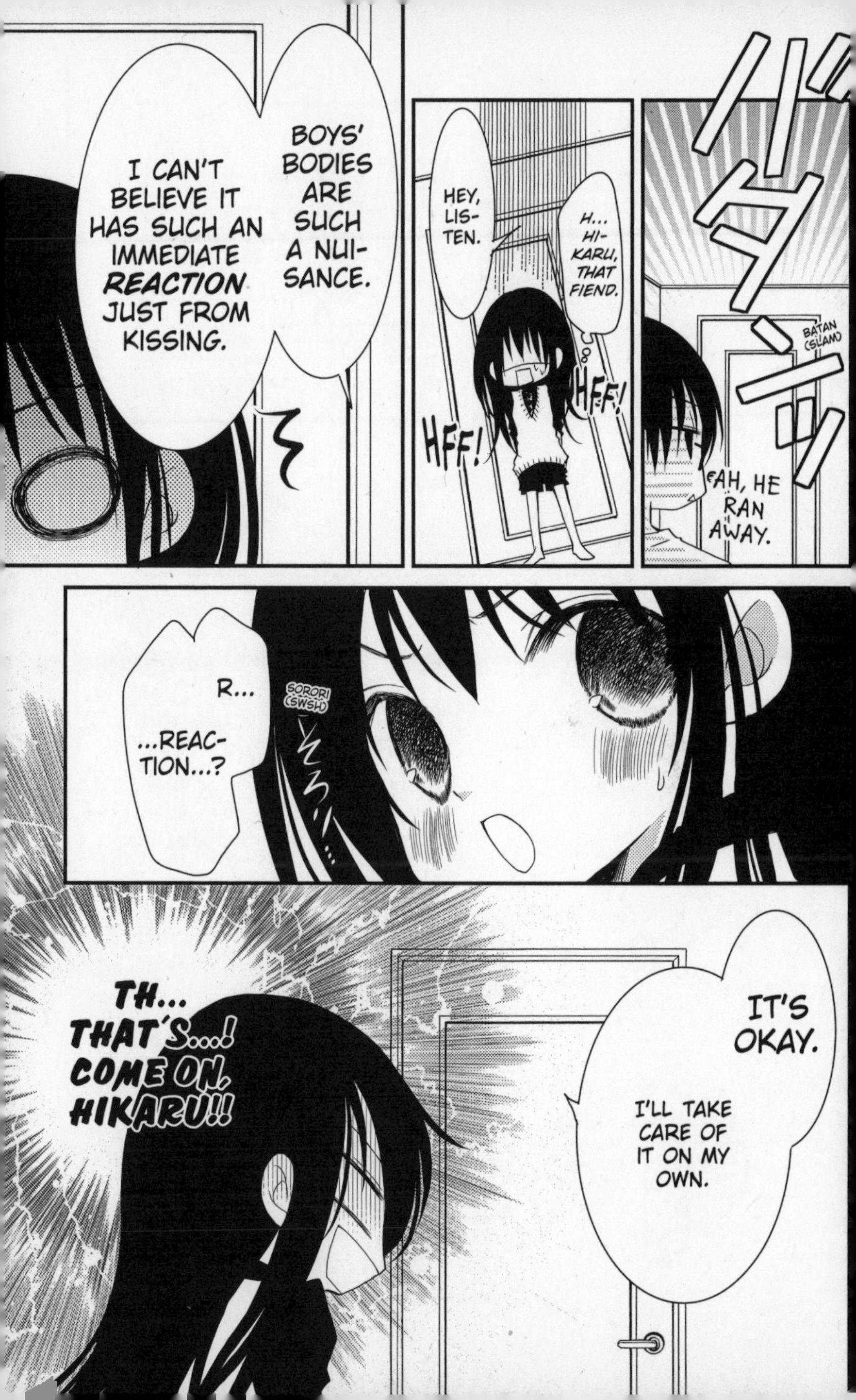
BATAN (SLAM)
AH, HE RAN AWAY.
H... HI-KARU, THAT FIEND.
HFF!
HFF!
HEY, LIS-TEN.
BOYS' BODIES ARE SUCH A NUI-SANCE.
I CAN'T BELIEVE IT HAS SUCH AN IMMEDIATE *REACTION* JUST FROM KISSING.
SORORI (SWSH)
R...
...REAC-TION...?
IT'S OKAY.
I'LL TAKE CARE OF IT ON MY OWN.
TH... THAT'S...! COME ON, HIKARU!!

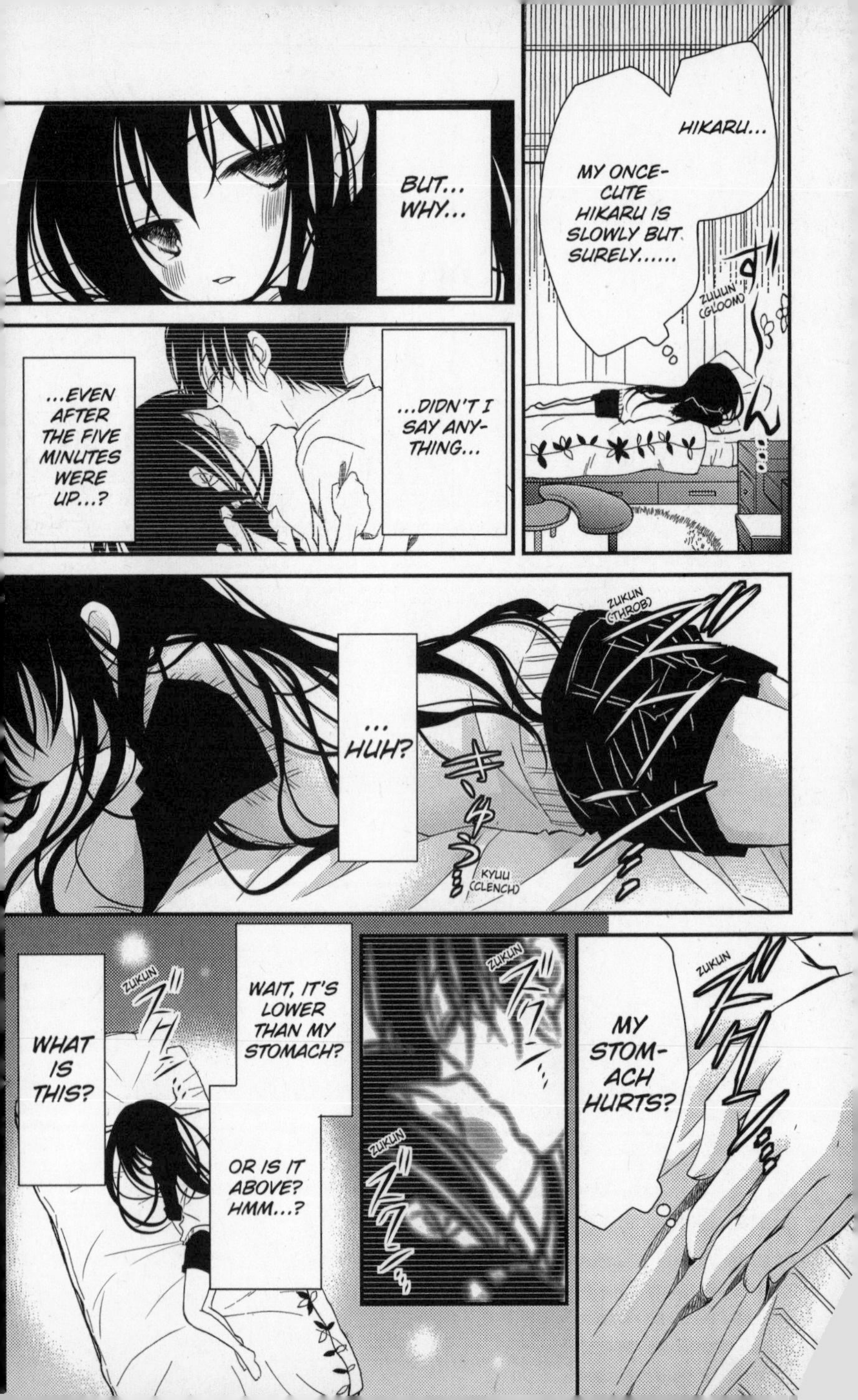

HIKARU...
MY ONCE-CUTE HIKARU IS SLOWLY BUT SURELY......
ZUUUN (GLOOM)
BUT... WHY...
...DIDN'T I SAY ANYTHING...
...EVEN AFTER THE FIVE MINUTES WERE UP...?
ZUKUN (THROB)
... HUH?
KYUU (CLENCH)
ZUKUN
MY STOMACH HURTS?
ZUKUN
ZUKUN
WAIT, IT'S LOWER THAN MY STOMACH?
ZUKUN
WHAT IS THIS?
OR IS IT ABOVE? HMM...?

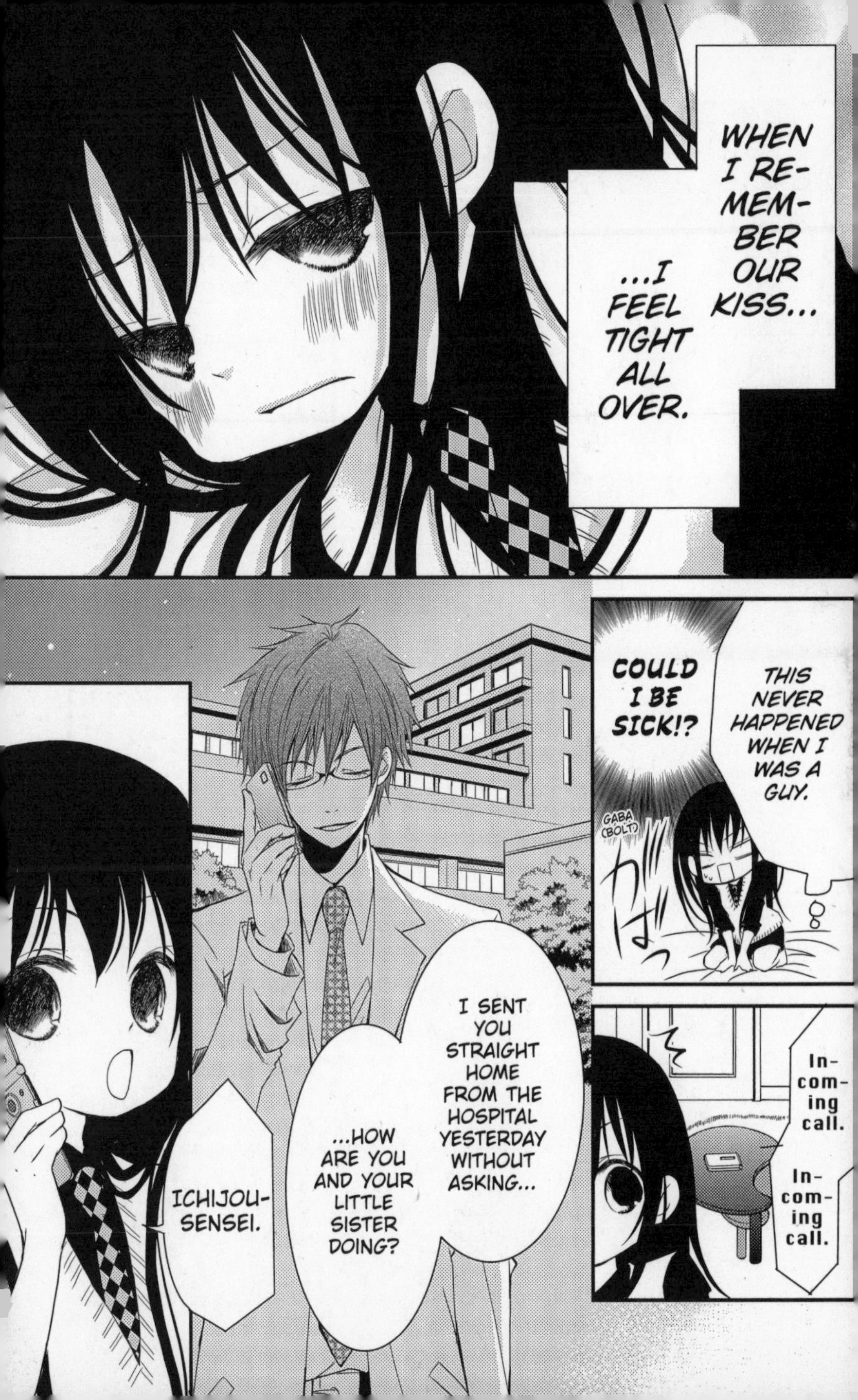
WHEN I RE-MEM-BER OUR KISS...
...I FEEL TIGHT ALL OVER.
THIS NEVER HAPPENED WHEN I WAS A GUY.
COULD I BE SICK!?
GABA (BOLT)
In-com-ing call.
In-com-ing call.
I SENT YOU STRAIGHT HOME FROM THE HOSPITAL YESTERDAY WITHOUT ASKING...
...HOW ARE YOU AND YOUR LITTLE SISTER DOING?
ICHIJOU-SENSEI.

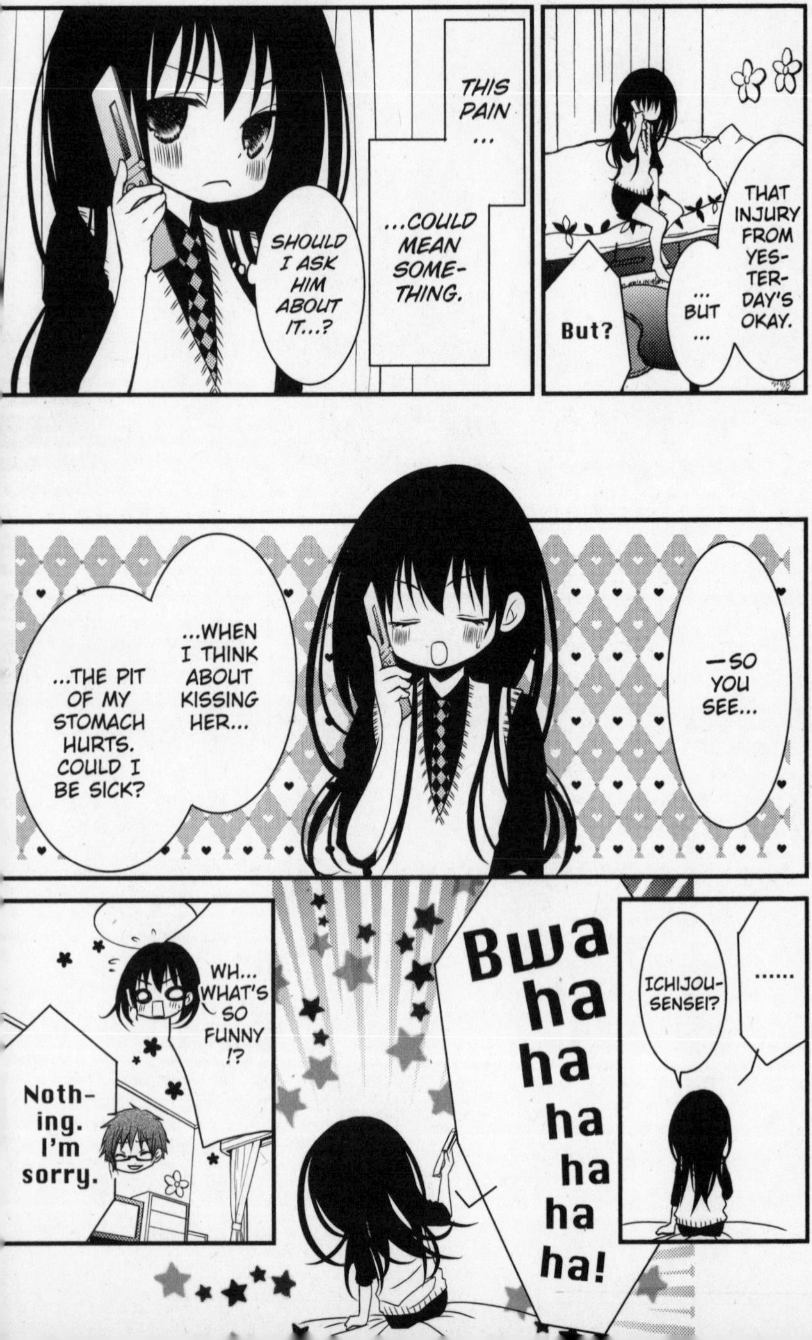
THAT INJURY FROM YESTERDAY'S OKAY.
... BUT ...
But?
THIS PAIN ...
...COULD MEAN SOMETHING.
SHOULD I ASK HIM ABOUT IT...?
—SO YOU SEE...
...WHEN I THINK ABOUT KISSING HER...
...THE PIT OF MY STOMACH HURTS. COULD I BE SICK?
......
ICHIJOU-SENSEI?
Bwa ha ha ha ha ha ha ha!
WH... WHAT'S SO FUNNY!?
Nothing. I'm sorry.

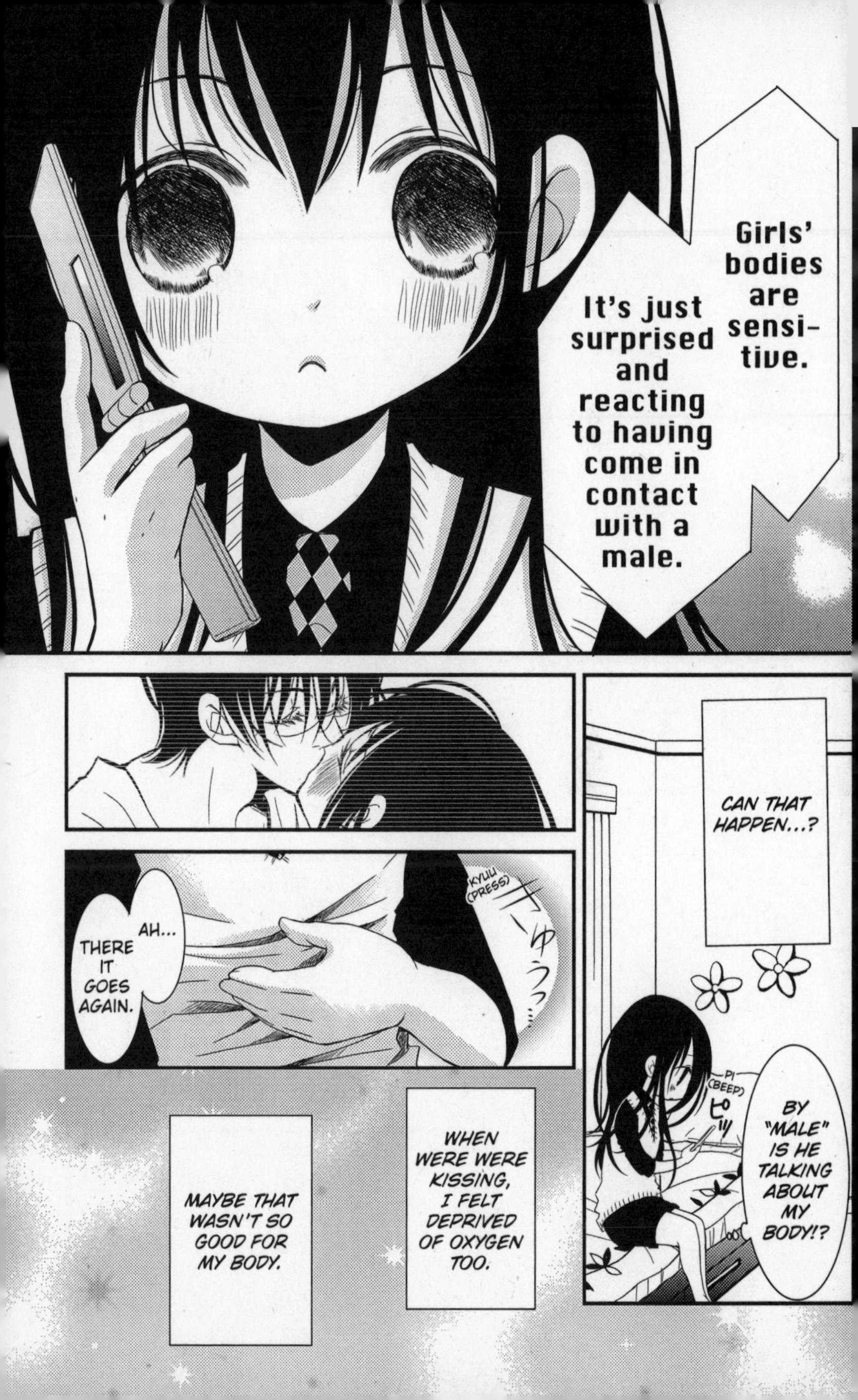
Girls' bodies are sensi-tive.
It's just surprised and reacting to having come in contact with a male.
CAN THAT HAPPEN...?
PI (BEEP)
BY "MALE" IS HE TALKING ABOUT MY BODY!?
KYUU (PRESS)
AH... THERE IT GOES AGAIN.
WHEN WERE WERE KISSING, I FELT DEPRIVED OF OXYGEN TOO.
MAYBE THAT WASN'T SO GOOD FOR MY BODY.

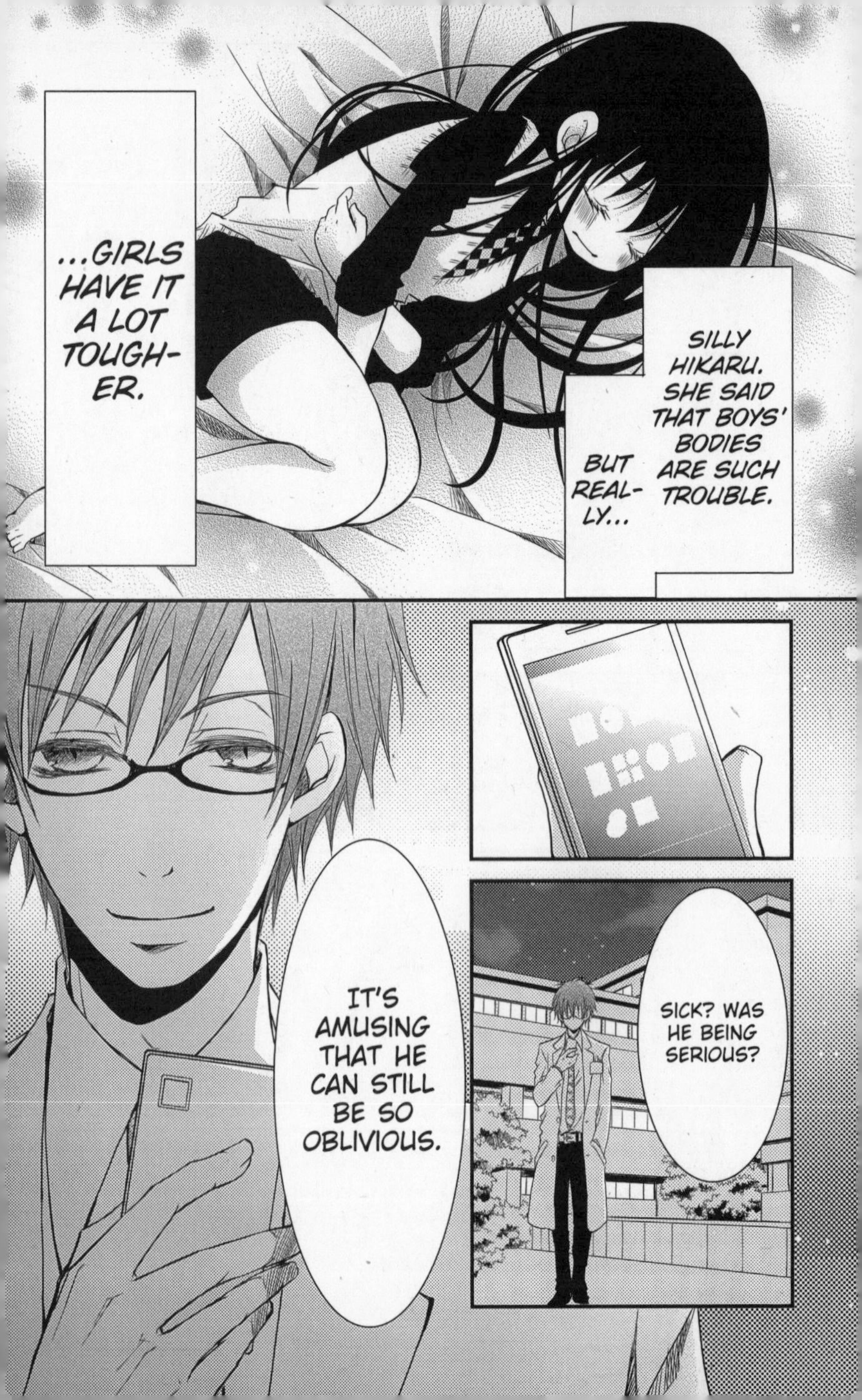
SILLY HIKARU. SHE SAID THAT BOYS' BODIES ARE SUCH TROUBLE.
BUT REALLY...
...GIRLS HAVE IT A LOT TOUGHER.
SICK? WAS HE BEING SERIOUS?
IT'S AMUSING THAT HE CAN STILL BE SO OBLIVIOUS.

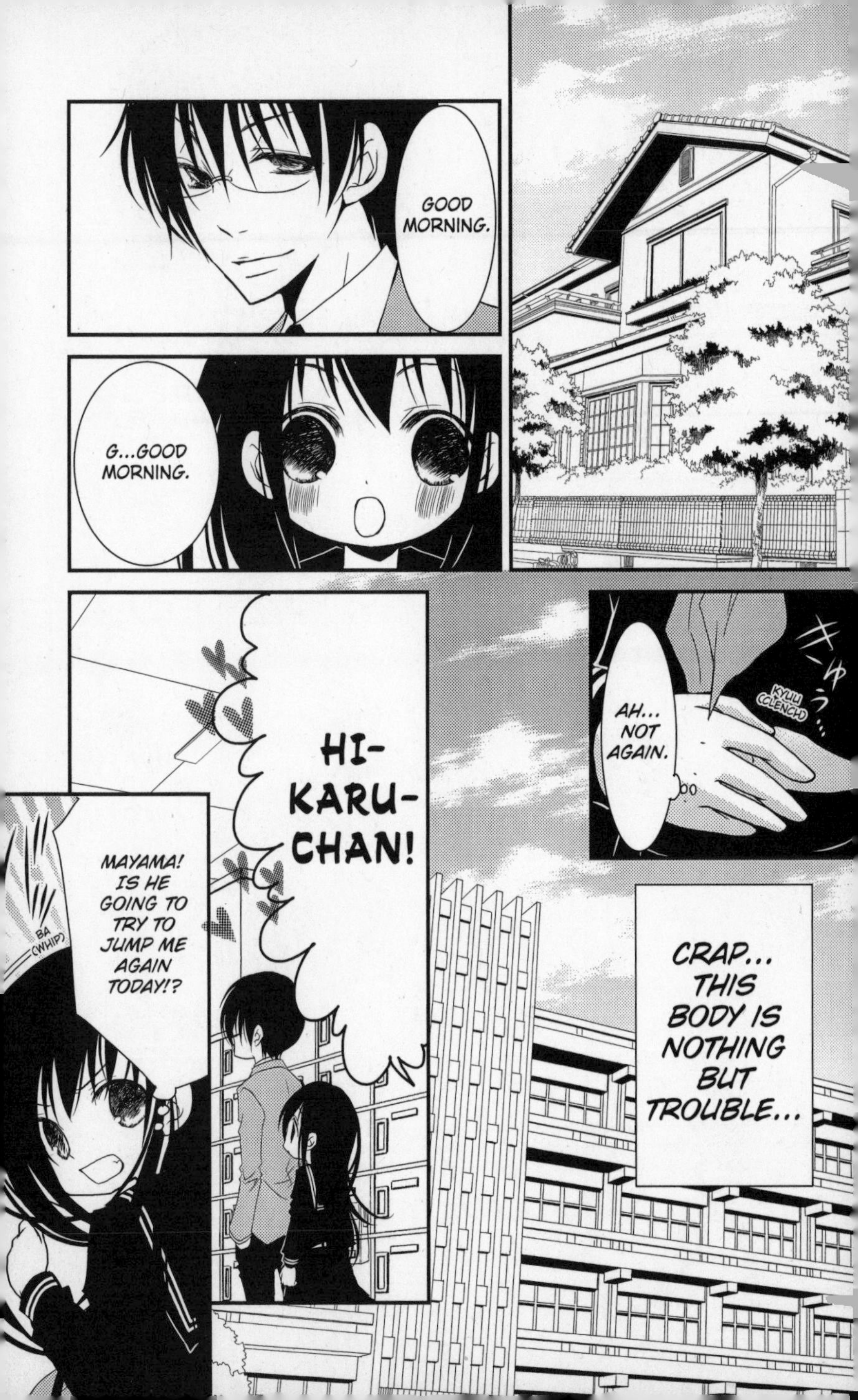
GOOD MORNING.
G...GOOD MORNING.
AH... NOT AGAIN.
きゅう...
KYUU (CLENCH)
CRAP... THIS BODY IS NOTHING BUT TROUBLE...
HI-KARU-CHAN!
MAYAMA! IS HE GOING TO TRY TO JUMP ME AGAIN TODAY!?
BA (WHIP)

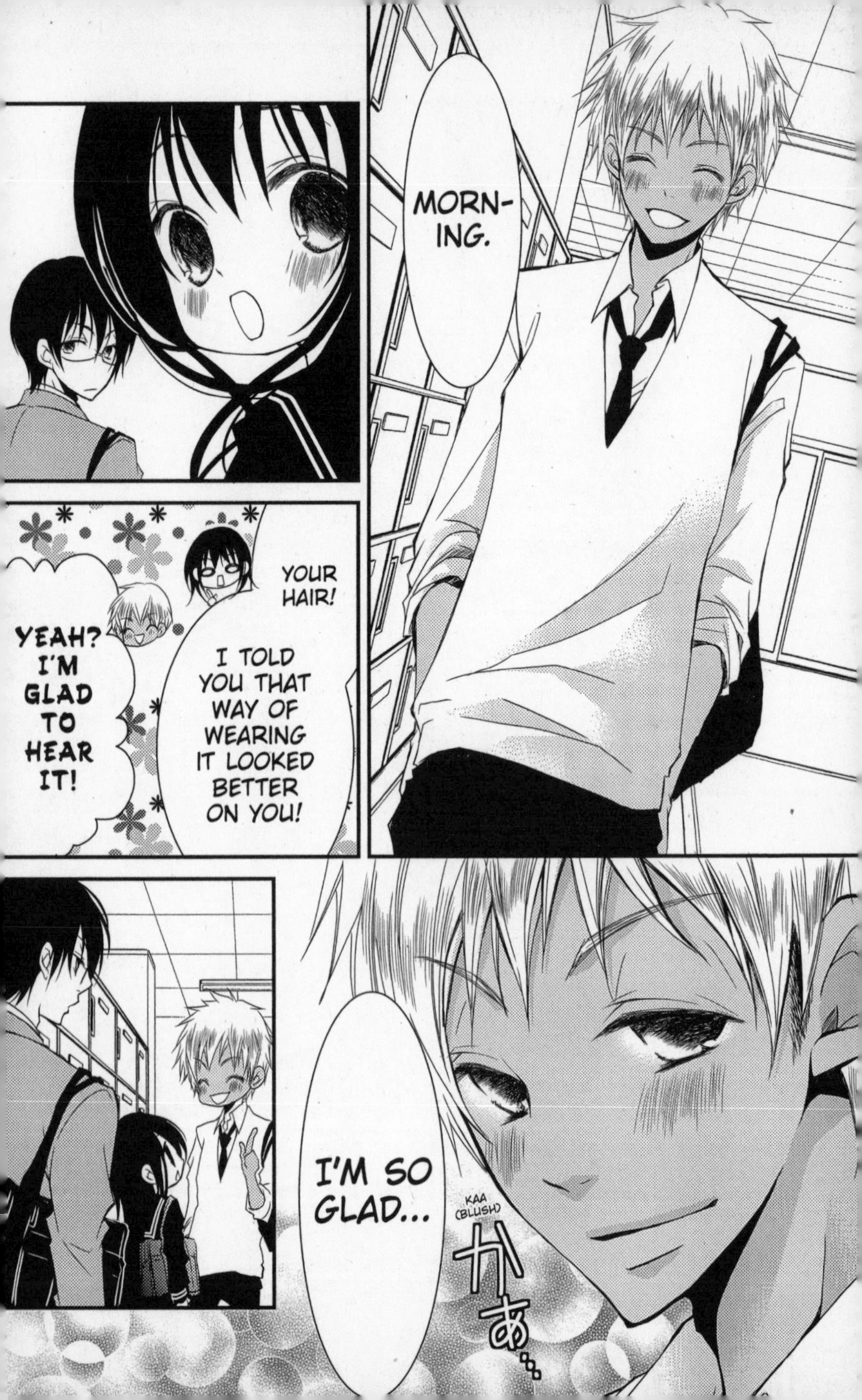
MORN-ING.
YOUR HAIR!
I TOLD YOU THAT WAY OF WEARING IT LOOKED BETTER ON YOU!
YEAH? I'M GLAD TO HEAR IT!
I'M SO GLAD...
KAA (BLUSH)
かぁ

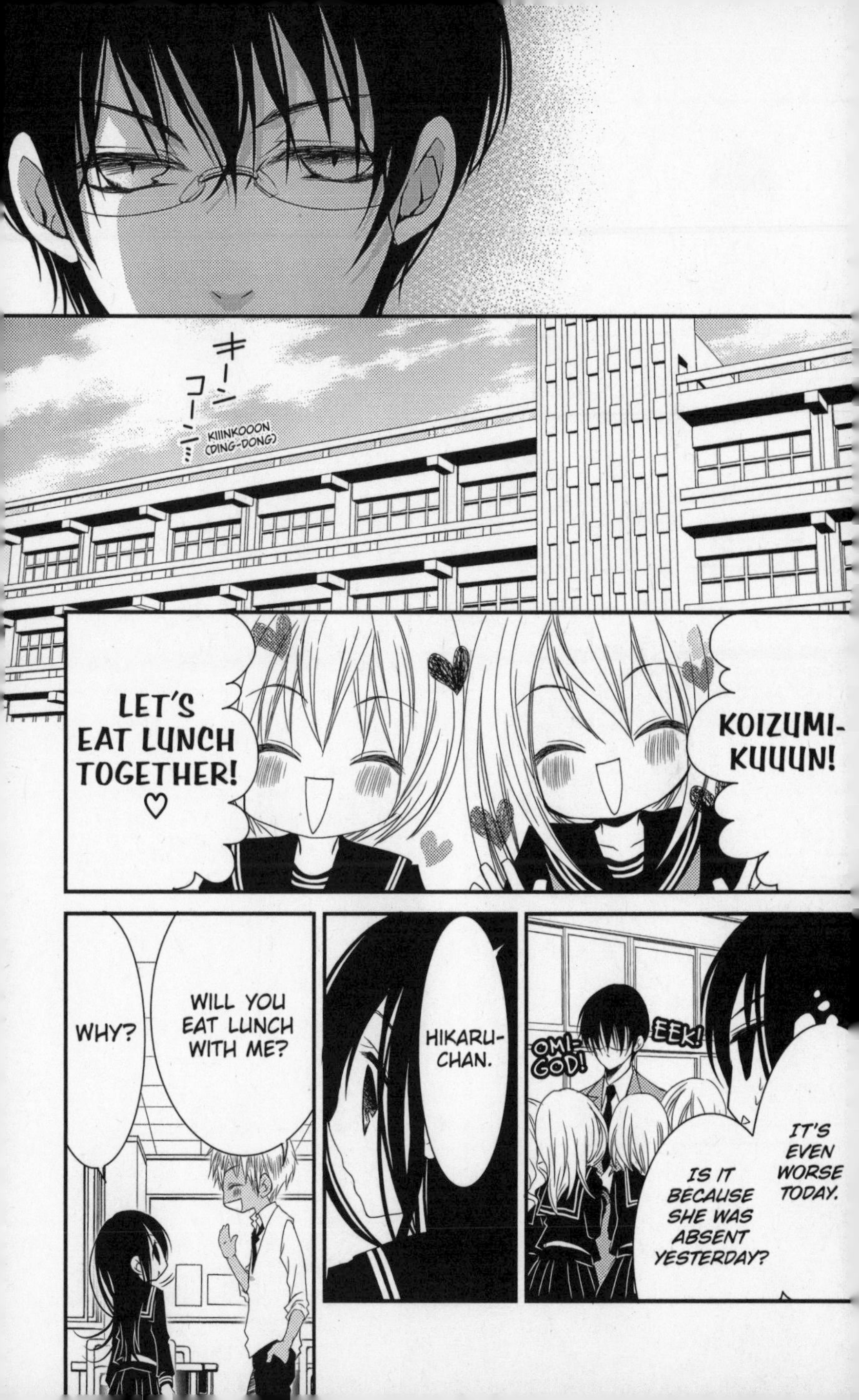

キーンコーン…
KIIINKOOON (DING-DONG)
KOIZUMI-KUUUN!
LET'S EAT LUNCH TOGETHER! ♡
EEK!
OMI-GOD!
IT'S EVEN WORSE TODAY.
IS IT BECAUSE SHE WAS ABSENT YESTERDAY?
HIKARU-CHAN.
WILL YOU EAT LUNCH WITH ME?
WHY?

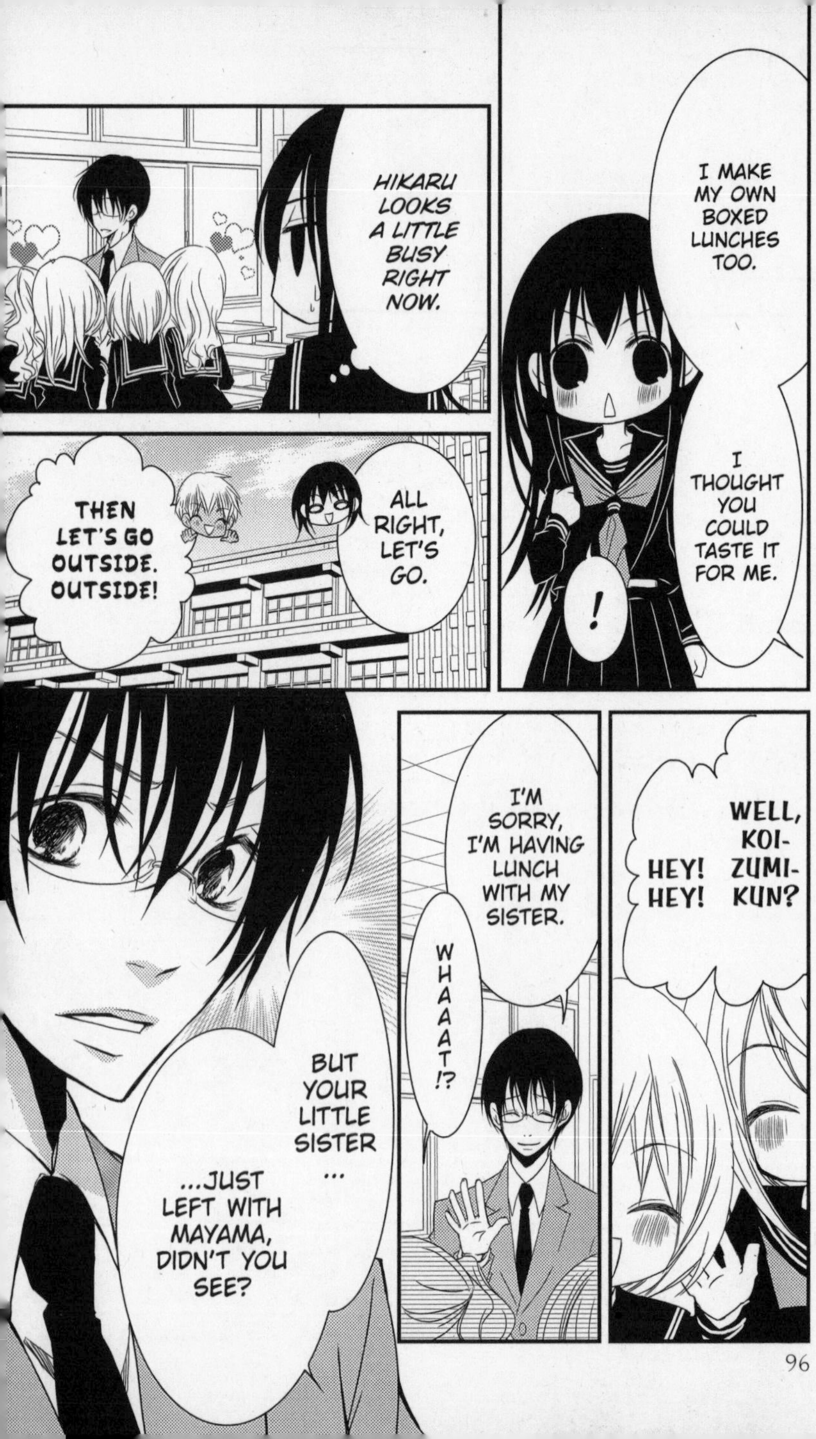
I MAKE MY OWN BOXED LUNCHES TOO.
I THOUGHT YOU COULD TASTE IT FOR ME.
!
HIKARU LOOKS A LITTLE BUSY RIGHT NOW.
ALL RIGHT, LET'S GO.
THEN LET'S GO OUTSIDE. OUTSIDE!
WELL, KOI-ZUMI-KUN?
HEY! HEY!
I'M SORRY, I'M HAVING LUNCH WITH MY SISTER.
WHAAAAT!?
BUT YOUR LITTLE SISTER...
...JUST LEFT WITH MAYAMA, DIDN'T YOU SEE?

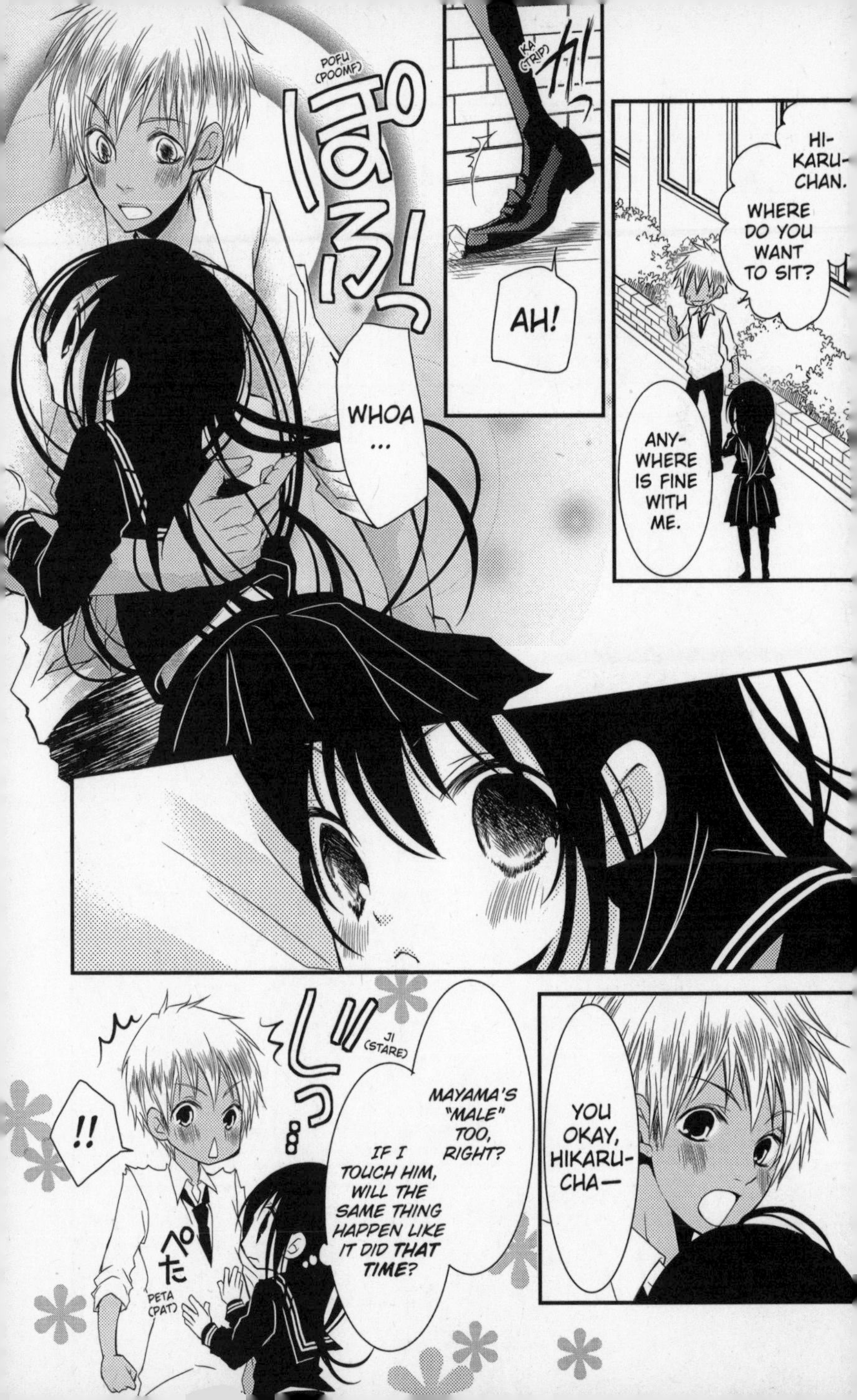
HI-KARU-CHAN. WHERE DO YOU WANT TO SIT?
ANY-WHERE IS FINE WITH ME.
KA (STRIP)
カ!
AH!
POFU (POOMF)
ぽふっ
WHOA ...
YOU OKAY, HIKARU CHA—
JI (STARE)
じーっ
MAYAMA'S "MALE" TOO, RIGHT?
IF I TOUCH HIM, WILL THE SAME THING HAPPEN LIKE IT DID THAT TIME?
!!
ぺた
PETA (PAT)

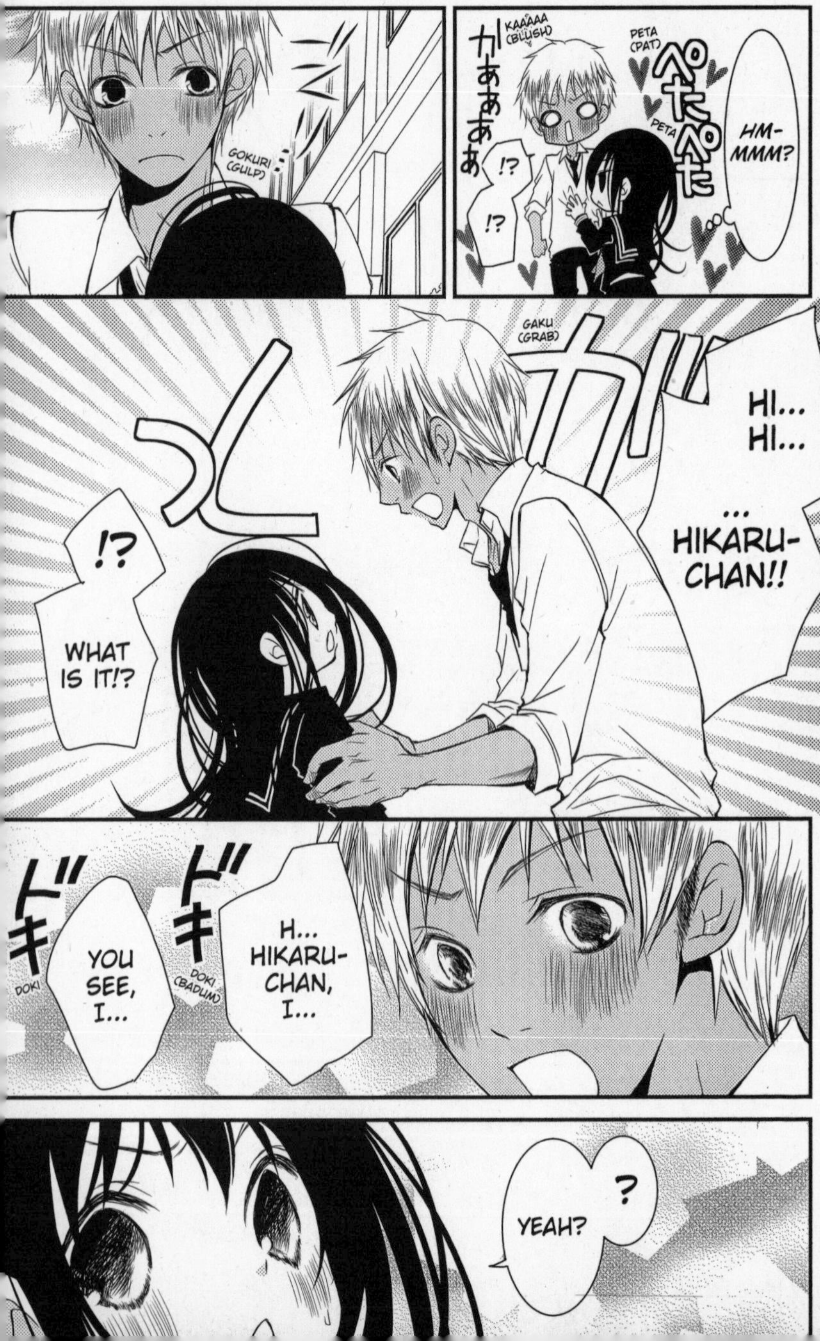
HM-MMM?
PETA (PAT)
ぺたぺた
PETA
KAAAAA (BLUSH)
かあああ
!?
!?
GOKURI (GULP)
HI... HI...
... HIKARU-CHAN!!
GAKU (GRAB)
!?
WHAT IS IT!?
H... HIKARU-CHAN, I...
ドキ
DOKI (BADUM)
YOU SEE, I...
ドキ
DOKI
?
YEAH?

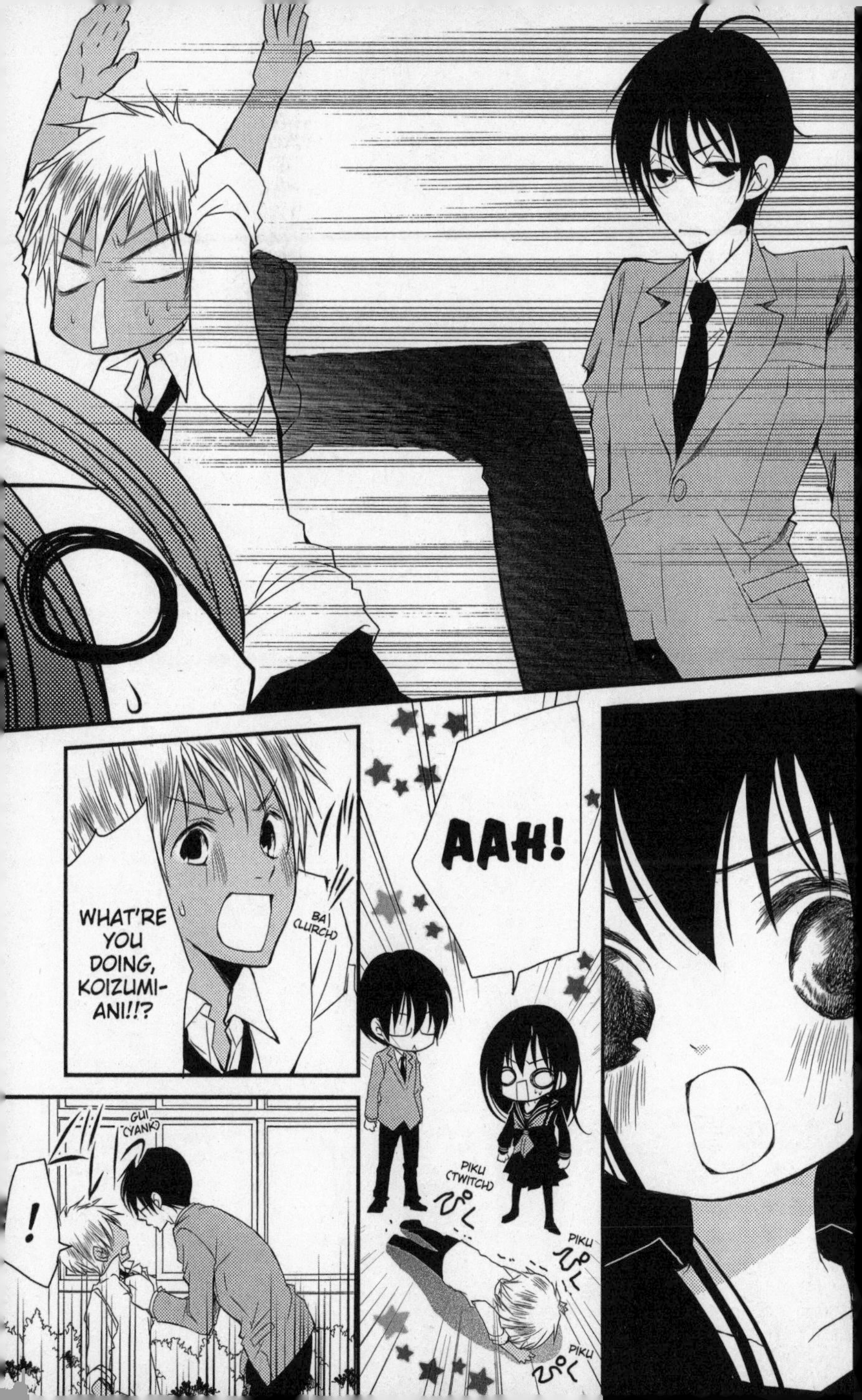

AAH!
PIKU (TWITCH)
ぴく
PIKU
ぴく
PIKU
ぴく
WHAT'RE YOU DOING, KOIZUMI-ANI!!?
BA (LURCH)
GUI (YANK)
!

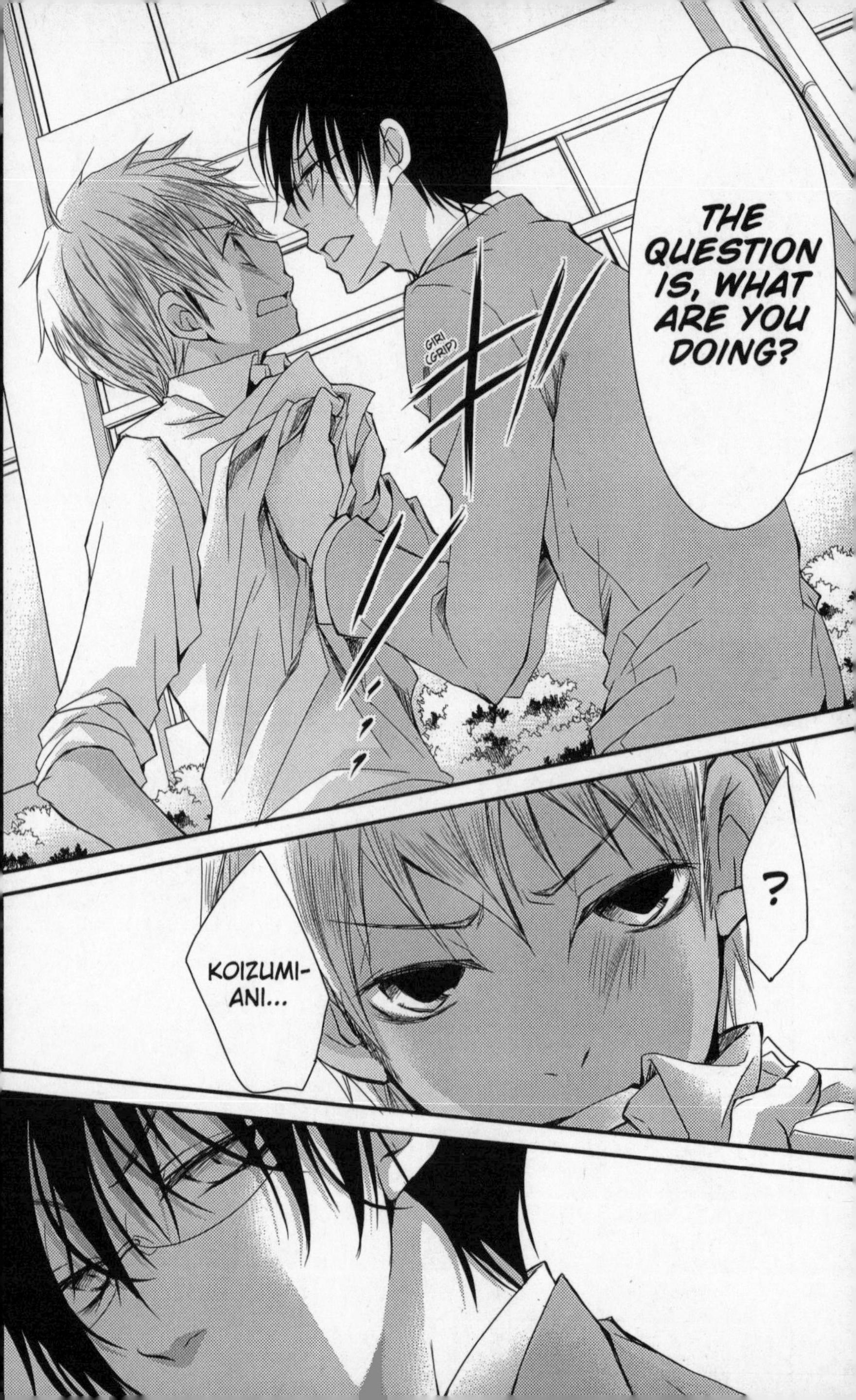
THE QUESTION IS, WHAT ARE YOU DOING?
GIRI (GRIP)
?
KOIZUMI-ANI...

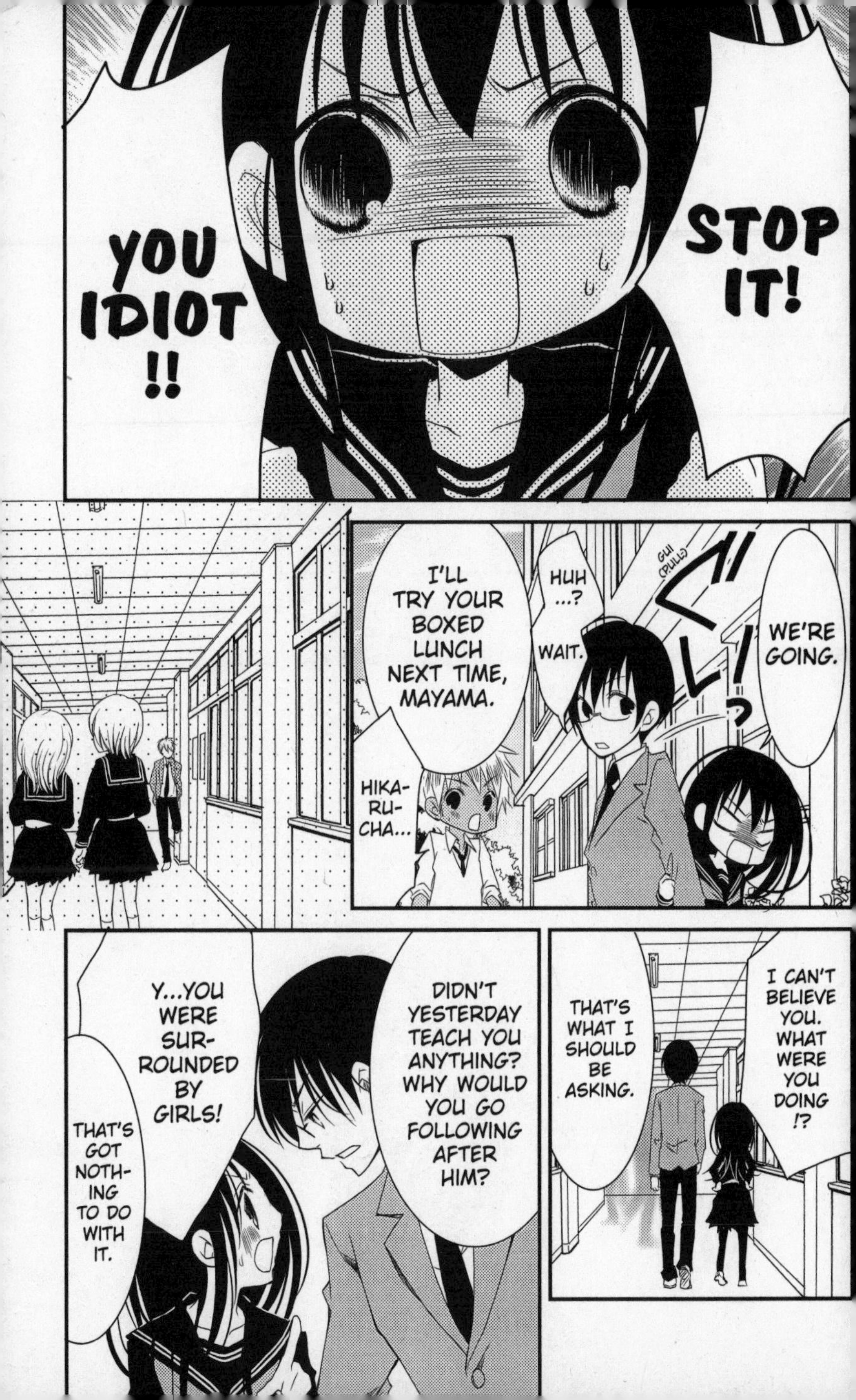
STOP IT!
YOU IDIOT!!
WE'RE GOING.
GUI (PULL)
HUH ...?
WAIT.
I'LL TRY YOUR BOXED LUNCH NEXT TIME, MAYAMA.
HIKA-RU-CHA...
I CAN'T BELIEVE YOU. WHAT WERE YOU DOING!?
THAT'S WHAT I SHOULD BE ASKING.
DIDN'T YESTERDAY TEACH YOU ANYTHING? WHY WOULD YOU GO FOLLOWING AFTER HIM?
Y...YOU WERE SUR-ROUNDED BY GIRLS!
THAT'S GOT NOTH-ING TO DO WITH IT.

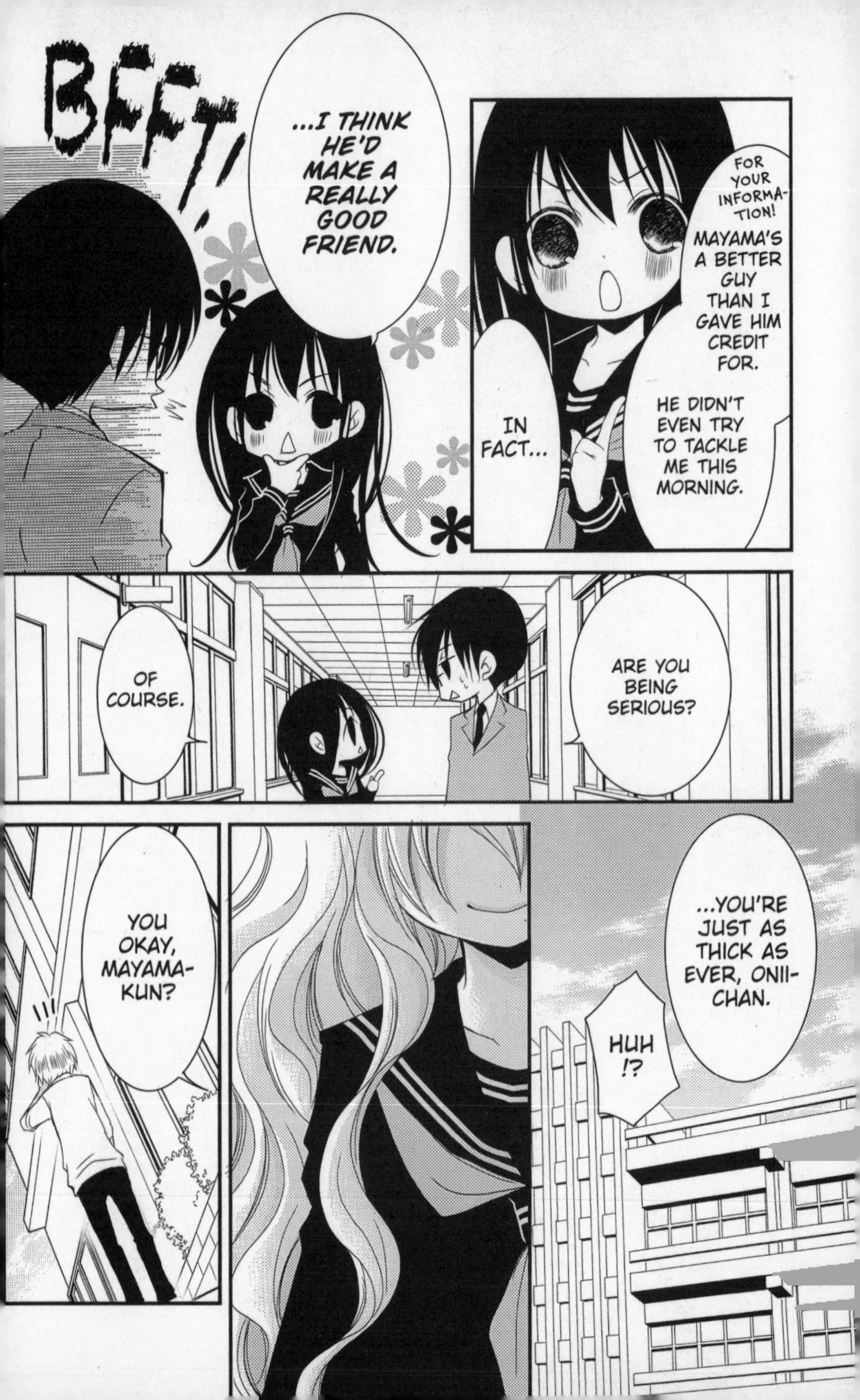
FOR YOUR INFORMATION! MAYAMA'S A BETTER GUY THAN I GAVE HIM CREDIT FOR.
HE DIDN'T EVEN TRY TO TACKLE ME THIS MORNING.
IN FACT...
...I THINK HE'D MAKE A REALLY GOOD FRIEND.
BFFT!!
ARE YOU BEING SERIOUS?
OF COURSE.
...YOU'RE JUST AS THICK AS EVER, ONII-CHAN.
HUH!?
YOU OKAY, MAYAMA-KUN?

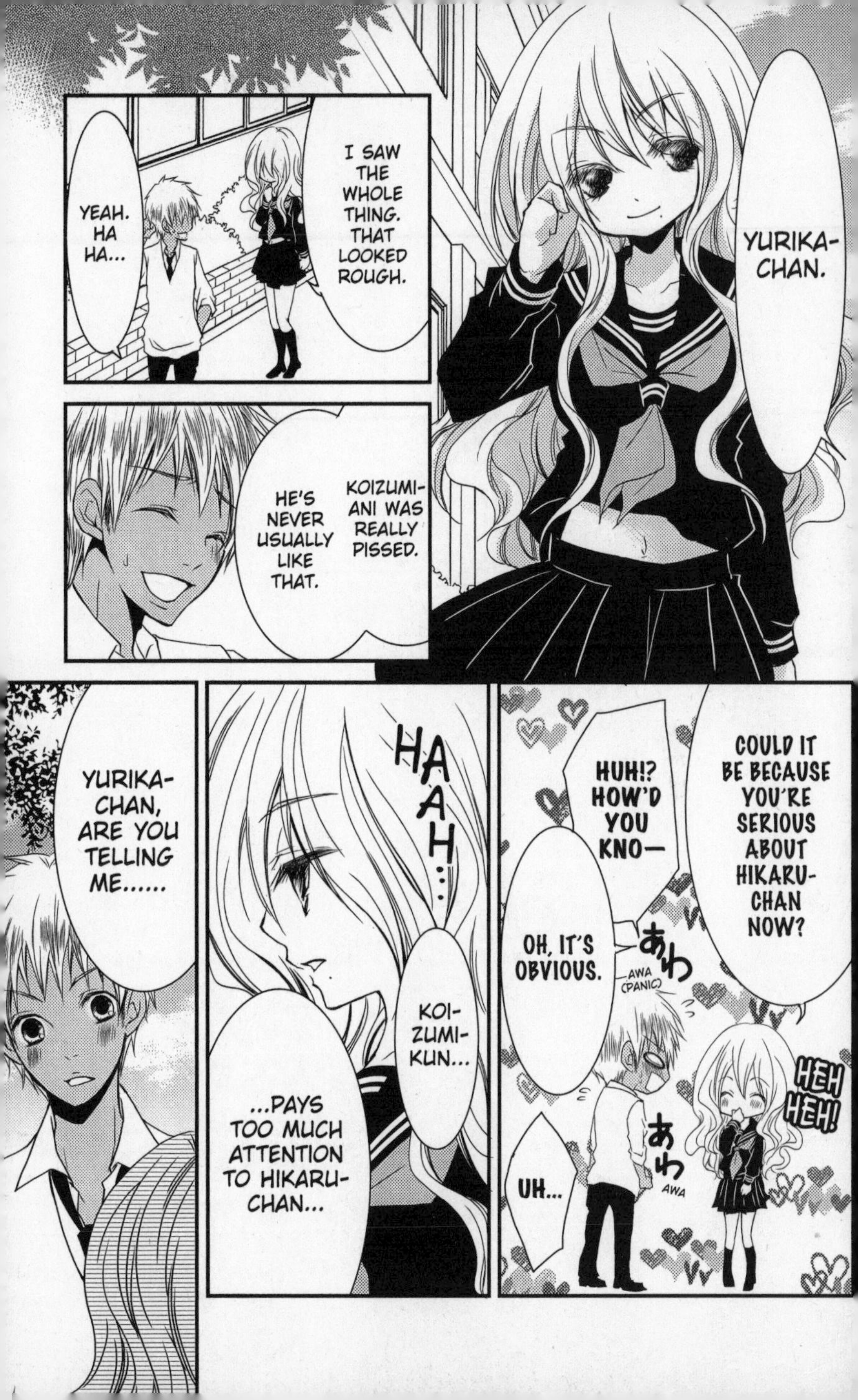
YURIKA-CHAN.
I SAW THE WHOLE THING. THAT LOOKED ROUGH.
YEAH. HA HA...
KOIZUMI-ANI WAS REALLY PISSED.
HE'S NEVER USUALLY LIKE THAT.
COULD IT BE BECAUSE YOU'RE SERIOUS ABOUT HIKARU-CHAN NOW?
HUH!? HOW'D YOU KNO—
あわ
AWA (PANIC)
OH, IT'S OBVIOUS.
HEH HEH!
UH...
あわ
AWA
HAAAH...
KOI-ZUMI-KUN...
...PAYS TOO MUCH ATTENTION TO HIKARU-CHAN...
YURIKA-CHAN, ARE YOU TELLING ME......

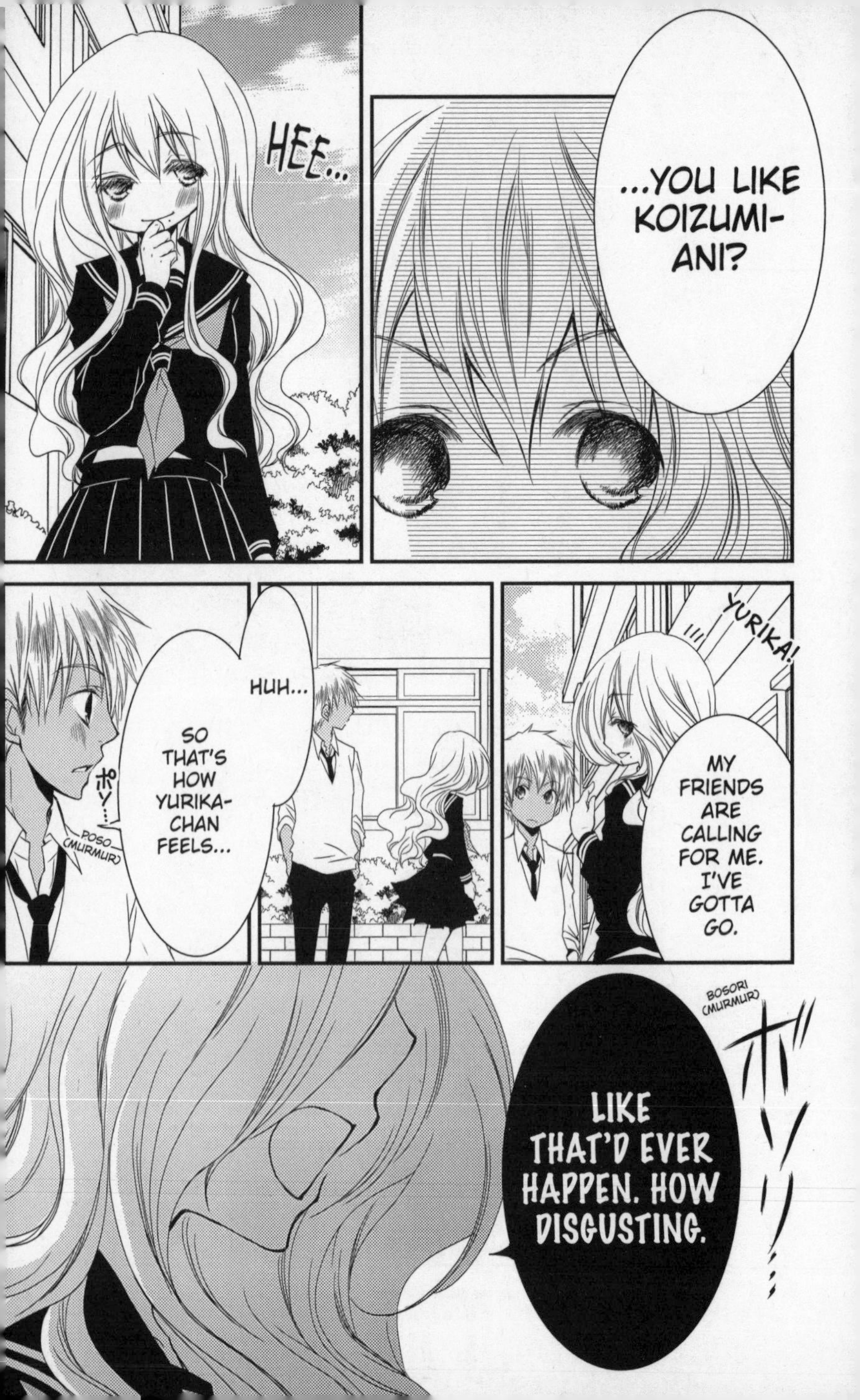
...YOU LIKE KOIZUMI-ANI?
HEE...
YURIKA!
MY FRIENDS ARE CALLING FOR ME. I'VE GOTTA GO.
HUH...
SO THAT'S HOW YURIKA-CHAN FEELS...
ポソ…
POSO (MURMUR)
BOSORI (MURMUR)
LIKE THAT'D EVER HAPPEN. HOW DISGUSTING.

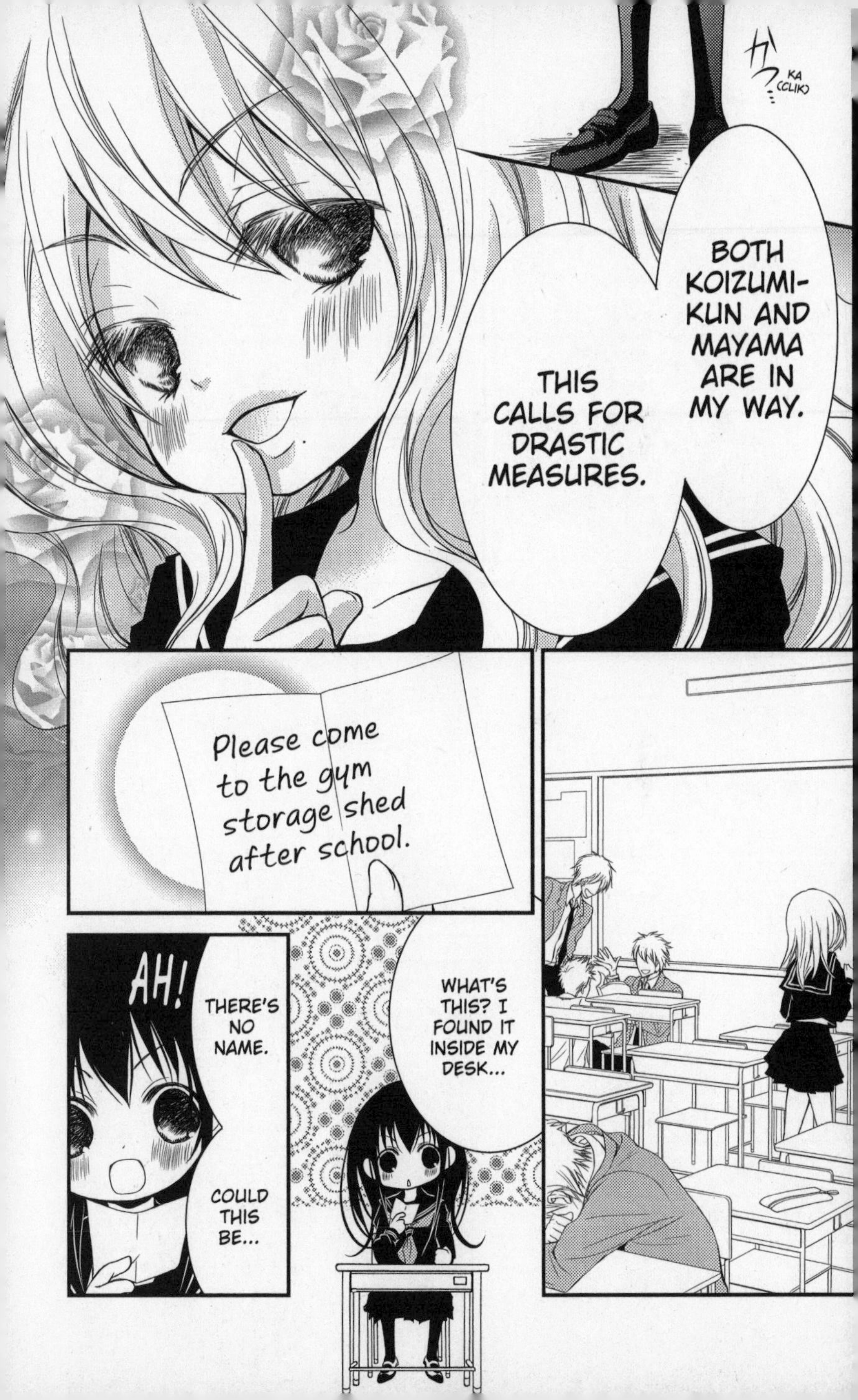

KA (CLIK)
BOTH KOIZUMI-KUN AND MAYAMA ARE IN MY WAY.
THIS CALLS FOR DRASTIC MEASURES.
Please come to the gym storage shed after school.
WHAT'S THIS? I FOUND IT INSIDE MY DESK...
AH!
THERE'S NO NAME.
COULD THIS BE...

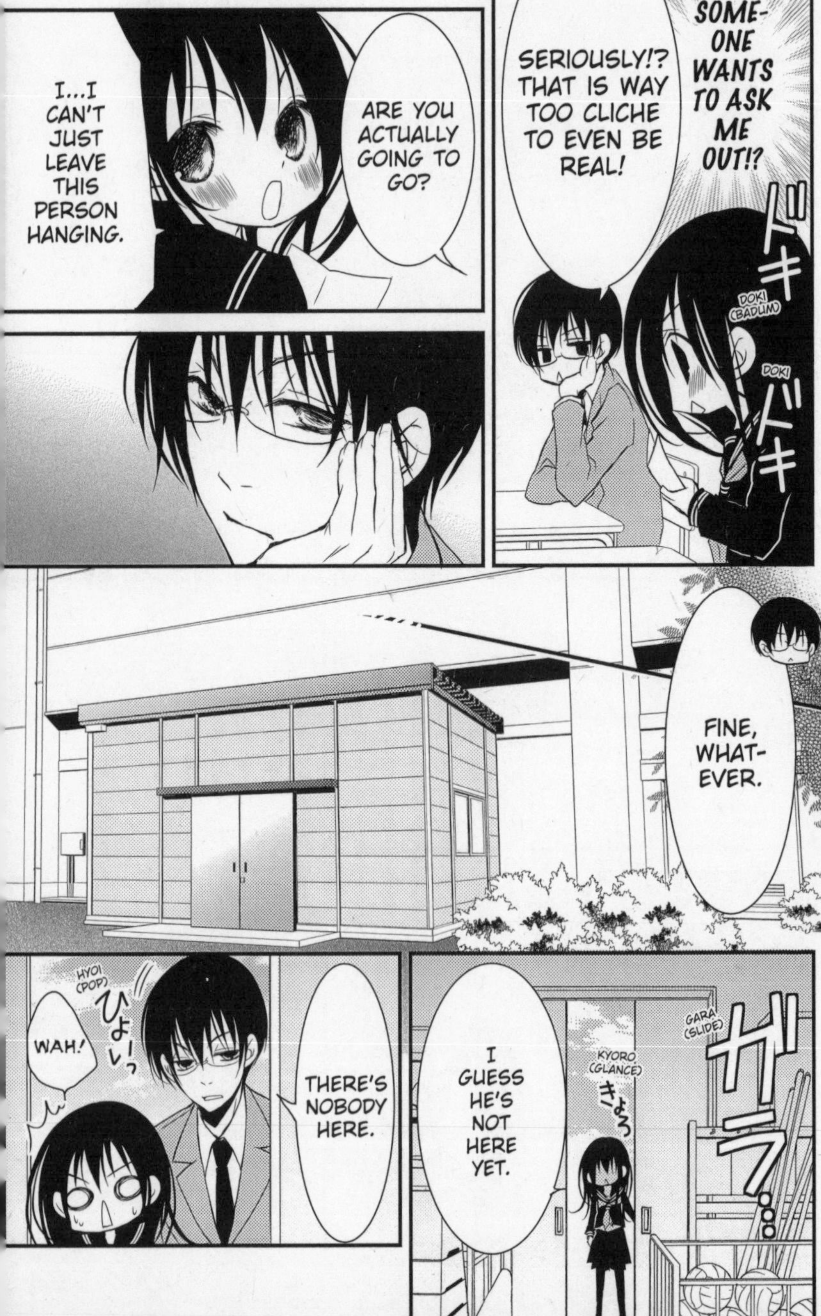
SOME-ONE WANTS TO ASK ME OUT!?
SERIOUSLY!? THAT IS WAY TOO CLICHE TO EVEN BE REAL!
ドキ
DOKI (BADUM)
ドキ
DOKI
ARE YOU ACTUALLY GOING TO GO?
I...I CAN'T JUST LEAVE THIS PERSON HANGING.
FINE, WHAT-EVER.
ガラ
GARA (SLIDE)
きょろ
KYORO (GLANCE)
I GUESS HE'S NOT HERE YET.
THERE'S NOBODY HERE.
ひょいっ
HYOI (POP)
WAH!

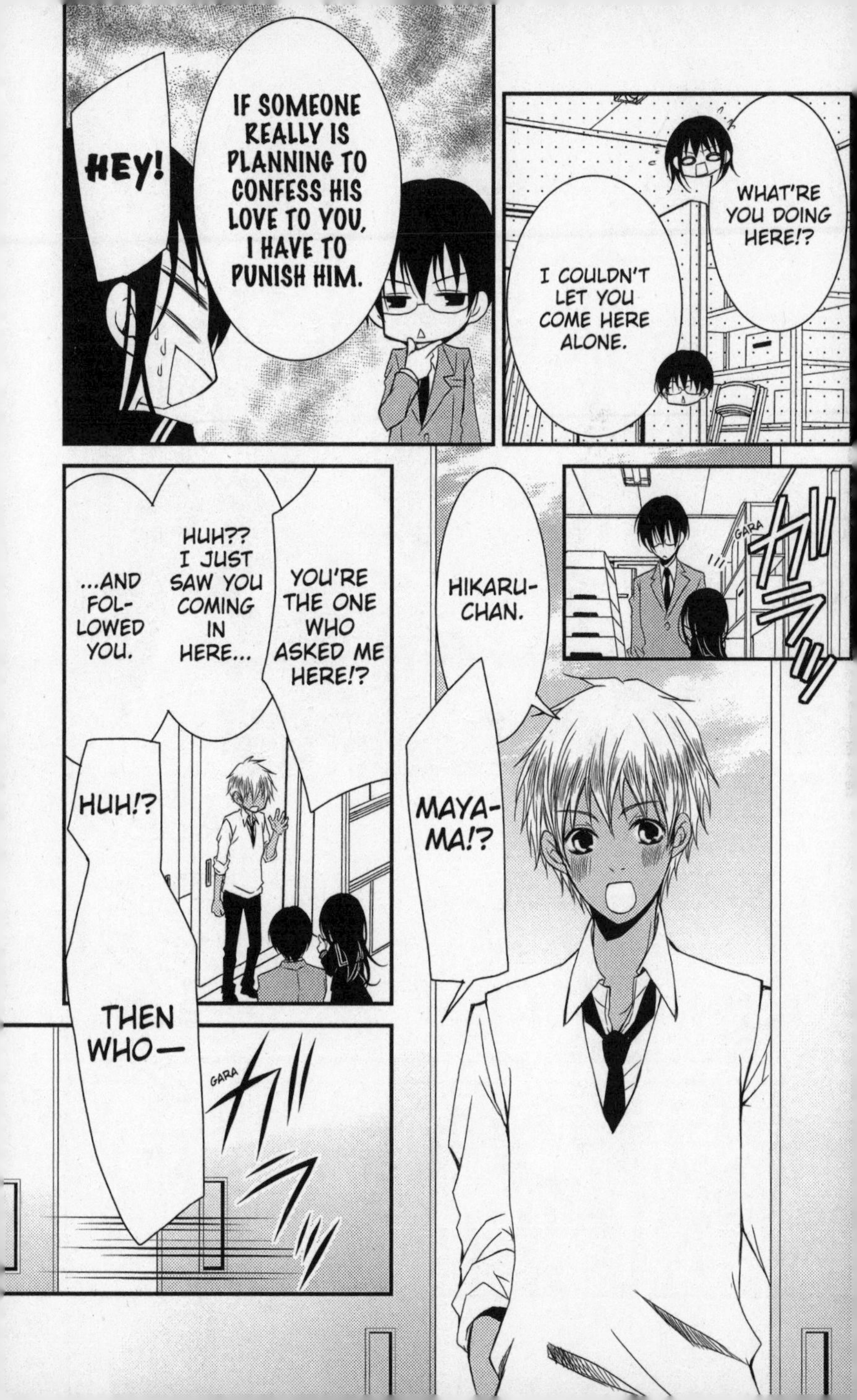
WHAT'RE YOU DOING HERE!?
I COULDN'T LET YOU COME HERE ALONE.
IF SOMEONE REALLY IS PLANNING TO CONFESS HIS LOVE TO YOU, I HAVE TO PUNISH HIM.
HEY!
GARA
HIKARU-CHAN.
MAYA-MA!?
YOU'RE THE ONE WHO ASKED ME HERE!?
HUH?? I JUST SAW YOU COMING IN HERE...
...AND FOL-LOWED YOU.
HUH!?
THEN WHO—
GARA

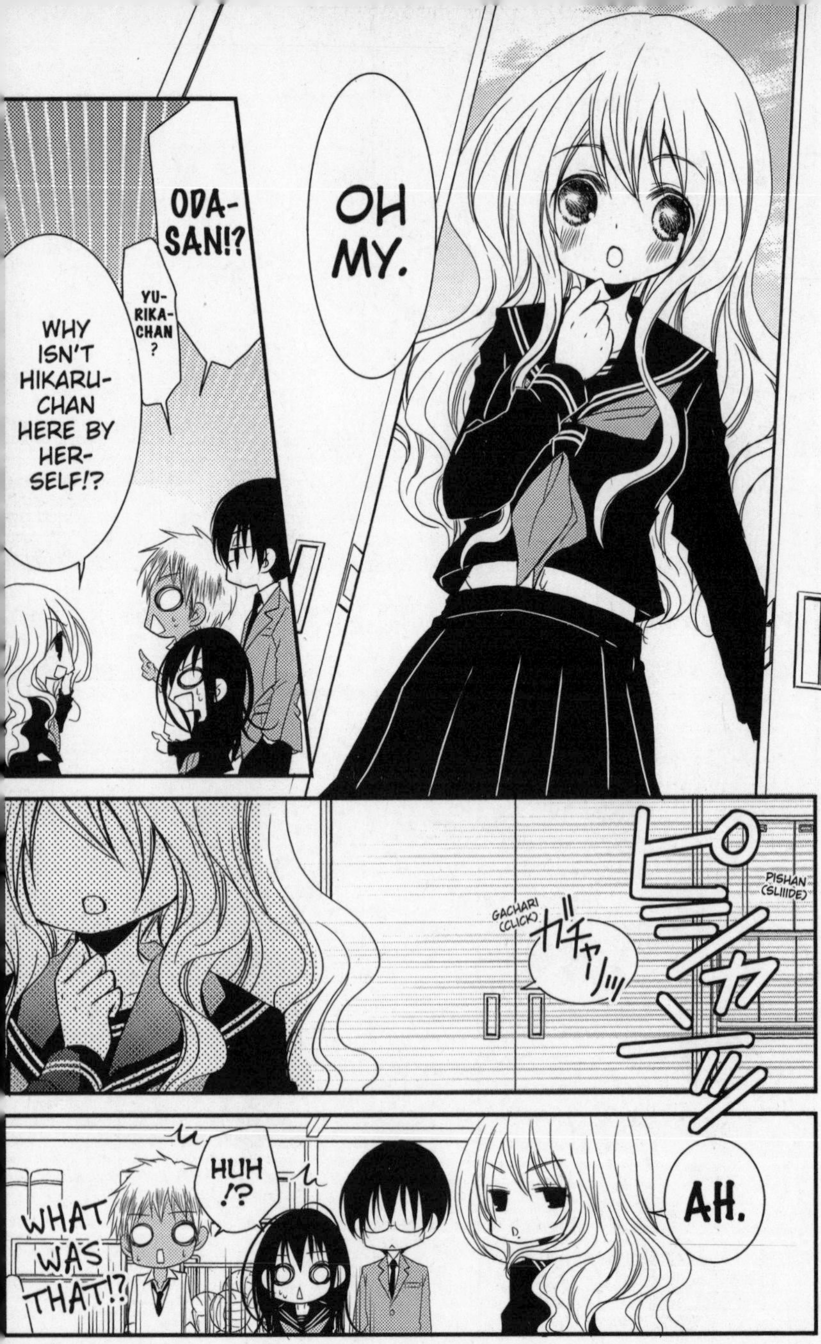
OH MY.
ODA-SAN!?
YU-RIKA-CHAN?
WHY ISN'T HIKARU-CHAN HERE BY HER-SELF!?
ピシャンッ
PISHAN (SLIIIDE)
ガチャリッ
GACHARI (CLICK)
AH.
HUH!?
WHAT WAS THAT!?

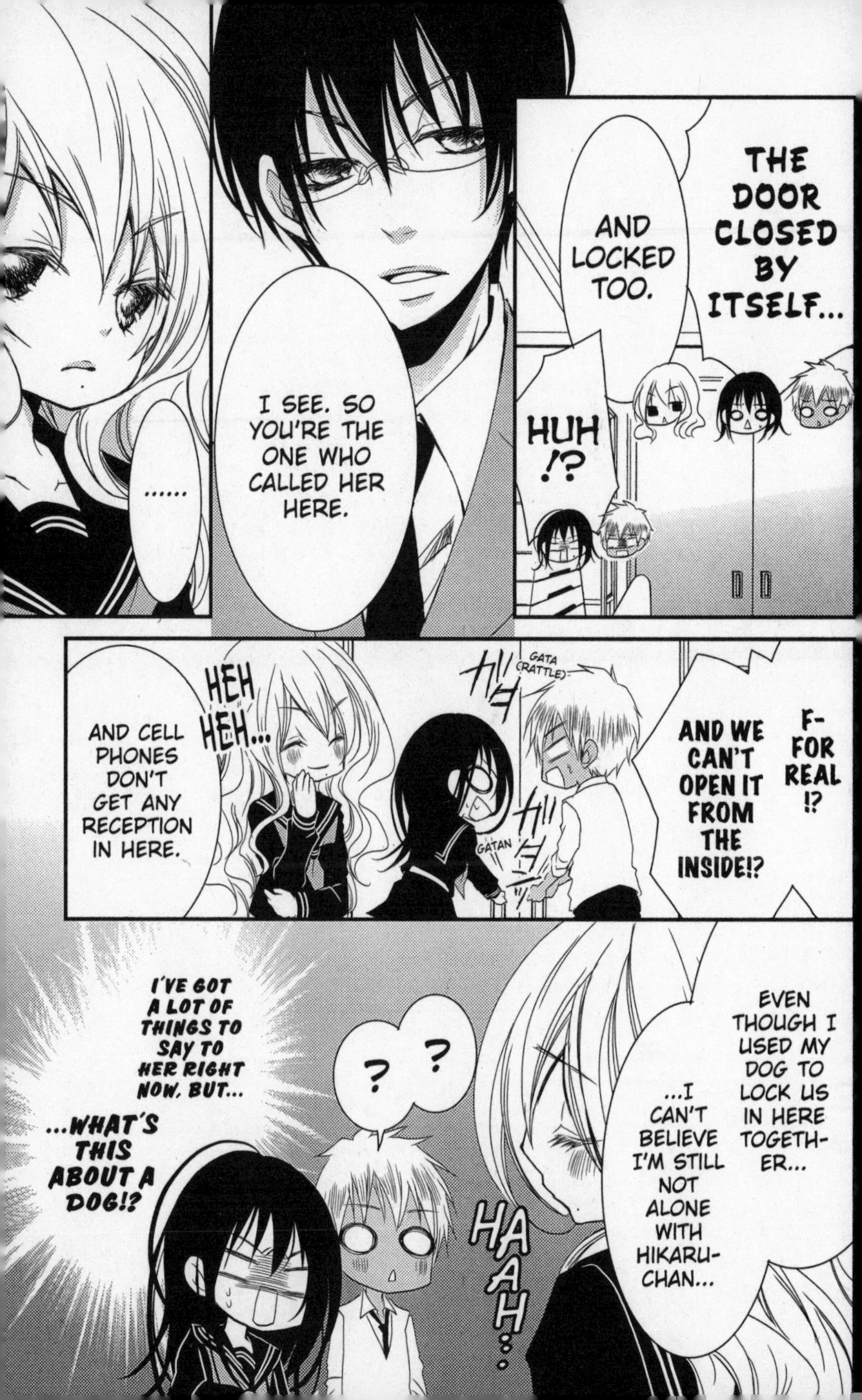
THE DOOR CLOSED BY ITSELF...
AND LOCKED TOO.
HUH!?
I SEE. SO YOU'RE THE ONE WHO CALLED HER HERE.
......
F-FOR REAL!?
AND WE CAN'T OPEN IT FROM THE INSIDE!?
GATA (RATTLE)
GATAN
HEH HEH...
AND CELL PHONES DON'T GET ANY RECEPTION IN HERE.
EVEN THOUGH I USED MY DOG TO LOCK US IN HERE TOGETH-ER...
...I CAN'T BELIEVE I'M STILL NOT ALONE WITH HIKARU-CHAN...
HAAAH...
? ?
I'VE GOT A LOT OF THINGS TO SAY TO HER RIGHT NOW, BUT...
...WHAT'S THIS ABOUT A DOG!?

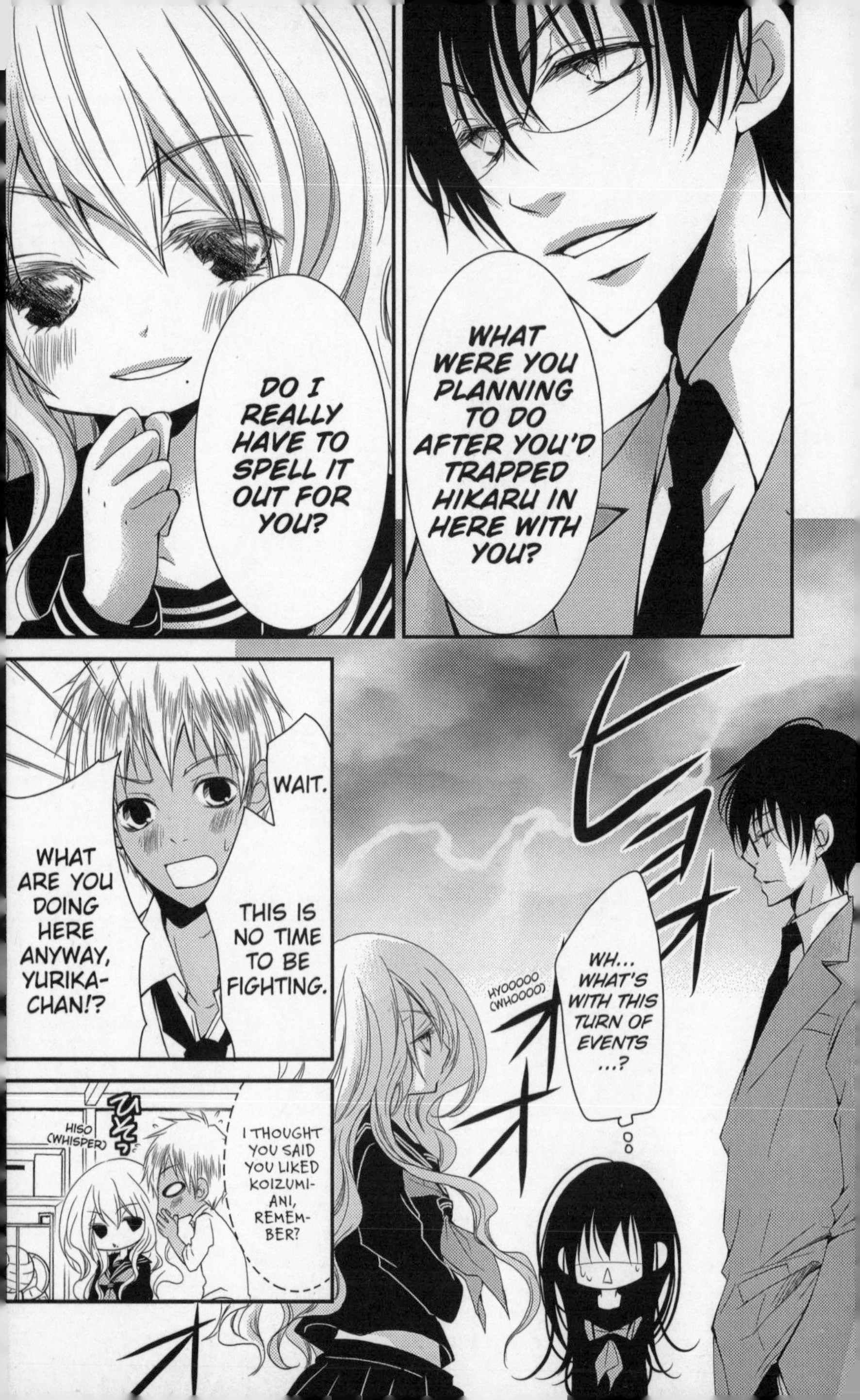
WHAT WERE YOU PLANNING TO DO AFTER YOU'D TRAPPED HIKARU IN HERE WITH YOU?
DO I REALLY HAVE TO SPELL IT OUT FOR YOU?
WH... WHAT'S WITH THIS TURN OF EVENTS ...?
HYOOOOO (WHOOOO)
WAIT.
THIS IS NO TIME TO BE FIGHTING.
WHAT ARE YOU DOING HERE ANYWAY, YURIKA-CHAN!?
I THOUGHT YOU SAID YOU LIKED KOIZUMI-ANI, REMEMBER?
HISO (WHISPER)

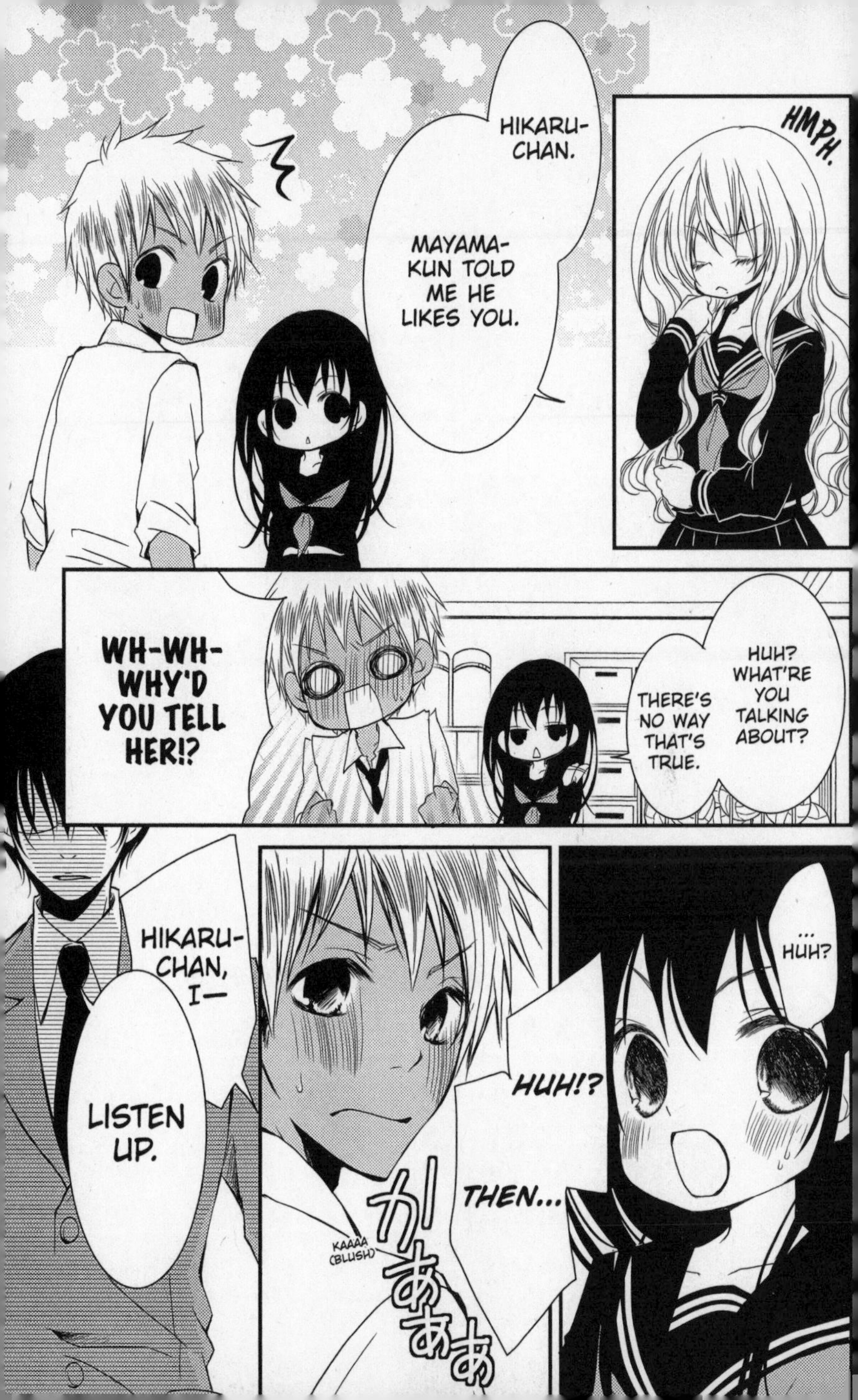
HMPH.
HIKARU-CHAN.
MAYAMA-KUN TOLD ME HE LIKES YOU.
HUH? WHAT'RE YOU TALKING ABOUT?
THERE'S NO WAY THAT'S TRUE.
WH-WH-WHY'D YOU TELL HER!?
... HUH?
HUH!?
THEN...
KAAAA (BLUSH)
HIKARU-CHAN, I—
LISTEN UP.

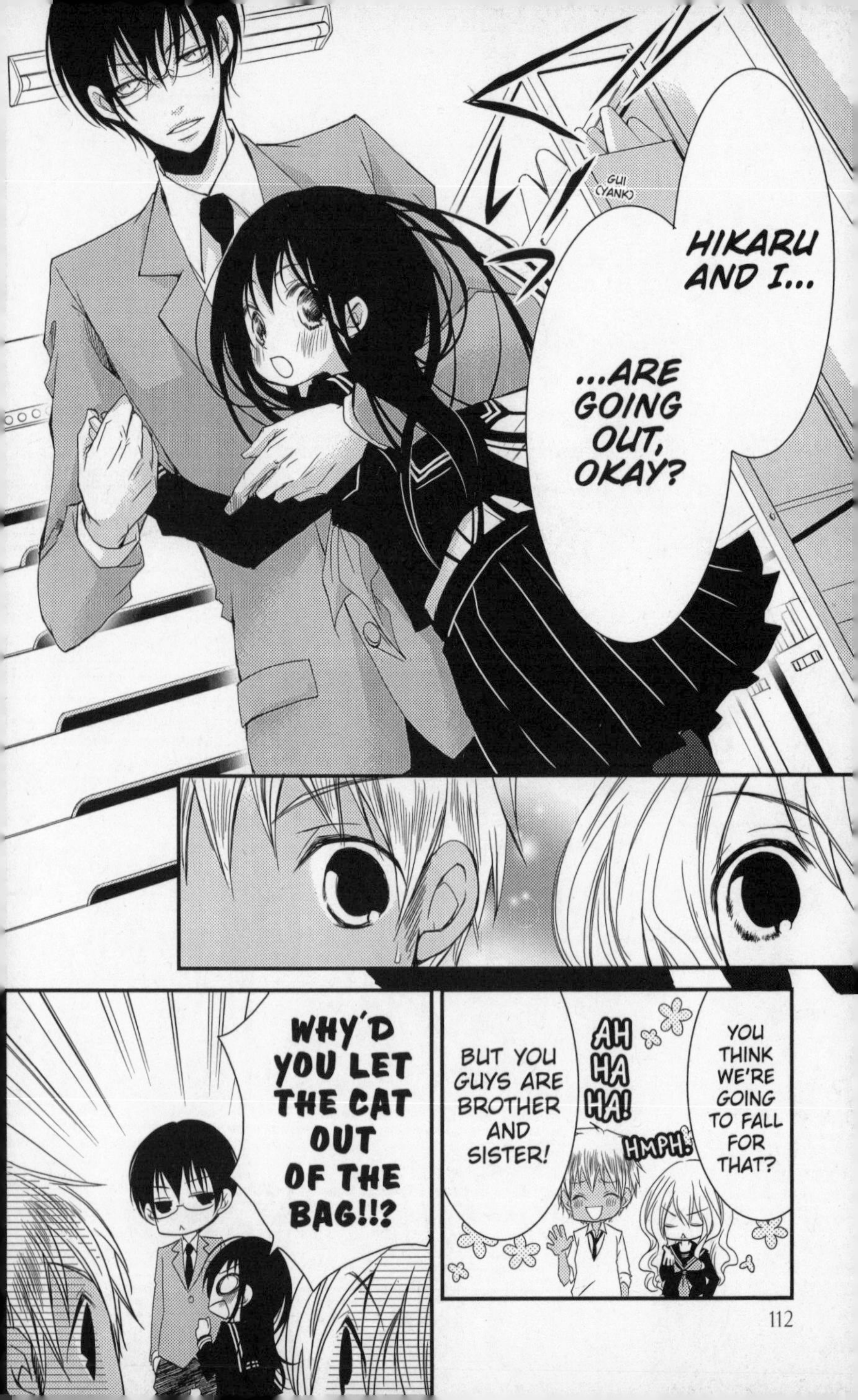
GUI (YANK)
HIKARU AND I...
...ARE GOING OUT, OKAY?
YOU THINK WE'RE GOING TO FALL FOR THAT?
HMPH!
AH HA HA!
BUT YOU GUYS ARE BROTHER AND SISTER!
WHY'D YOU LET THE CAT OUT OF THE BAG!!?

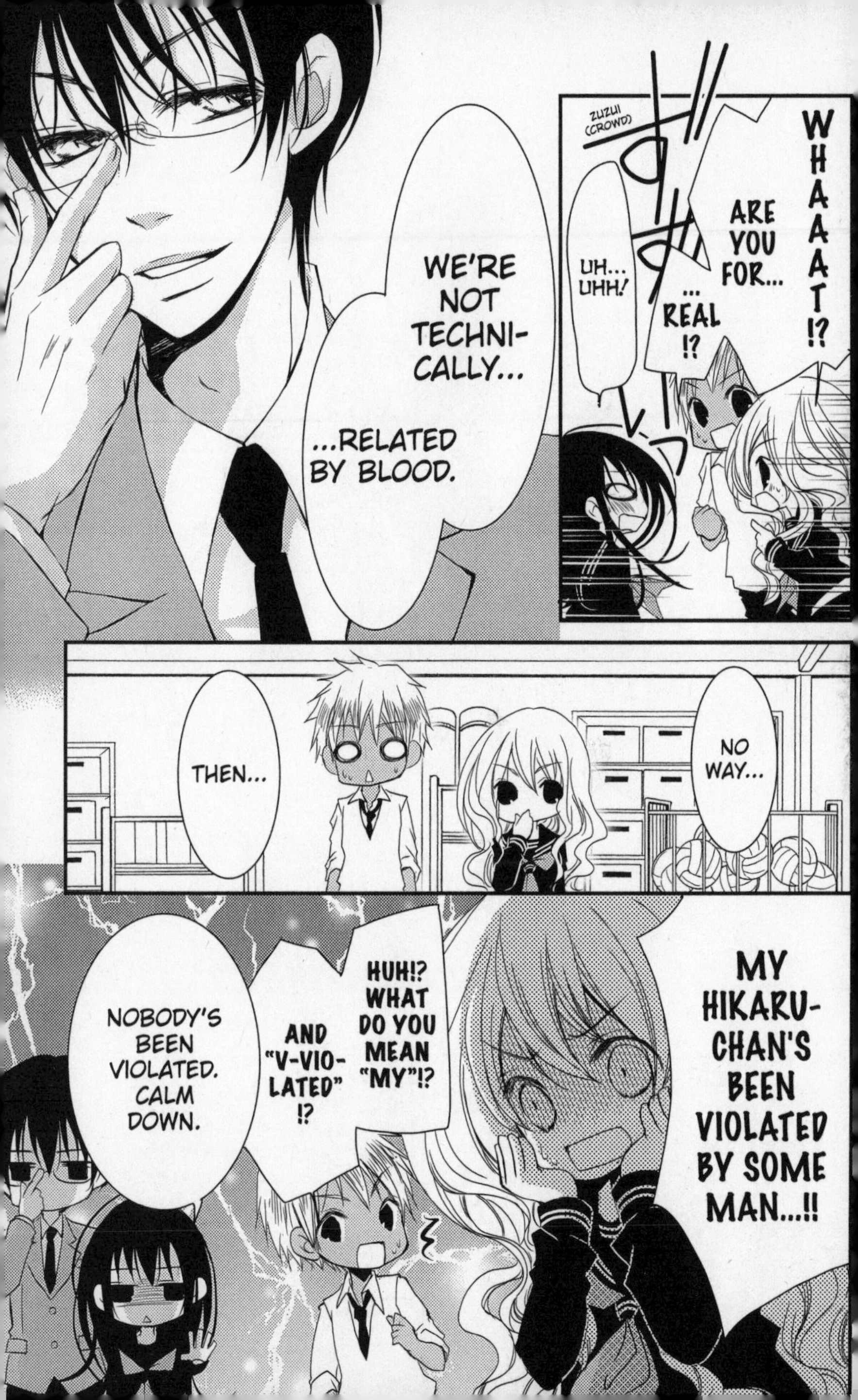
WHAAAT!?
ARE YOU FOR...
...REAL!?
ZUZUI (CROWD)
UH... UHH!
WE'RE NOT TECHNICALLY...
...RELATED BY BLOOD.
NO WAY...
THEN...
MY HIKARU-CHAN'S BEEN VIOLATED BY SOME MAN...!!
HUH!? WHAT DO YOU MEAN "MY"!?
AND "V-VIOLATED"!?
NOBODY'S BEEN VIOLATED. CALM DOWN.

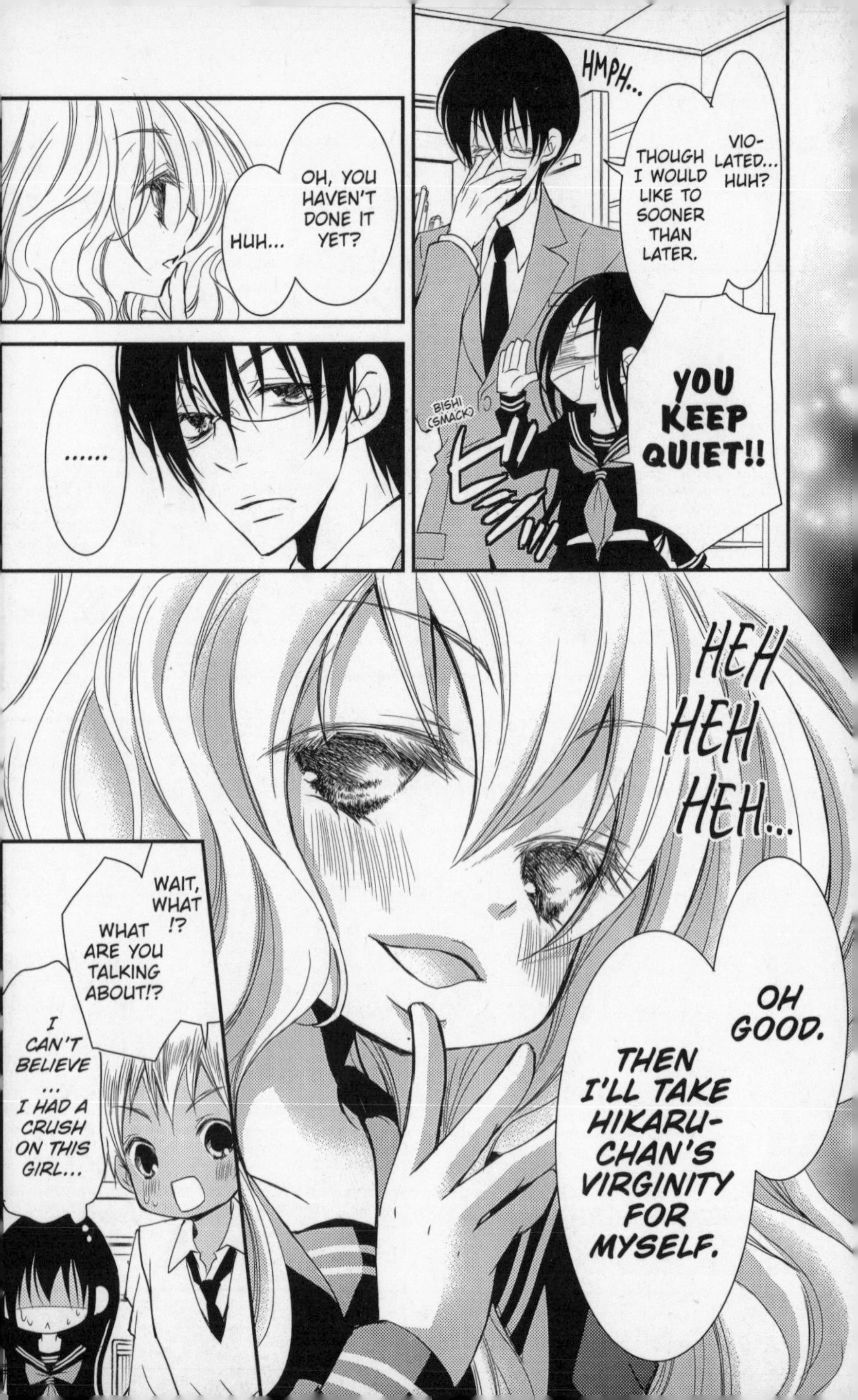
HMPH...
VIO-LATED... HUH?
THOUGH I WOULD LIKE TO SOONER THAN LATER.
BISHI (SMACK)
YOU KEEP QUIET!!
OH, YOU HAVEN'T DONE IT YET?
HUH...
......
HEH HEH HEH...
OH GOOD.
THEN I'LL TAKE HIKARU-CHAN'S VIRGINITY FOR MYSELF.
WAIT, WHAT!?
WHAT ARE YOU TALKING ABOUT!?
I CAN'T BELIEVE... I HAD A CRUSH ON THIS GIRL...

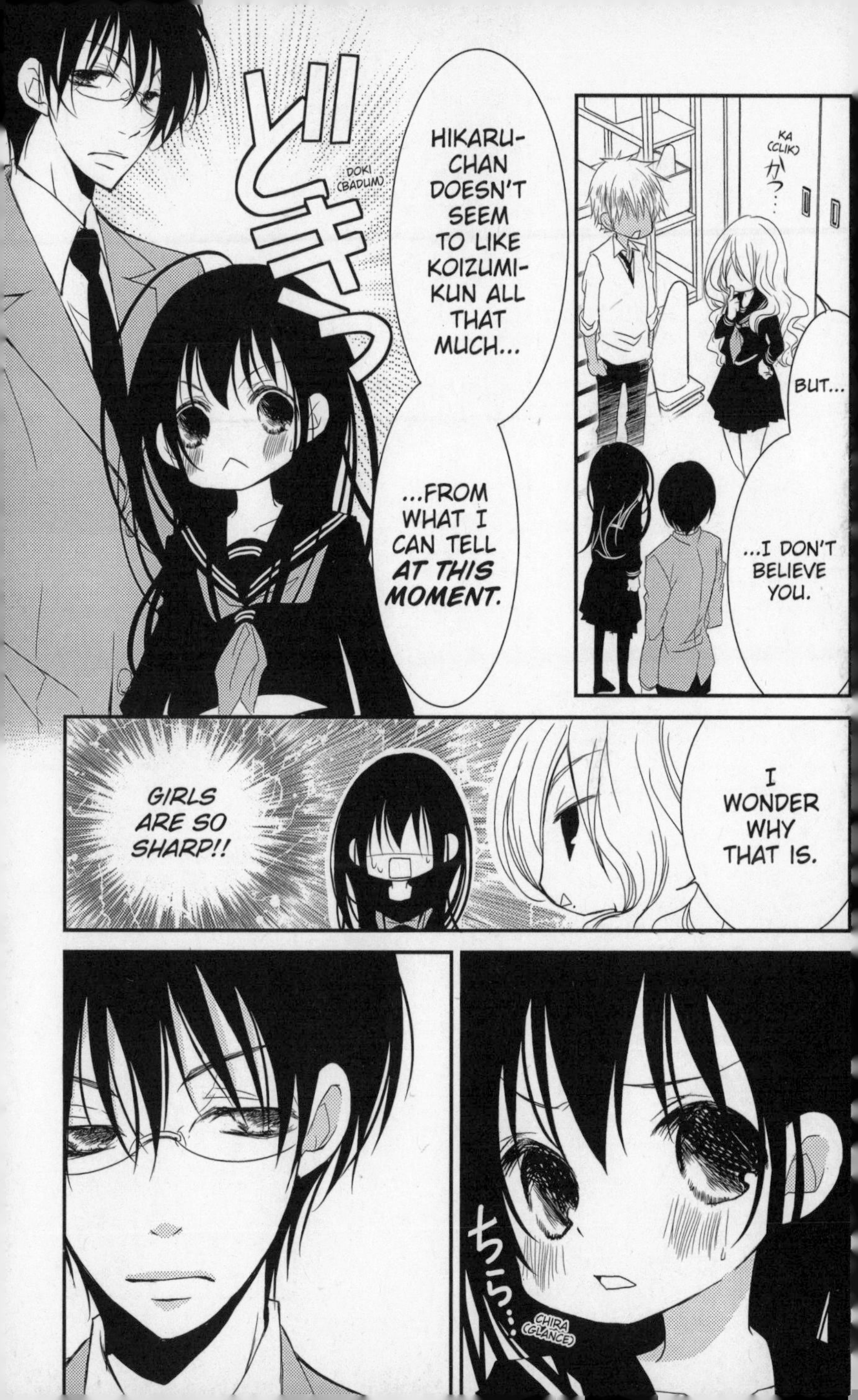
KA (CLIK)
かっ…
BUT...
...I DON'T BELIEVE YOU.
HIKARU-CHAN DOESN'T SEEM TO LIKE KOIZUMI-KUN ALL THAT MUCH...
...FROM WHAT I CAN TELL *AT THIS MOMENT.*
どきっ
DOKI (BADUM)
I WONDER WHY THAT IS.
GIRLS ARE SO SHARP!!
ちら…
CHIRA (GLANCE)

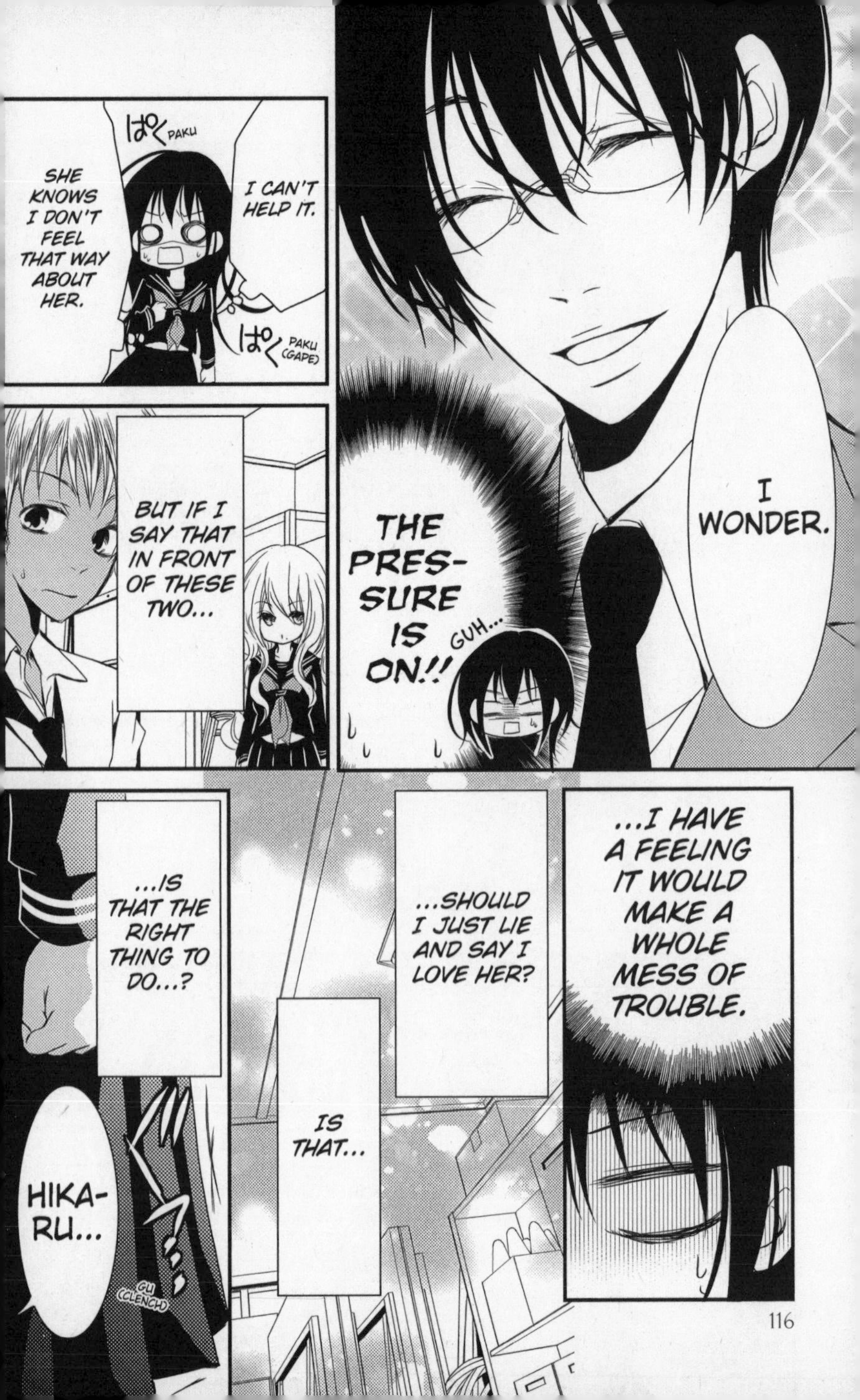
I WONDER.
THE PRES-SURE IS ON!!
GUH...
ぱく PAKU
I CAN'T HELP IT.
SHE KNOWS I DON'T FEEL THAT WAY ABOUT HER.
ぱく PAKU (GAPE)
BUT IF I SAY THAT IN FRONT OF THESE TWO...
...I HAVE A FEELING IT WOULD MAKE A WHOLE MESS OF TROUBLE.
...SHOULD I JUST LIE AND SAY I LOVE HER?
IS THAT...
...IS THAT THE RIGHT THING TO DO...?
HIKA-RU...
GU (CLENCH)

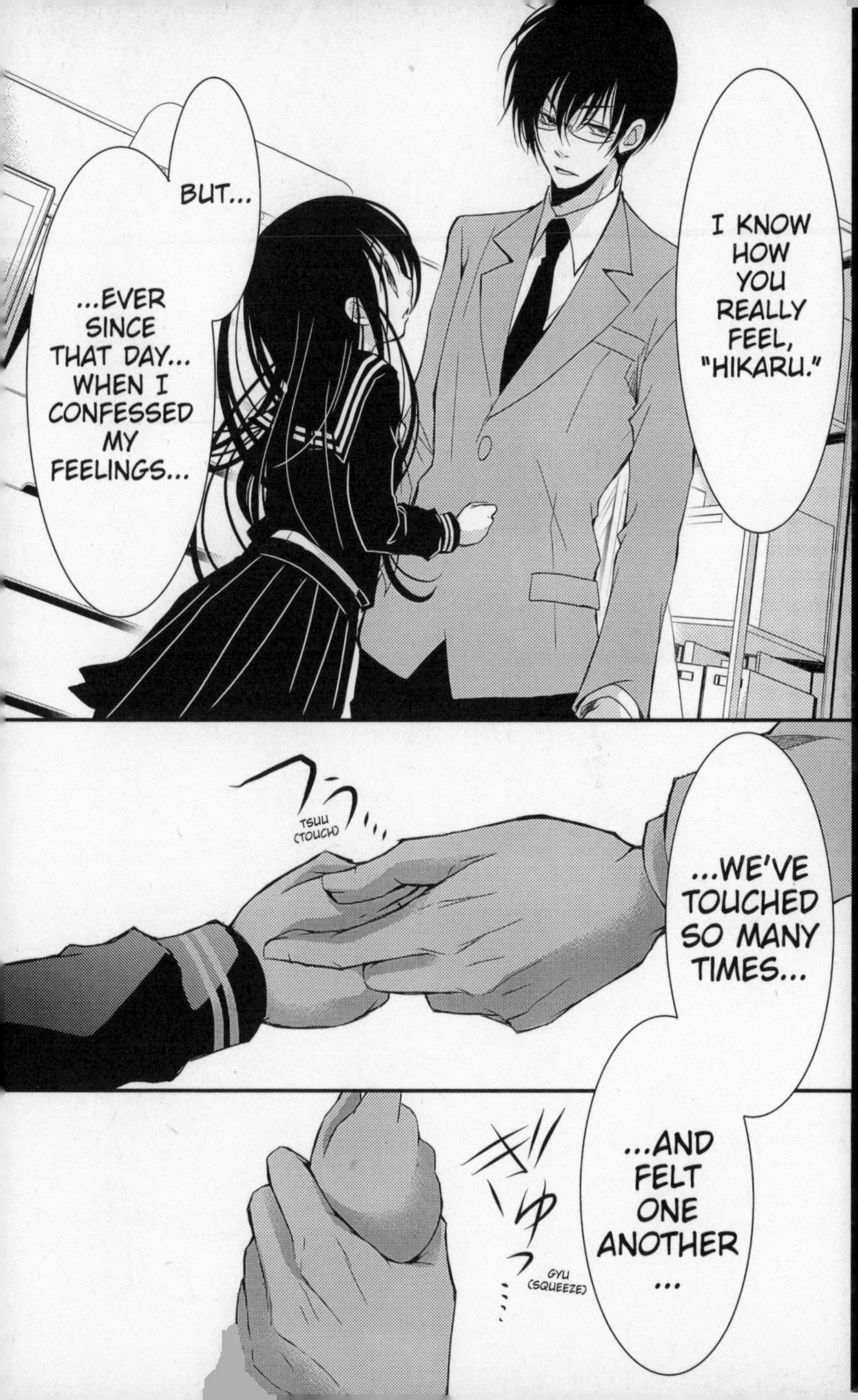
I KNOW HOW YOU REALLY FEEL, "HIKARU."
BUT...
...EVER SINCE THAT DAY... WHEN I CONFESSED MY FEELINGS...
...WE'VE TOUCHED SO MANY TIMES...
TSUU (TOUCH)
...AND FELT ONE ANOTHER ...
GYU (SQUEEZE)

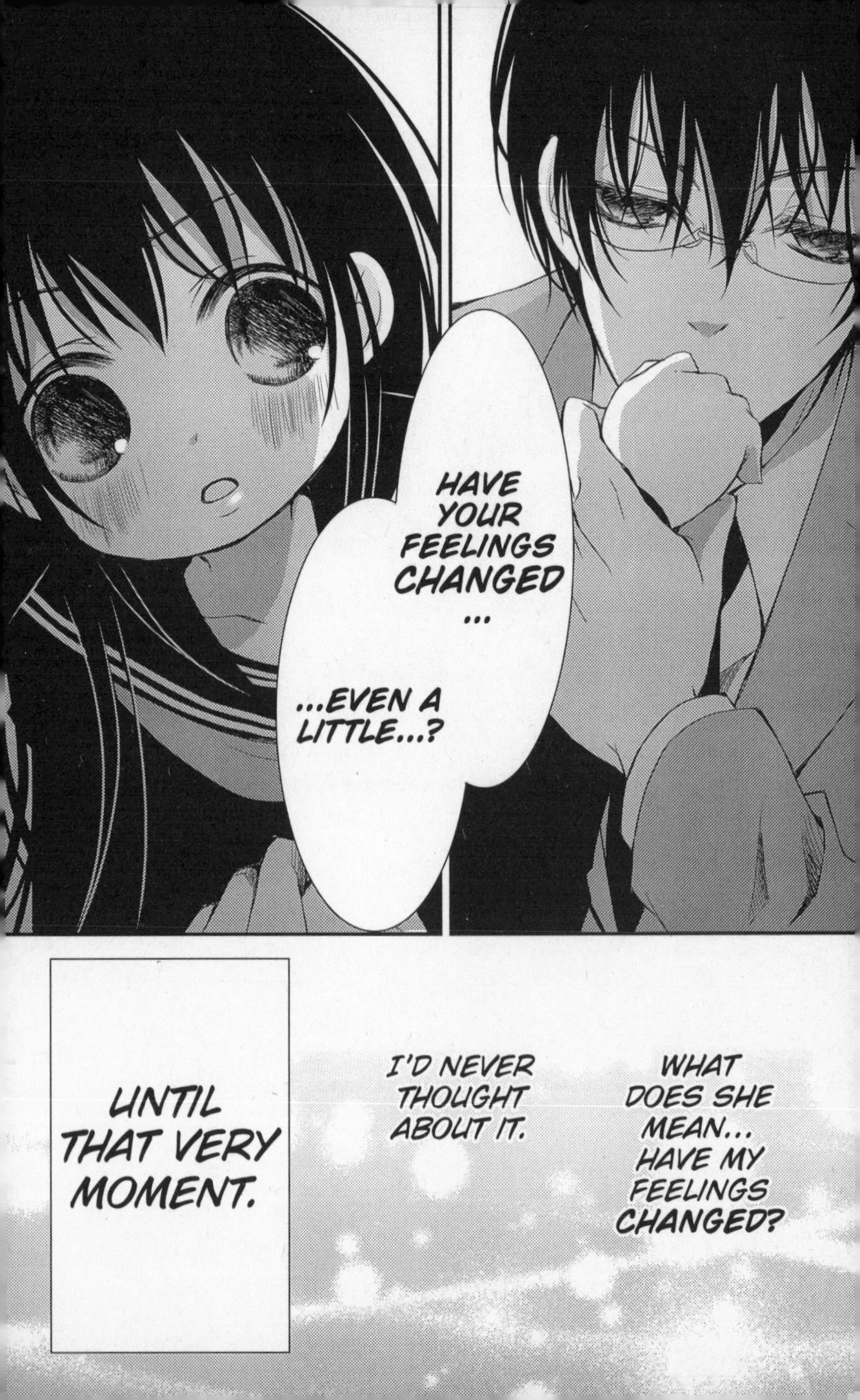
HAVE YOUR FEELINGS CHANGED ...
...EVEN A LITTLE...?
WHAT DOES SHE MEAN... HAVE MY FEELINGS CHANGED?
I'D NEVER THOUGHT ABOUT IT.
UNTIL THAT VERY MOMENT.

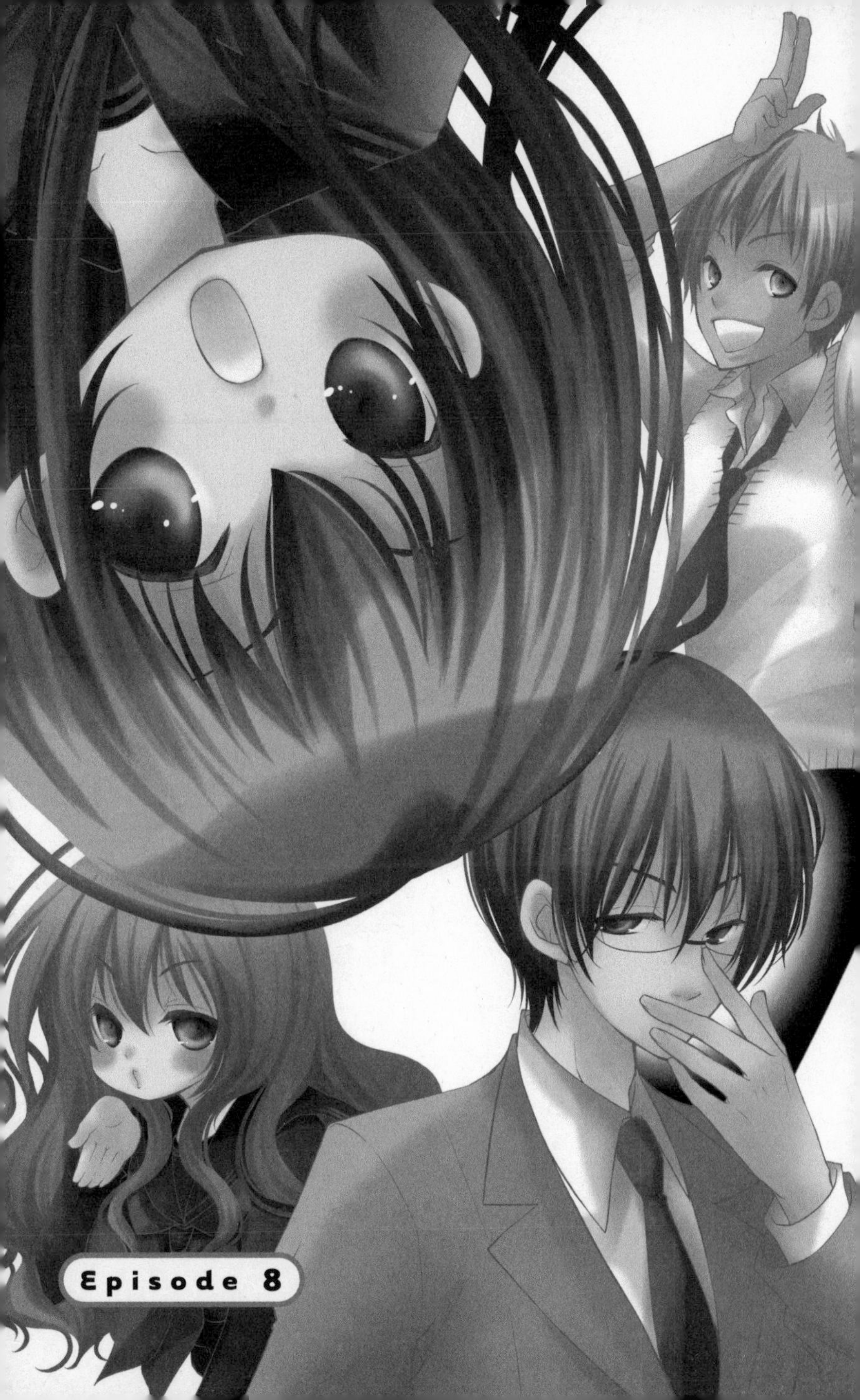
Episode 8

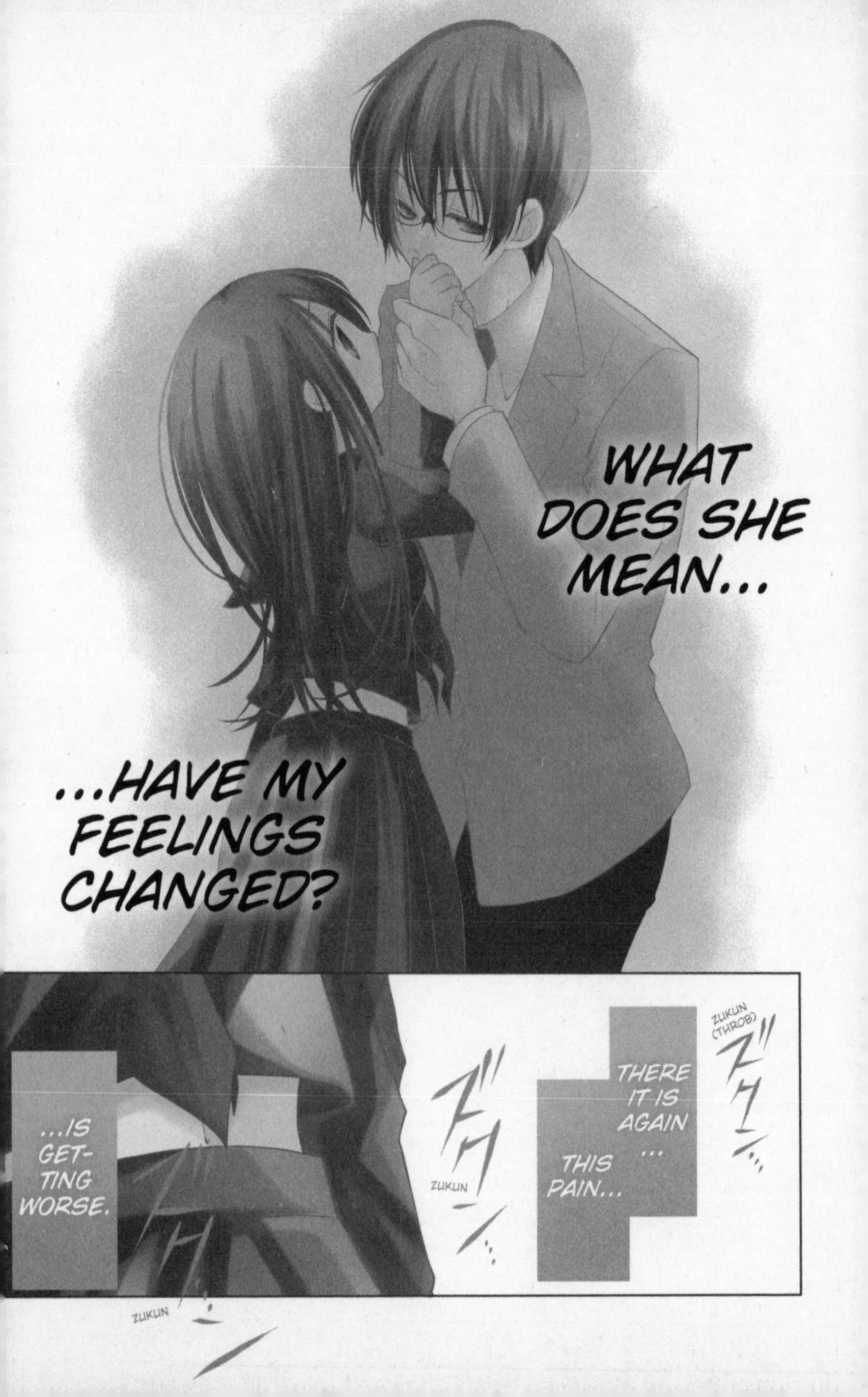
WHAT DOES SHE MEAN...
...HAVE MY FEELINGS CHANGED?
ZUKUN (THROB)
THERE IT IS AGAIN...
THIS PAIN...
ZUKUN
...IS GET-TING WORSE.
ZUKUN

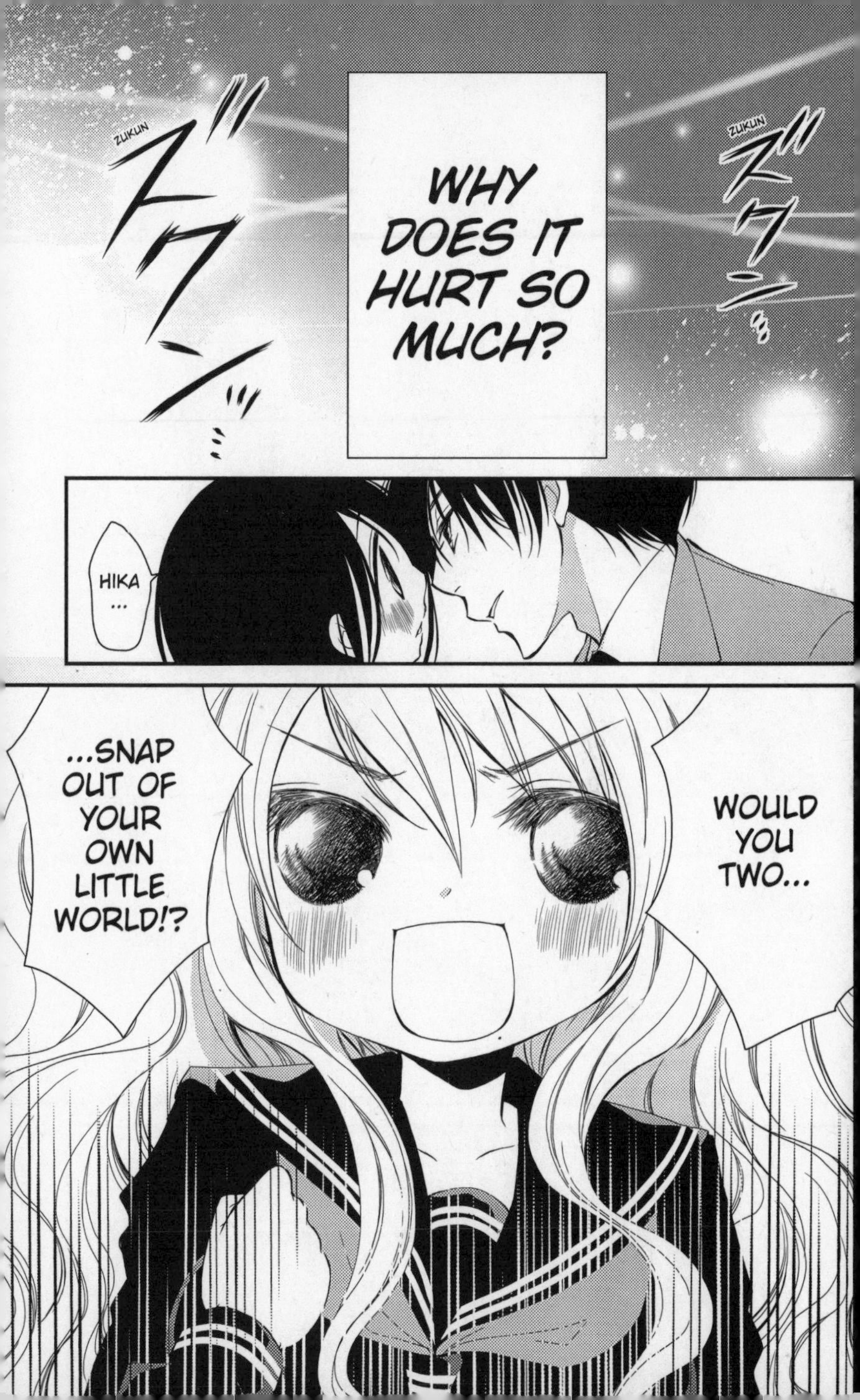
ZUKUN
WHY DOES IT HURT SO MUCH?
ZUKUN
HIKA ...
WOULD YOU TWO...
...SNAP OUT OF YOUR OWN LITTLE WORLD!?

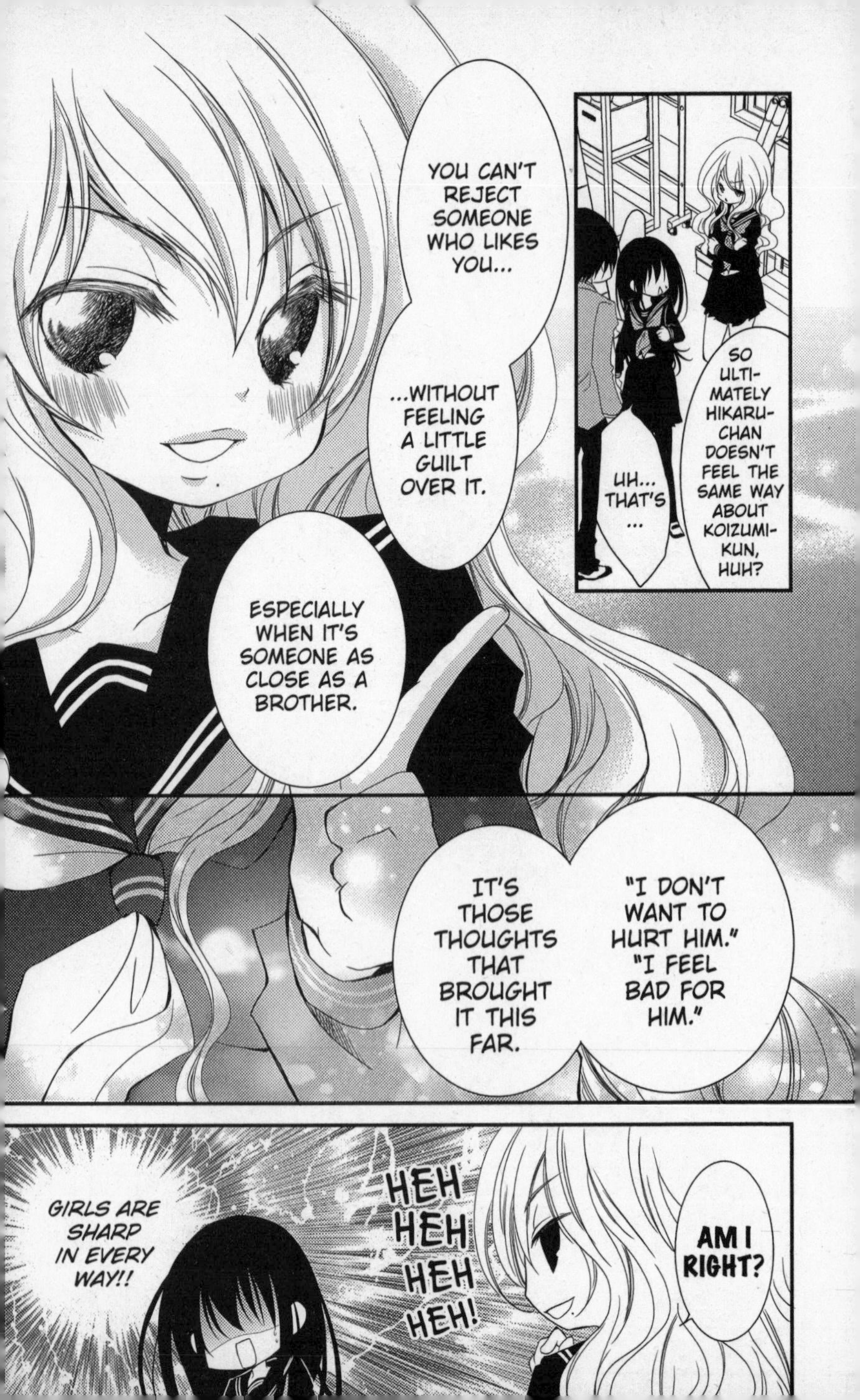
SO ULTI-MATELY HIKARU-CHAN DOESN'T FEEL THE SAME WAY ABOUT KOIZUMI-KUN, HUH?
UH... THAT'S ...
YOU CAN'T REJECT SOMEONE WHO LIKES YOU...
...WITHOUT FEELING A LITTLE GUILT OVER IT.
ESPECIALLY WHEN IT'S SOMEONE AS CLOSE AS A BROTHER.
"I DON'T WANT TO HURT HIM." "I FEEL BAD FOR HIM."
IT'S THOSE THOUGHTS THAT BROUGHT IT THIS FAR.
AM I RIGHT?
HEH HEH HEH HEH!
GIRLS ARE SHARP IN EVERY WAY!!

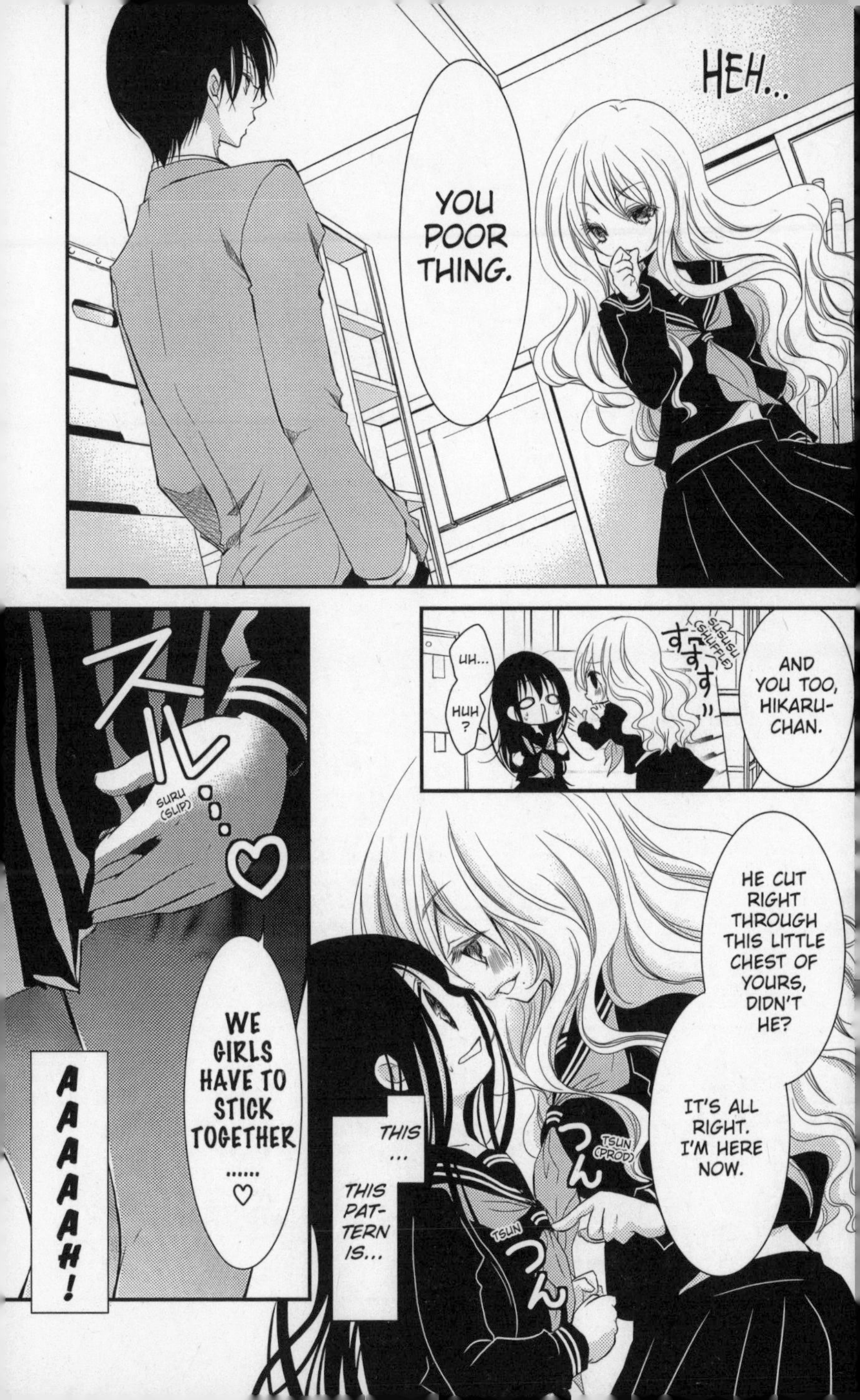
HEH...
YOU POOR THING.
AND YOU TOO, HIKARU-CHAN.
すすす
SUSUSU (SHUFFLE)
UH...
HUH?
HE CUT RIGHT THROUGH THIS LITTLE CHEST OF YOURS, DIDN'T HE?
IT'S ALL RIGHT. I'M HERE NOW.
つん
TSUN (PROD)
つん
TSUN
THIS... THIS PATTERN IS...
スル
SURU (SLIP)
♡
WE GIRLS HAVE TO STICK TOGETHER......♡
AAAAAAH!

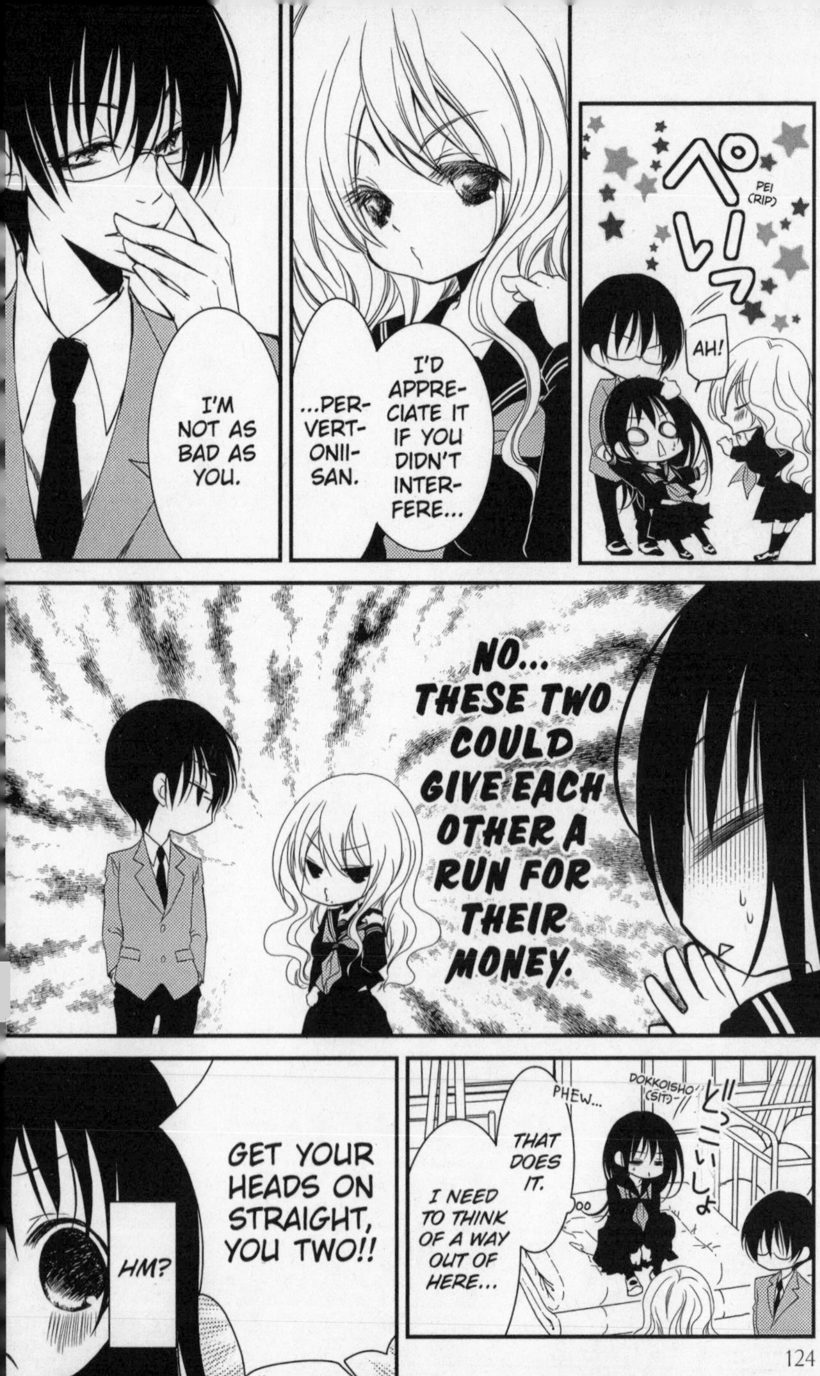
ぺりっ
PEI (RIP)
AH!
I'D APPRECIATE IT IF YOU DIDN'T INTERFERE...
...PERVERT-ONII-SAN.
I'M NOT AS BAD AS YOU.
NO... THESE TWO COULD GIVE EACH OTHER A RUN FOR THEIR MONEY.
どっこいしょ
DOKKOISHO (SIT)
PHEW...
THAT DOES IT.
I NEED TO THINK OF A WAY OUT OF HERE...
GET YOUR HEADS ON STRAIGHT, YOU TWO!!
HM?

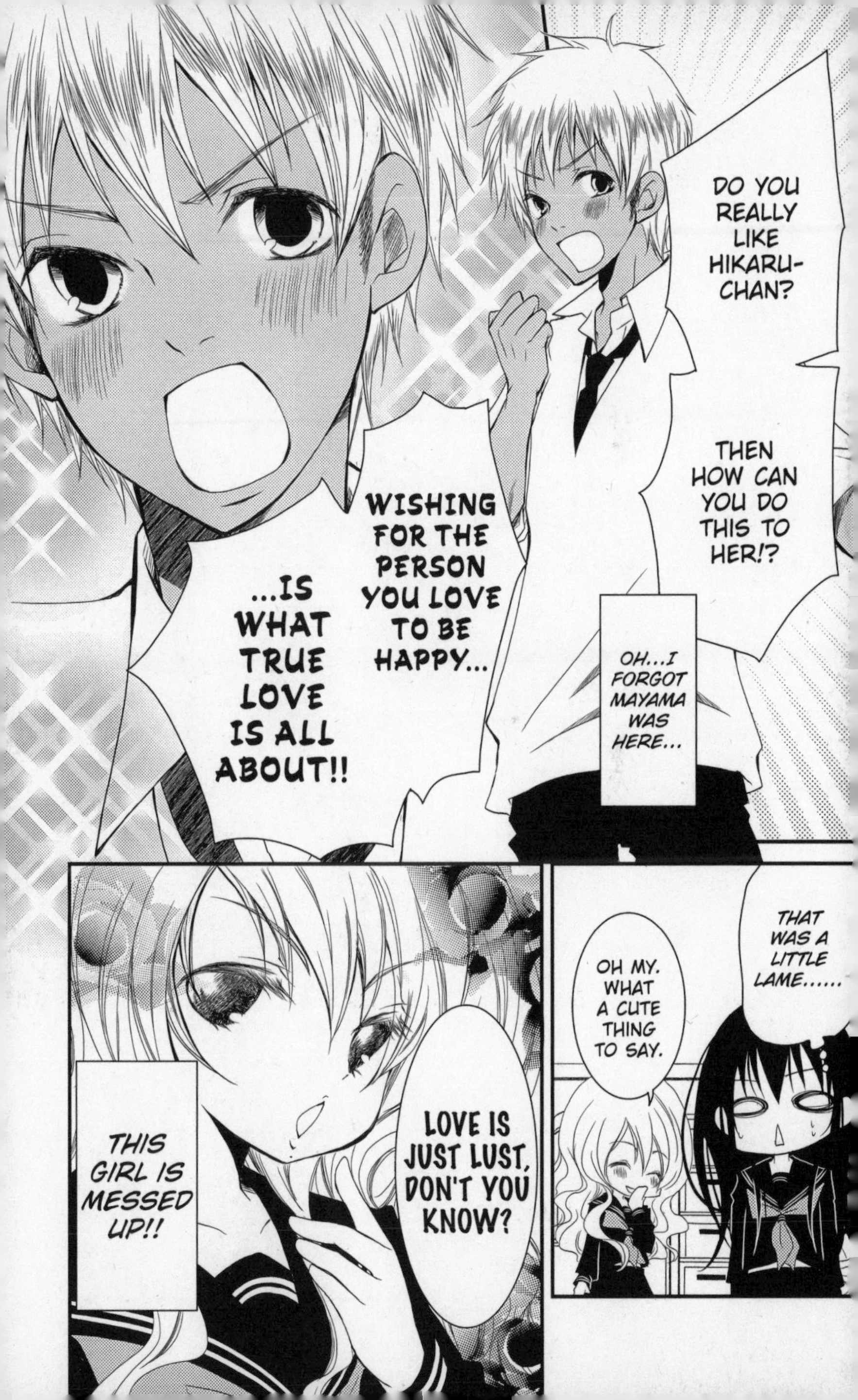
DO YOU REALLY LIKE HIKARU-CHAN?
THEN HOW CAN YOU DO THIS TO HER!?
OH...I FORGOT MAYAMA WAS HERE...
WISHING FOR THE PERSON YOU LOVE TO BE HAPPY...
...IS WHAT TRUE LOVE IS ALL ABOUT!!
THAT WAS A LITTLE LAME......
OH MY. WHAT A CUTE THING TO SAY.
LOVE IS JUST LUST, DON'T YOU KNOW?
THIS GIRL IS MESSED UP!!

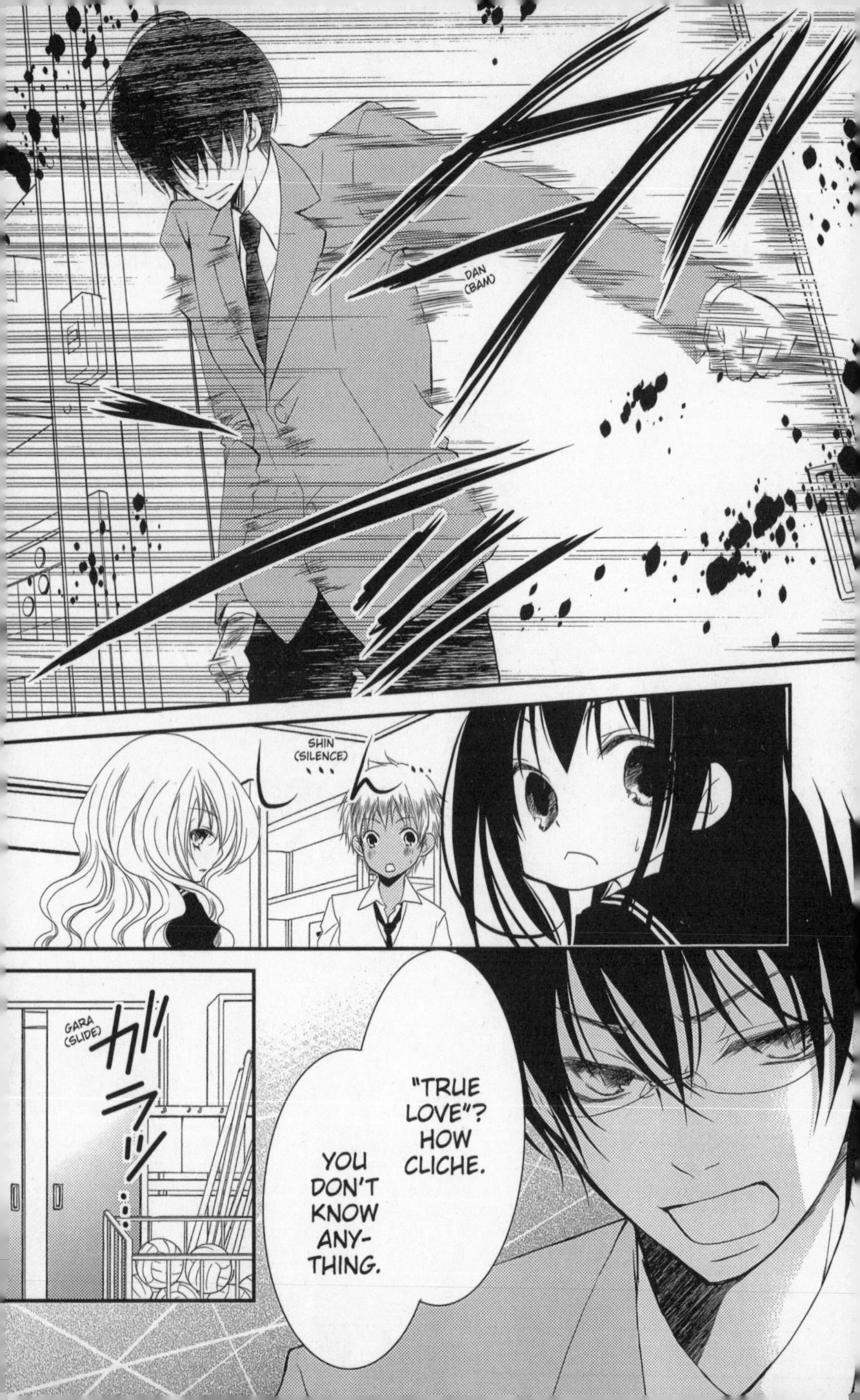
DAN (BAM)
SHIN (SILENCE)
...
GARA (SLIDE)
ガラッ
...
"TRUE LOVE"? HOW CLICHE.
YOU DON'T KNOW ANY-THING.

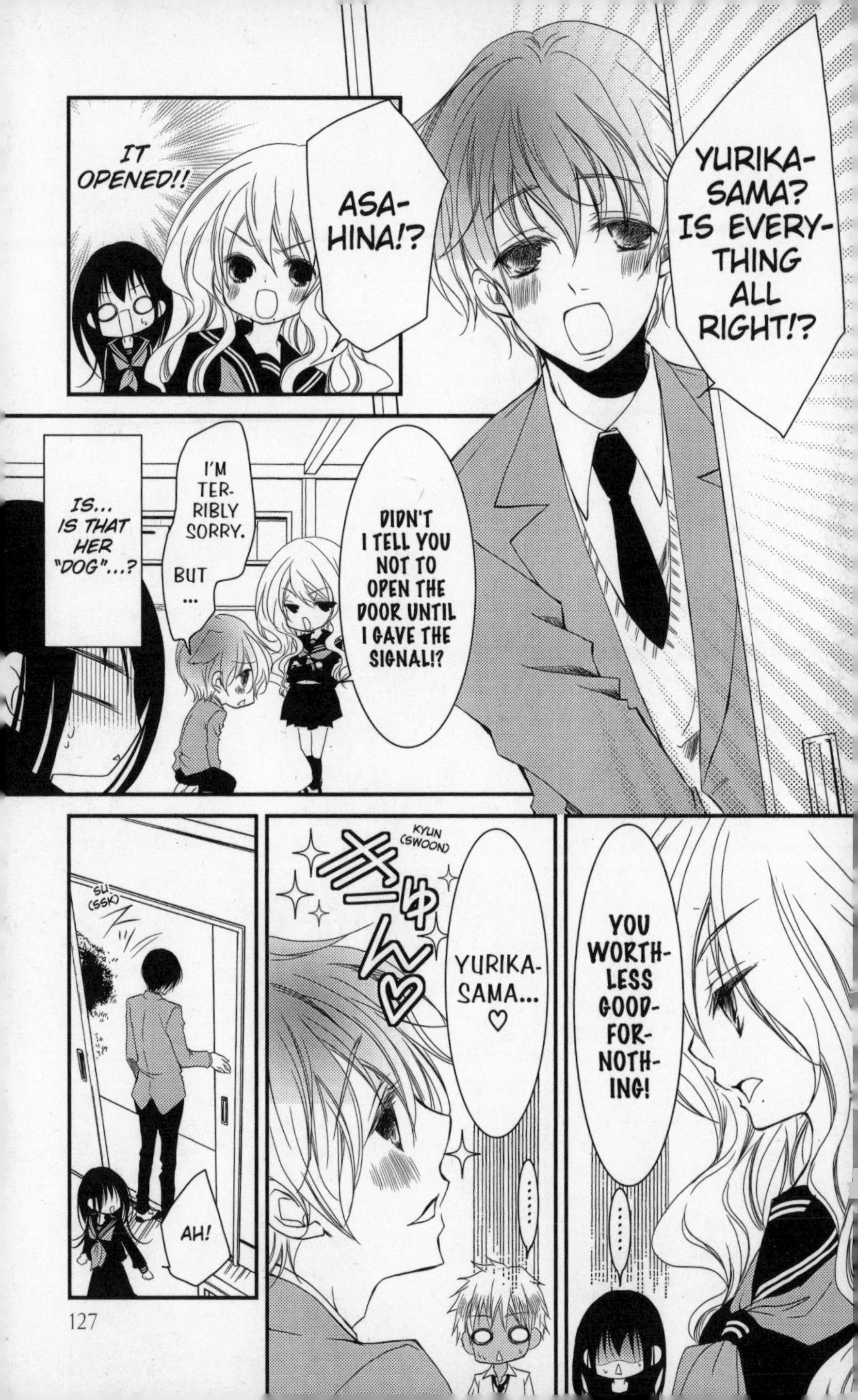
YURIKA-SAMA? IS EVERYTHING ALL RIGHT!?
ASA-HINA!?
IT OPENED!!
DIDN'T I TELL YOU NOT TO OPEN THE DOOR UNTIL I GAVE THE SIGNAL!?
I'M TER-RIBLY SORRY.
BUT ...
IS... IS THAT HER "DOG"...?
YOU WORTH-LESS GOOD-FOR-NOTH-ING!
......
KYUN (SWOON)
YURIKA-SAMA... ♡
......
SU (SSK)
AH!

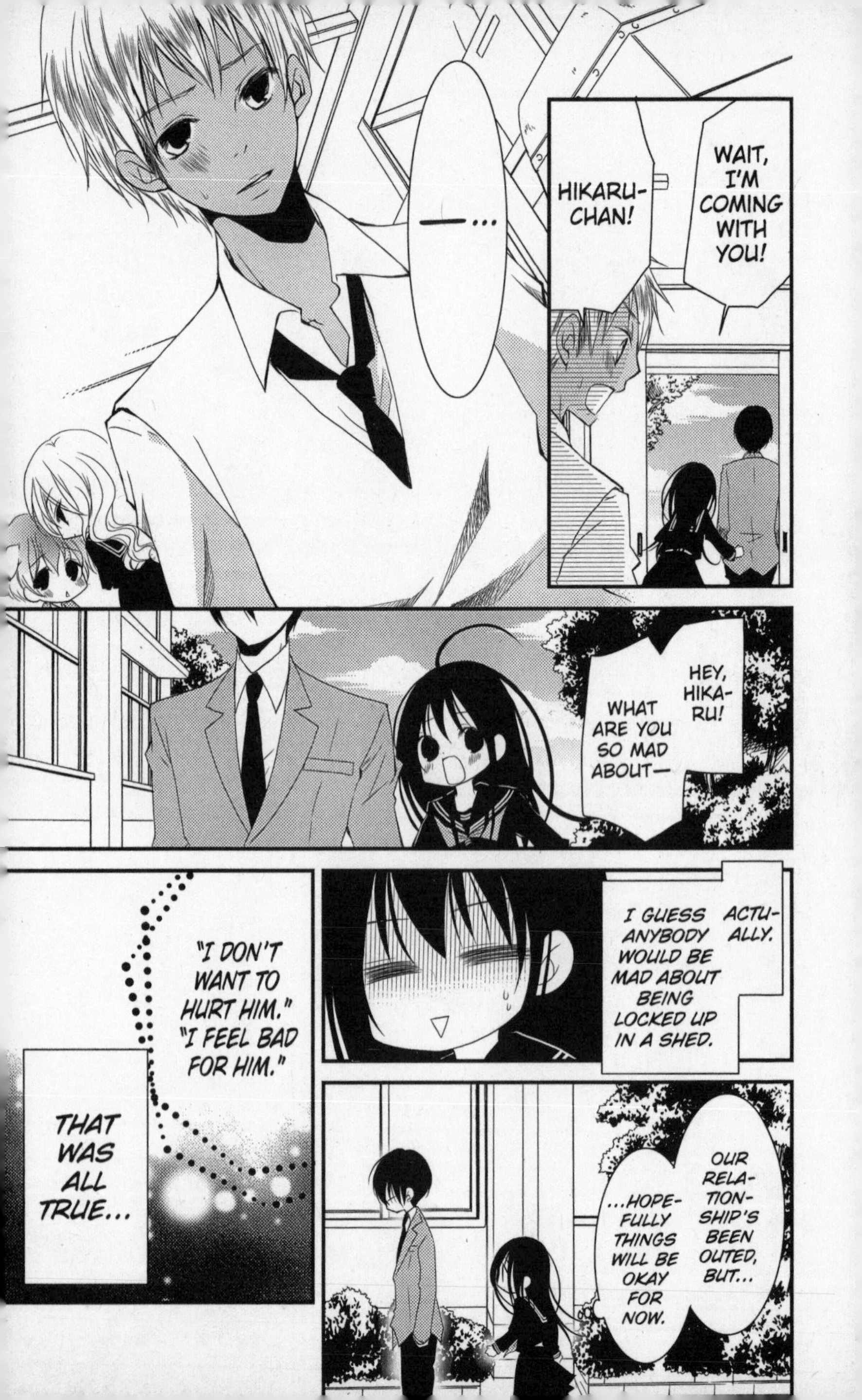
WAIT, I'M COMING WITH YOU!
HIKARU-CHAN!
—...
HEY, HIKARU!
WHAT ARE YOU SO MAD ABOUT—
ACTUALLY.
I GUESS ANYBODY WOULD BE MAD ABOUT BEING LOCKED UP IN A SHED.
OUR RELATIONSHIP'S BEEN OUTED, BUT...
...HOPEFULLY THINGS WILL BE OKAY FOR NOW.
"I DON'T WANT TO HURT HIM."
"I FEEL BAD FOR HIM."
THAT WAS ALL TRUE...

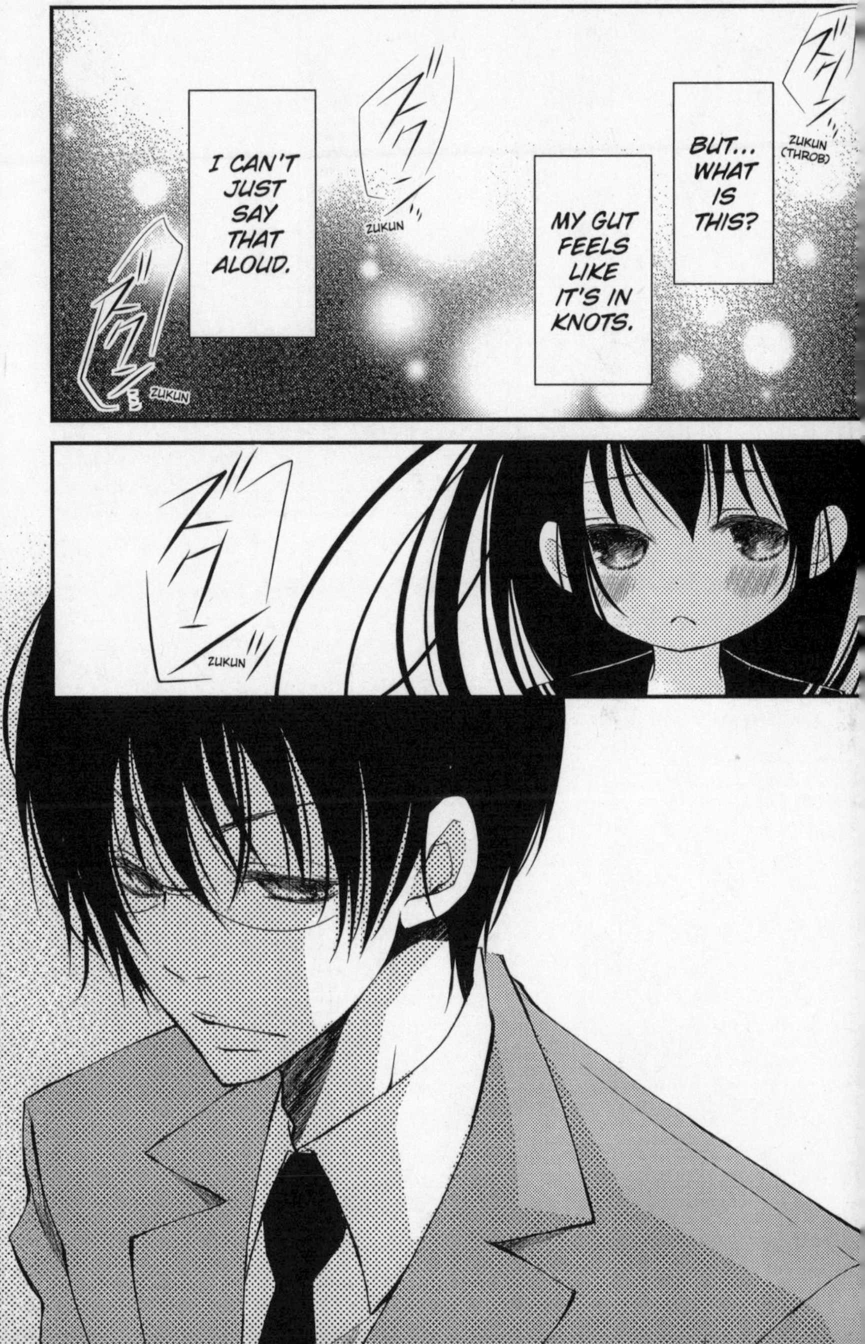
ZUKUN (THROB)
BUT... WHAT IS THIS?
MY GUT FEELS LIKE IT'S IN KNOTS.
ZUKUN
I CAN'T JUST SAY THAT ALOUD.
ZUKUN
ZUKUN

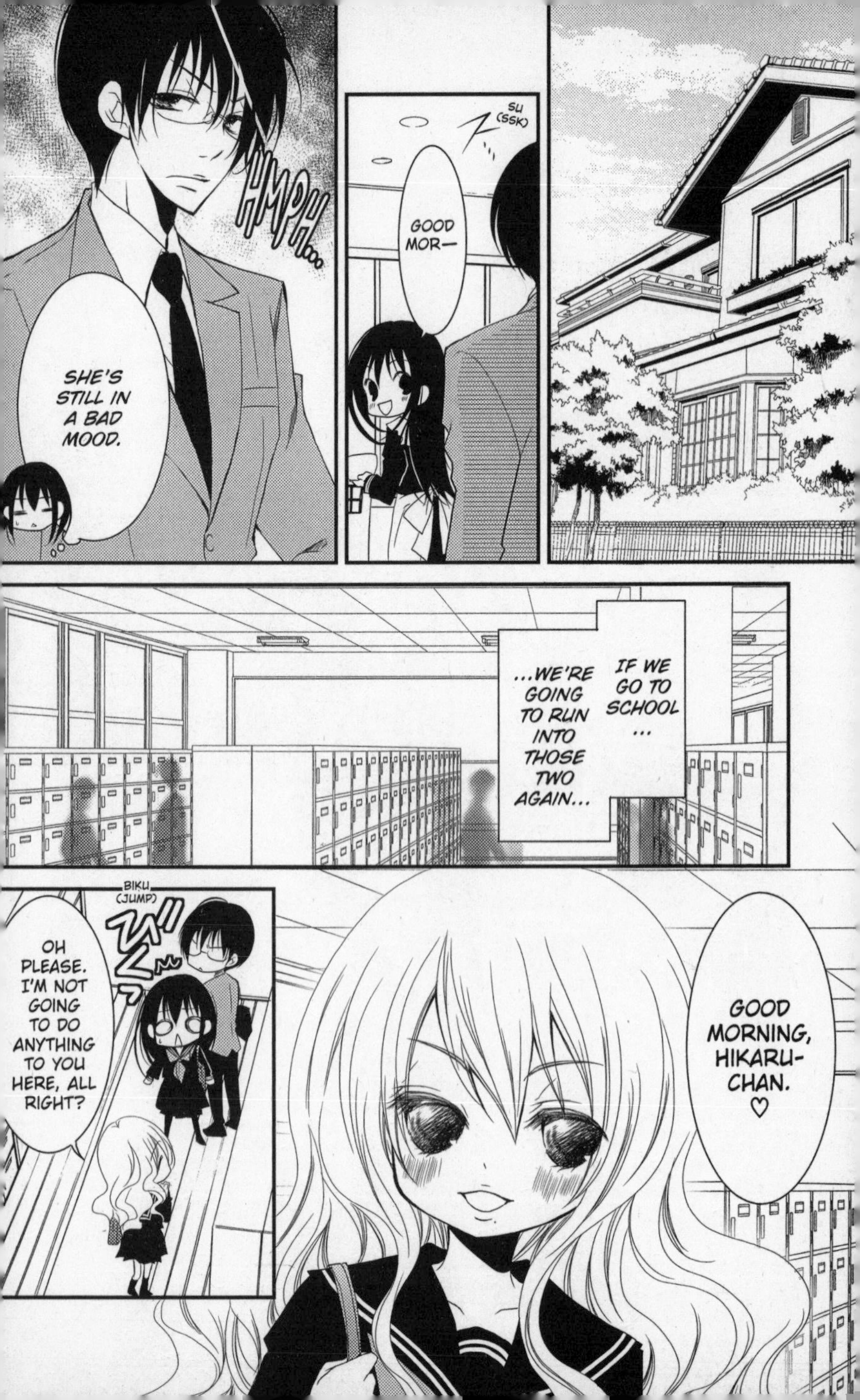
SU (SSK)
GOOD MOR—
HMPH...
SHE'S STILL IN A BAD MOOD.
IF WE GO TO SCHOOL ...
...WE'RE GOING TO RUN INTO THOSE TWO AGAIN...
GOOD MORNING, HIKARU-CHAN. ♡
BIKU (JUMP)
OH PLEASE. I'M NOT GOING TO DO ANYTHING TO YOU HERE, ALL RIGHT?

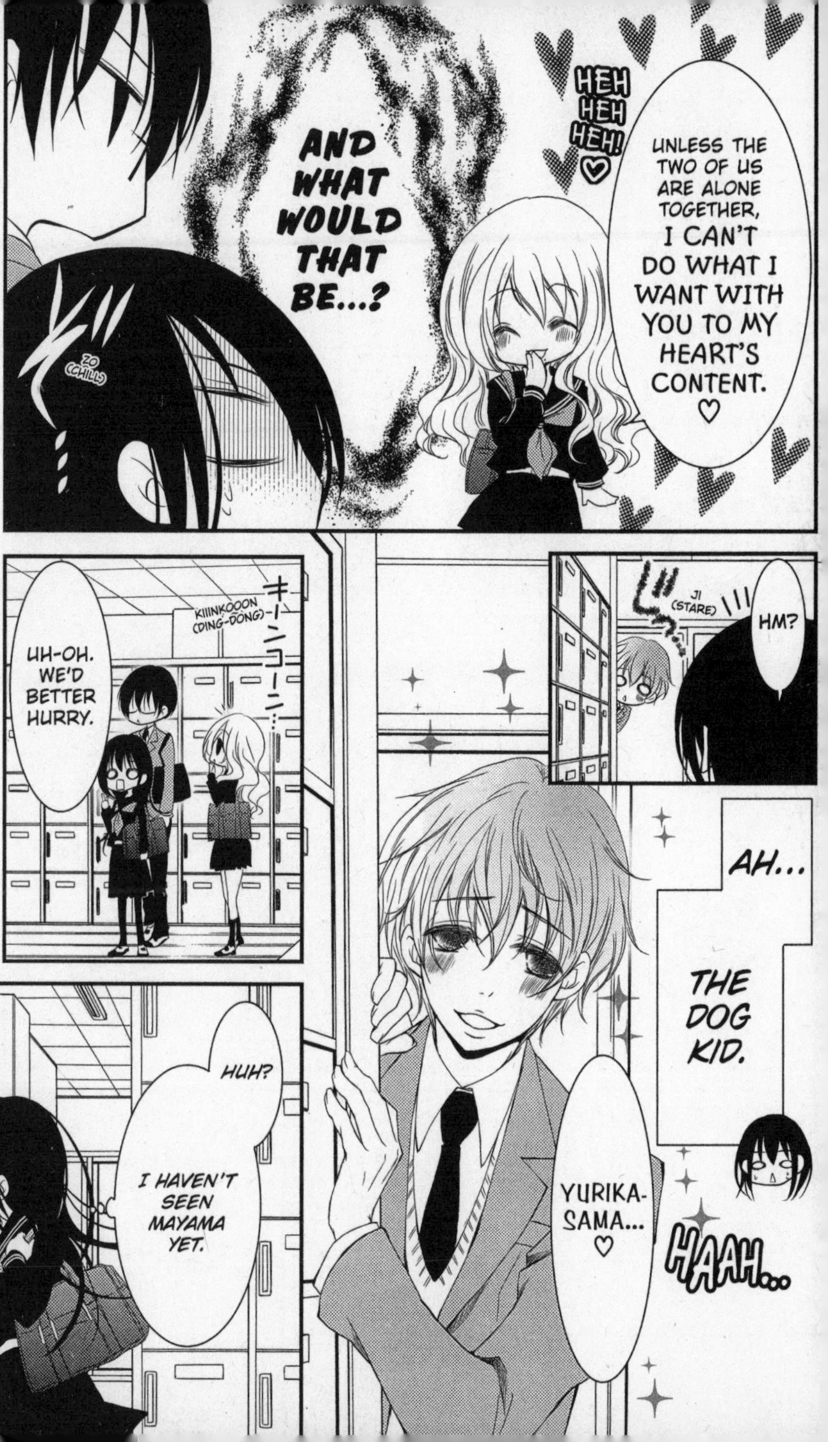
HEH HEH HEH! ♡
UNLESS THE TWO OF US ARE ALONE TOGETHER, I CAN'T DO WHAT I WANT WITH YOU TO MY HEART'S CONTENT. ♡
AND WHAT WOULD THAT BE...?
ZO (CHILL)
JI (STARE)
HM?
AH...
THE DOG KID.
YURIKA-SAMA... ♡
HAAH...
KIIINKOOON (DING-DONG)
UH-OH. WE'D BETTER HURRY.
HUH?
I HAVEN'T SEEN MAYAMA YET.

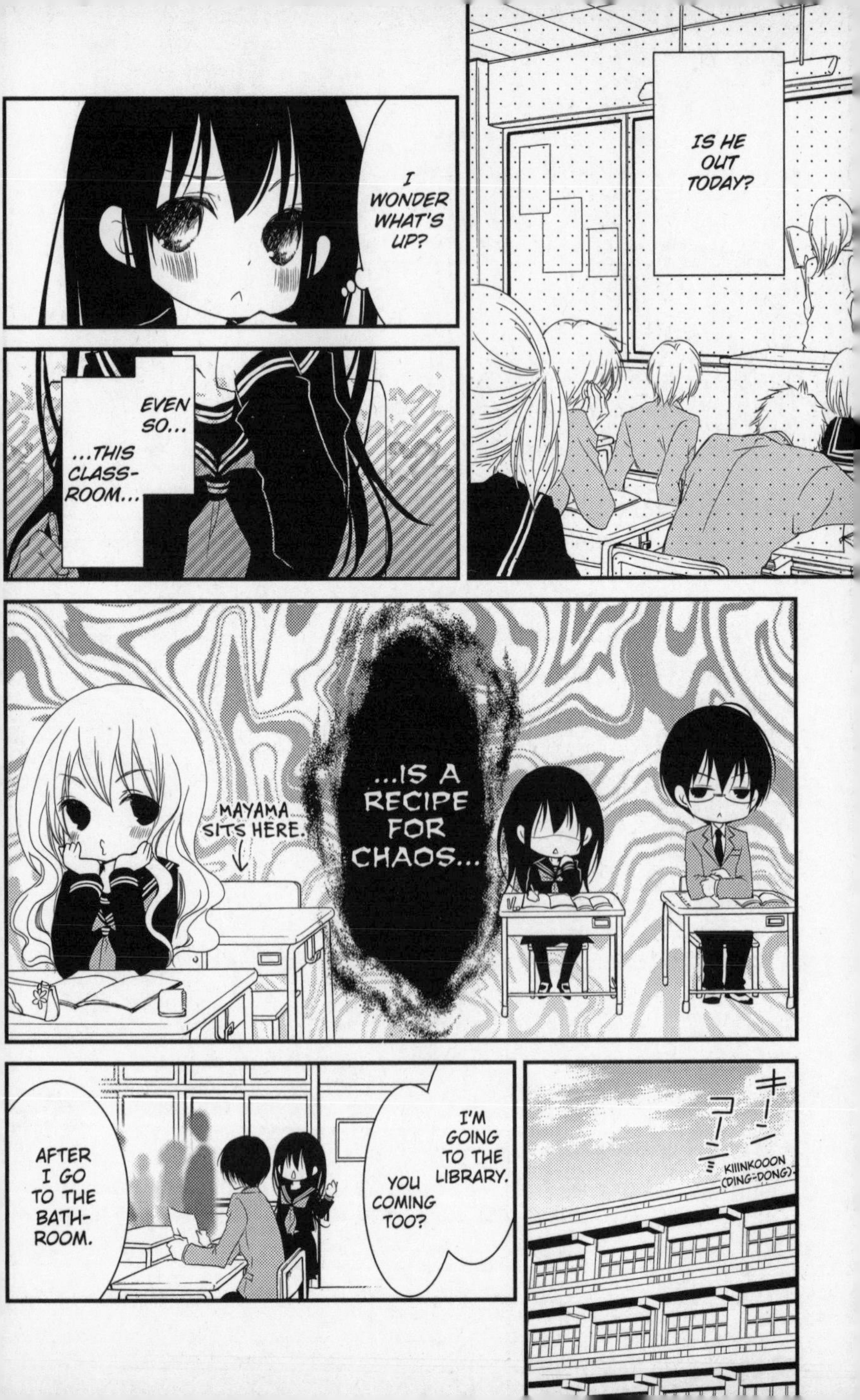
IS HE OUT TODAY?
I WONDER WHAT'S UP?
EVEN SO...
...THIS CLASS-ROOM...
...IS A RECIPE FOR CHAOS...
MAYAMA SITS HERE.
キーンコーン
KIIINKOOON (DING-DONG)
I'M GOING TO THE LIBRARY.
YOU COMING TOO?
AFTER I GO TO THE BATH-ROOM.

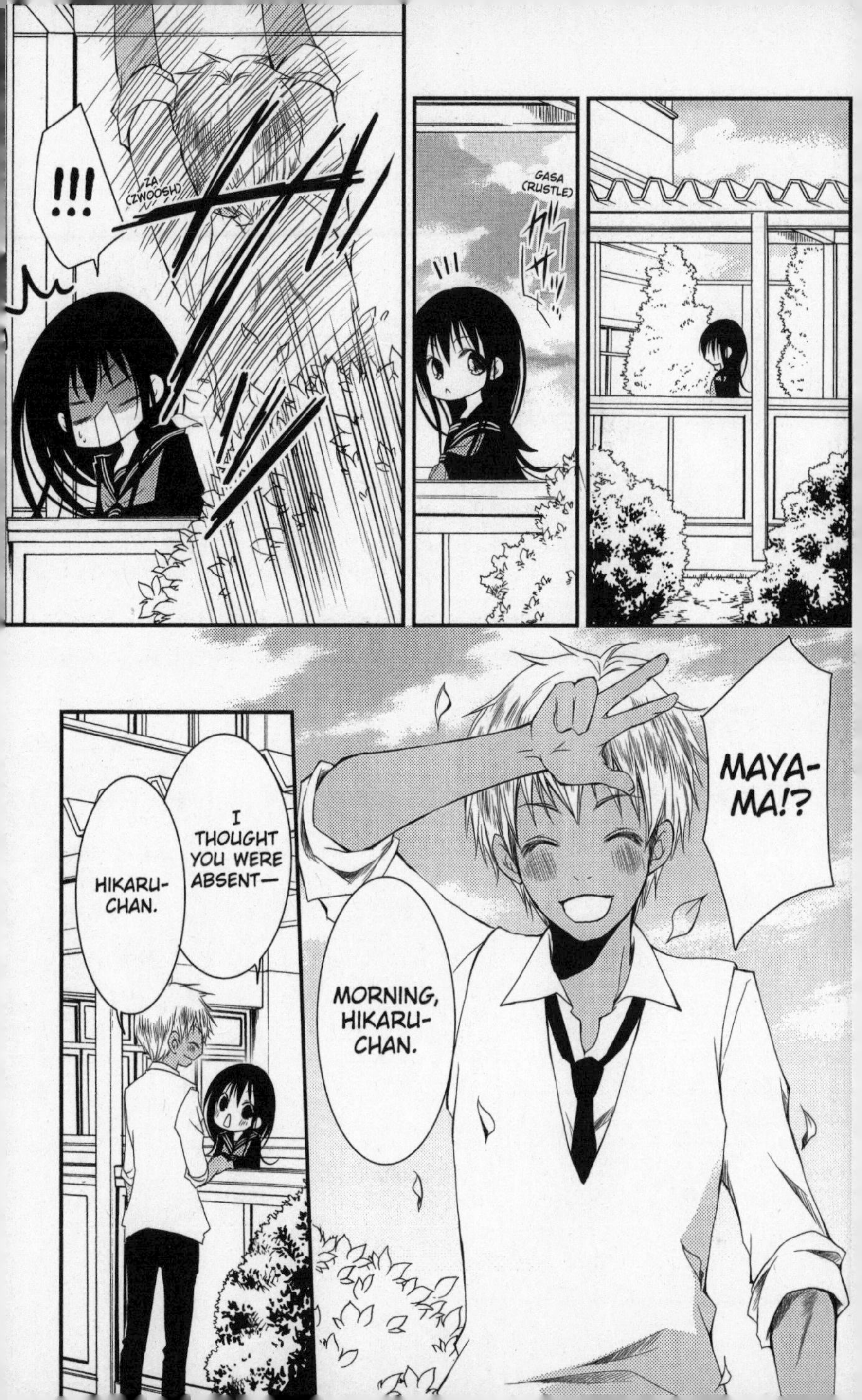
GASA (RUSTLE)
!!!
ZA (ZWOOSH)
MAYAMA!?
MORNING, HIKARU-CHAN.
I THOUGHT YOU WERE ABSENT—
HIKARU-CHAN.

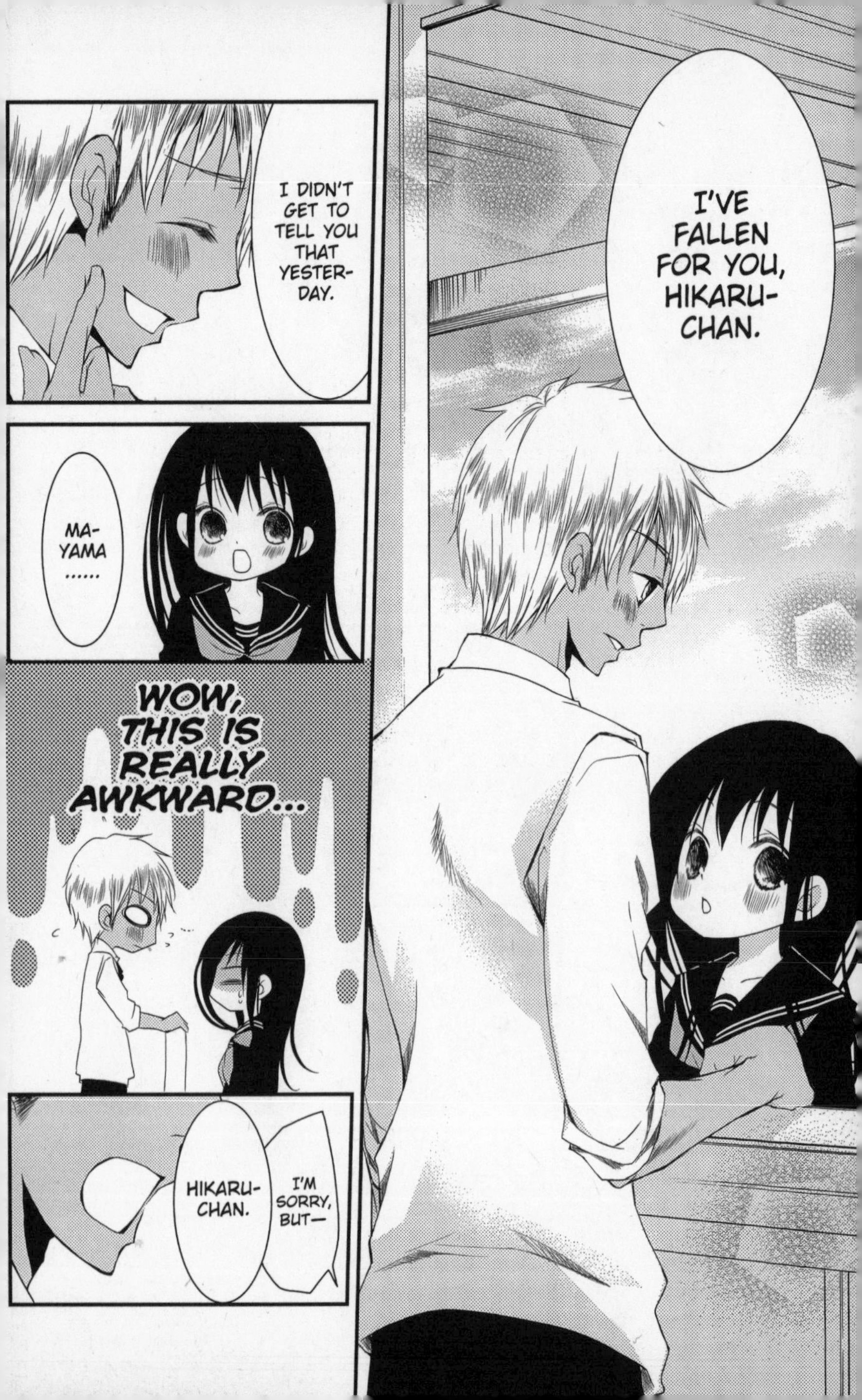
I'VE FALLEN FOR YOU, HIKARU-CHAN.
I DIDN'T GET TO TELL YOU THAT YESTER-DAY.
MA-YAMA ......
WOW, THIS IS REALLY AWKWARD...
HIKARU-CHAN.
I'M SORRY, BUT—

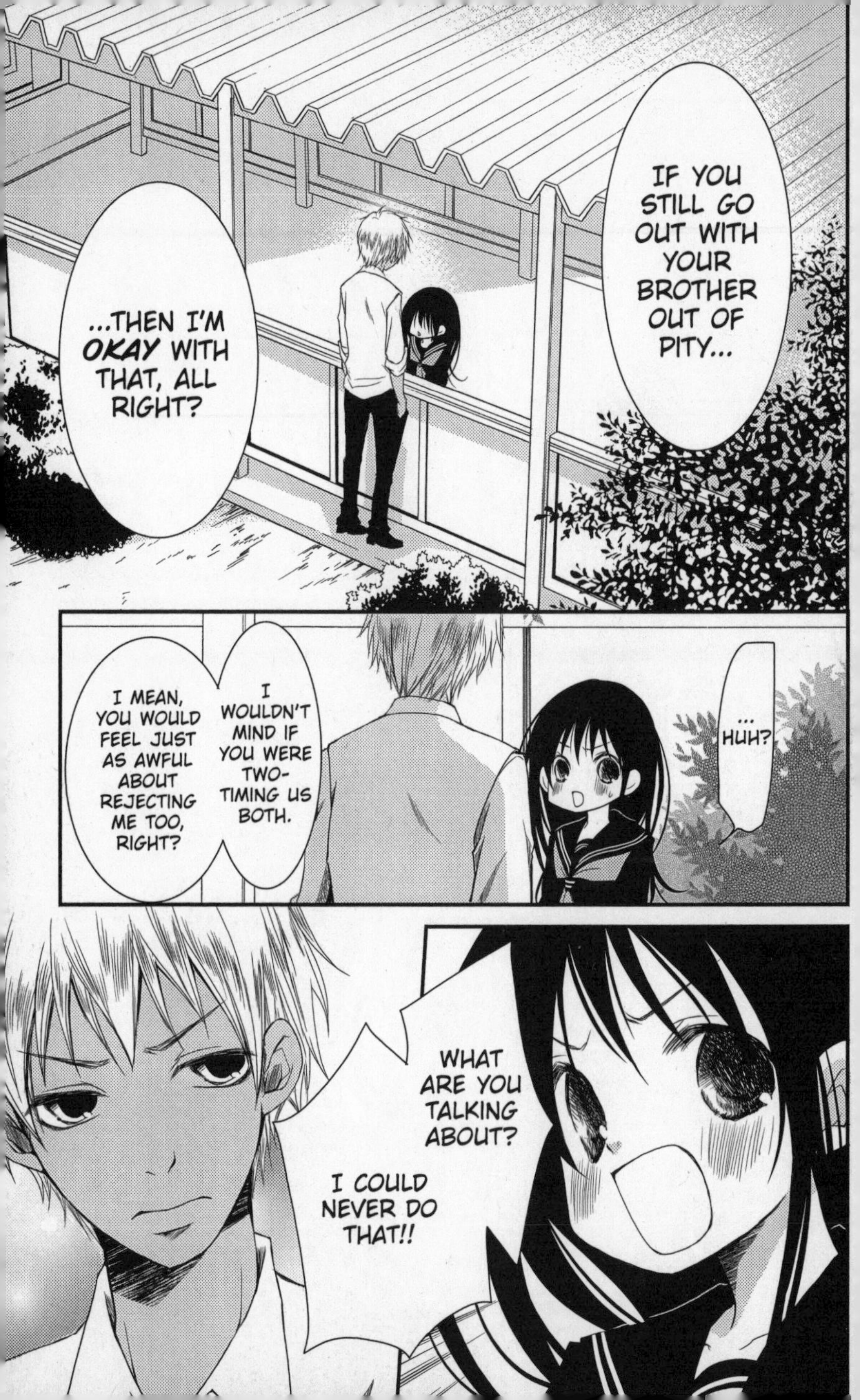
IF YOU STILL GO OUT WITH YOUR BROTHER OUT OF PITY...
...THEN I'M *OKAY* WITH THAT, ALL RIGHT?
... HUH?
I WOULDN'T MIND IF YOU WERE TWO-TIMING US BOTH.
I MEAN, YOU WOULD FEEL JUST AS AWFUL ABOUT REJECTING ME TOO, RIGHT?
WHAT ARE YOU TALKING ABOUT?
I COULD NEVER DO THAT!!

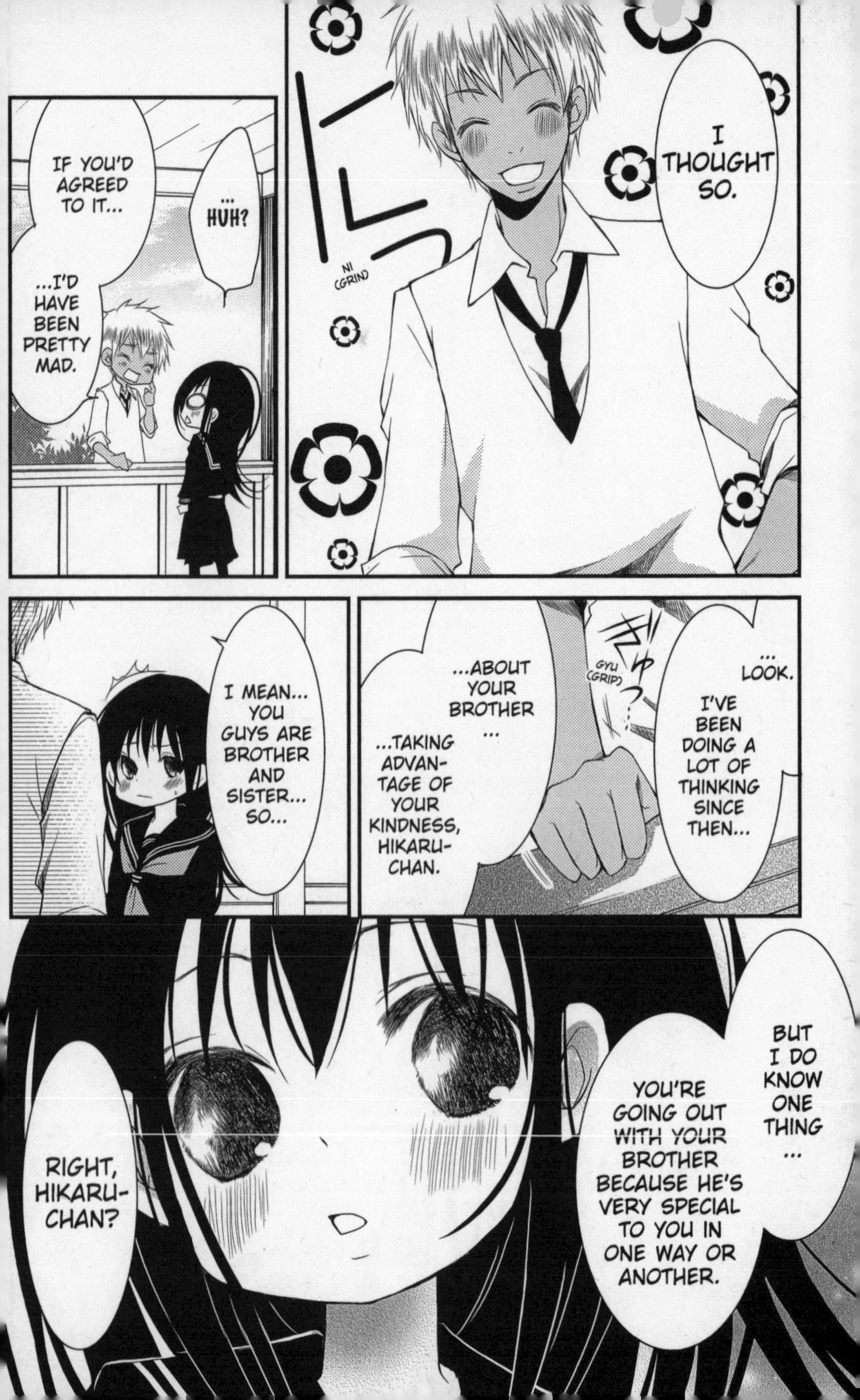
I THOUGHT SO.
NI (GRIN)
... HUH?
IF YOU'D AGREED TO IT...
...I'D HAVE BEEN PRETTY MAD.
... LOOK.
I'VE BEEN DOING A LOT OF THINKING SINCE THEN...
GYU (GRIP)
...ABOUT YOUR BROTHER ...
...TAKING ADVANTAGE OF YOUR KINDNESS, HIKARU-CHAN.
I MEAN... YOU GUYS ARE BROTHER AND SISTER... SO...
BUT I DO KNOW ONE THING ...
YOU'RE GOING OUT WITH YOUR BROTHER BECAUSE HE'S VERY SPECIAL TO YOU IN ONE WAY OR ANOTHER.
RIGHT, HIKARU-CHAN?

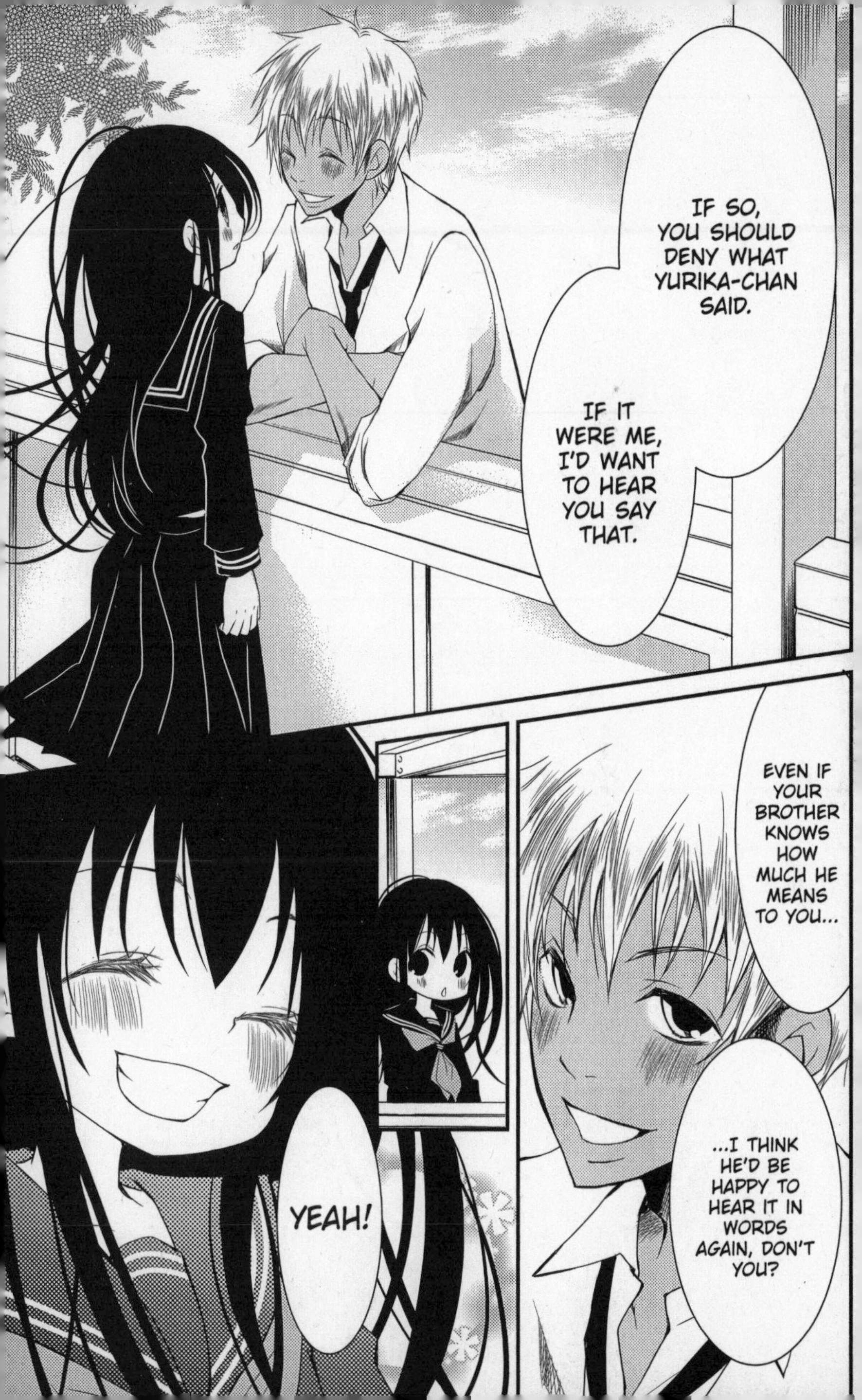
IF SO, YOU SHOULD DENY WHAT YURIKA-CHAN SAID.
IF IT WERE ME, I'D WANT TO HEAR YOU SAY THAT.
EVEN IF YOUR BROTHER KNOWS HOW MUCH HE MEANS TO YOU...
...I THINK HE'D BE HAPPY TO HEAR IT IN WORDS AGAIN, DON'T YOU?
YEAH!

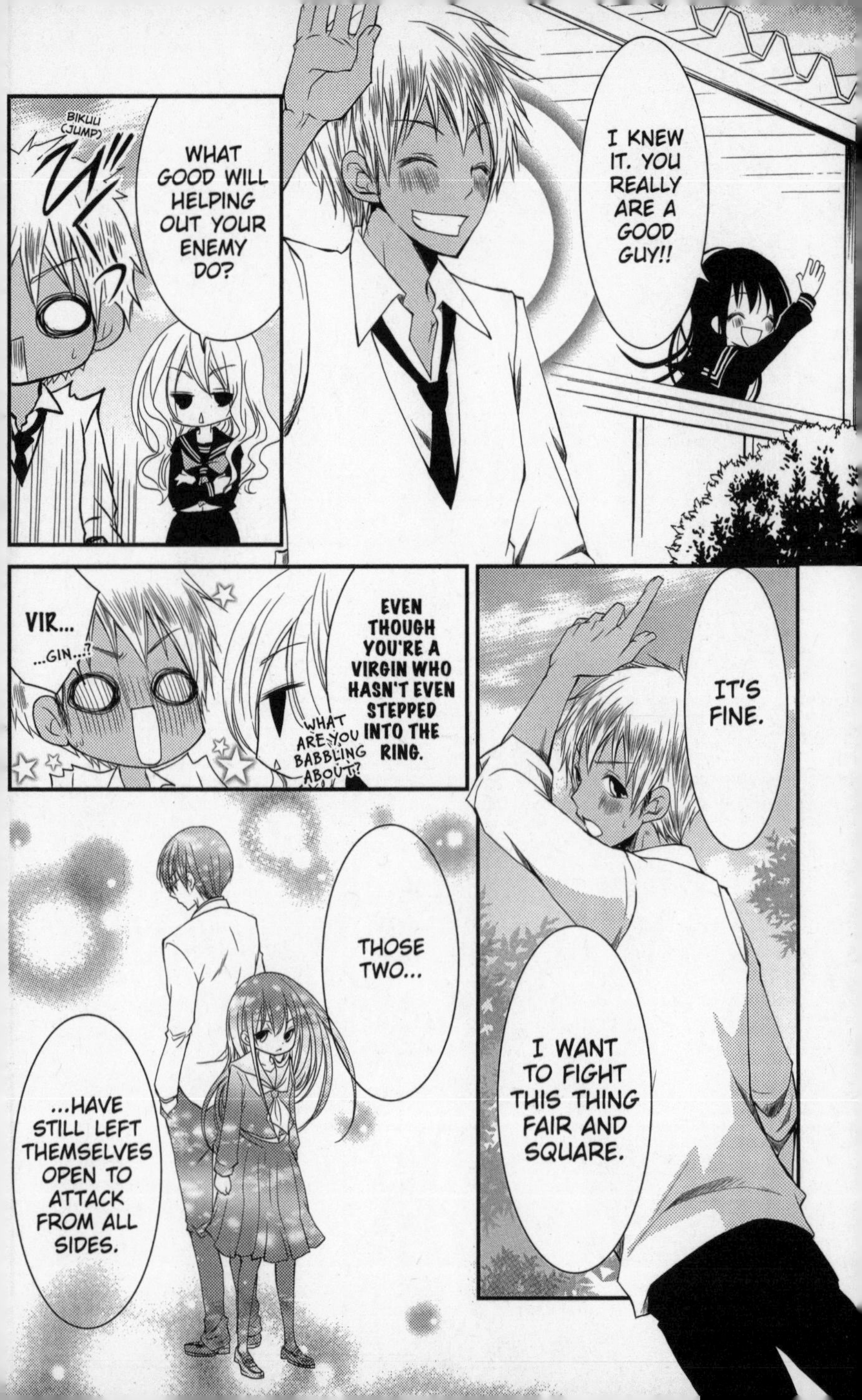
I KNEW IT. YOU REALLY ARE A GOOD GUY!!
BIKUU (JUMP)
WHAT GOOD WILL HELPING OUT YOUR ENEMY DO?
IT'S FINE.
I WANT TO FIGHT THIS THING FAIR AND SQUARE.
EVEN THOUGH YOU'RE A VIRGIN WHO HASN'T EVEN STEPPED INTO THE RING.
VIR...
...GIN...?
WHAT ARE YOU BABBLING ABOUT?!
THOSE TWO...
...HAVE STILL LEFT THEMSELVES OPEN TO ATTACK FROM ALL SIDES.

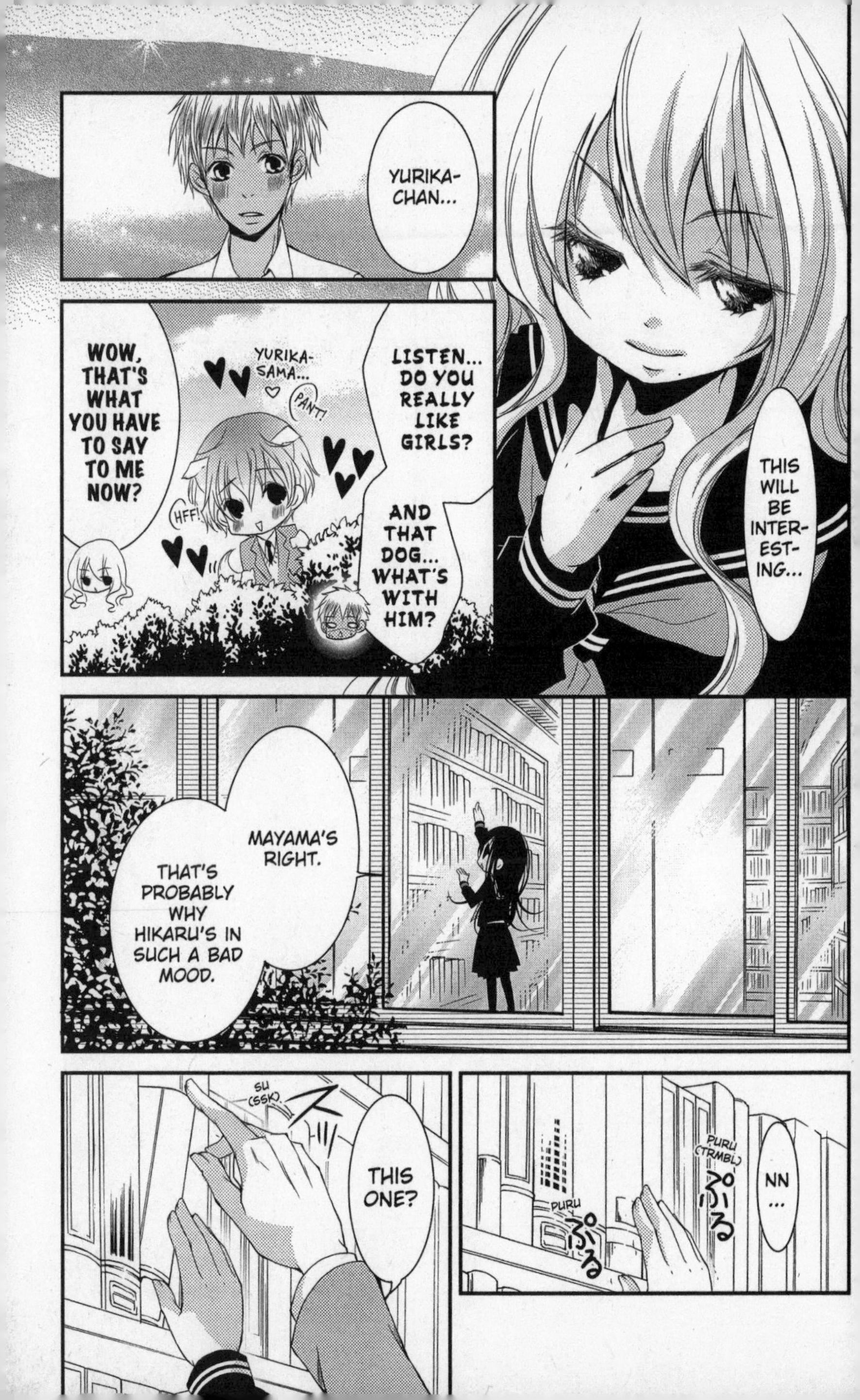
THIS WILL BE INTER-EST-ING...
YURIKA-CHAN...
LISTEN... DO YOU REALLY LIKE GIRLS?
AND THAT DOG... WHAT'S WITH HIM?
YURIKA-SAMA...
PANT!
HFF!
WOW, THAT'S WHAT YOU HAVE TO SAY TO ME NOW?
MAYAMA'S RIGHT.
THAT'S PROBABLY WHY HIKARU'S IN SUCH A BAD MOOD.
NN ...
PURU (TRMBL) ぷるぷる
PURU ぷるぷる
THIS ONE?
SU (SSK) ス

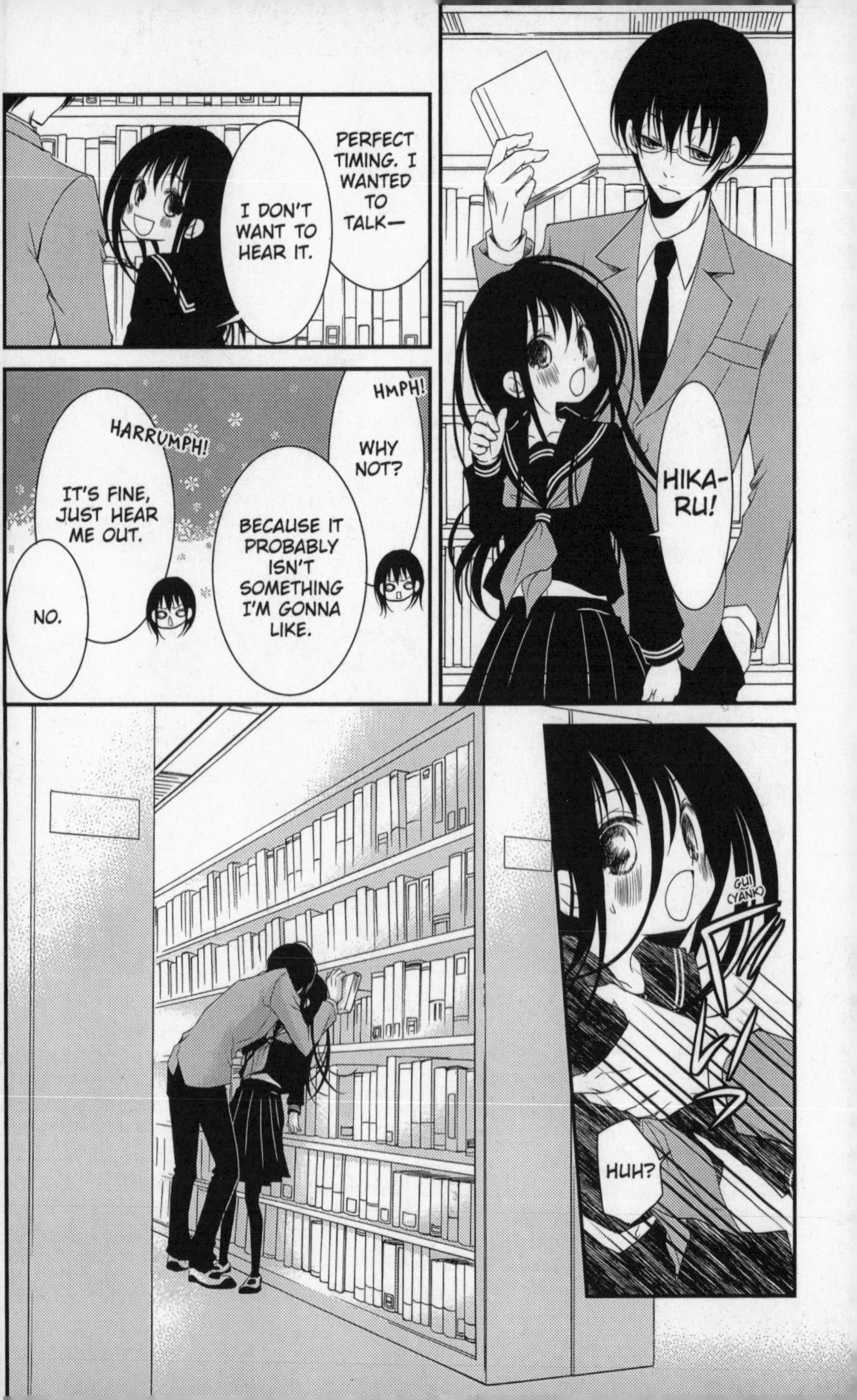
HIKA-RU!
PERFECT TIMING. I WANTED TO TALK—
I DON'T WANT TO HEAR IT.
HMPH!
WHY NOT?
BECAUSE IT PROBABLY ISN'T SOMETHING I'M GONNA LIKE.
HARRUMPH!
IT'S FINE, JUST HEAR ME OUT.
NO.
GUI (YANK)
HUH?

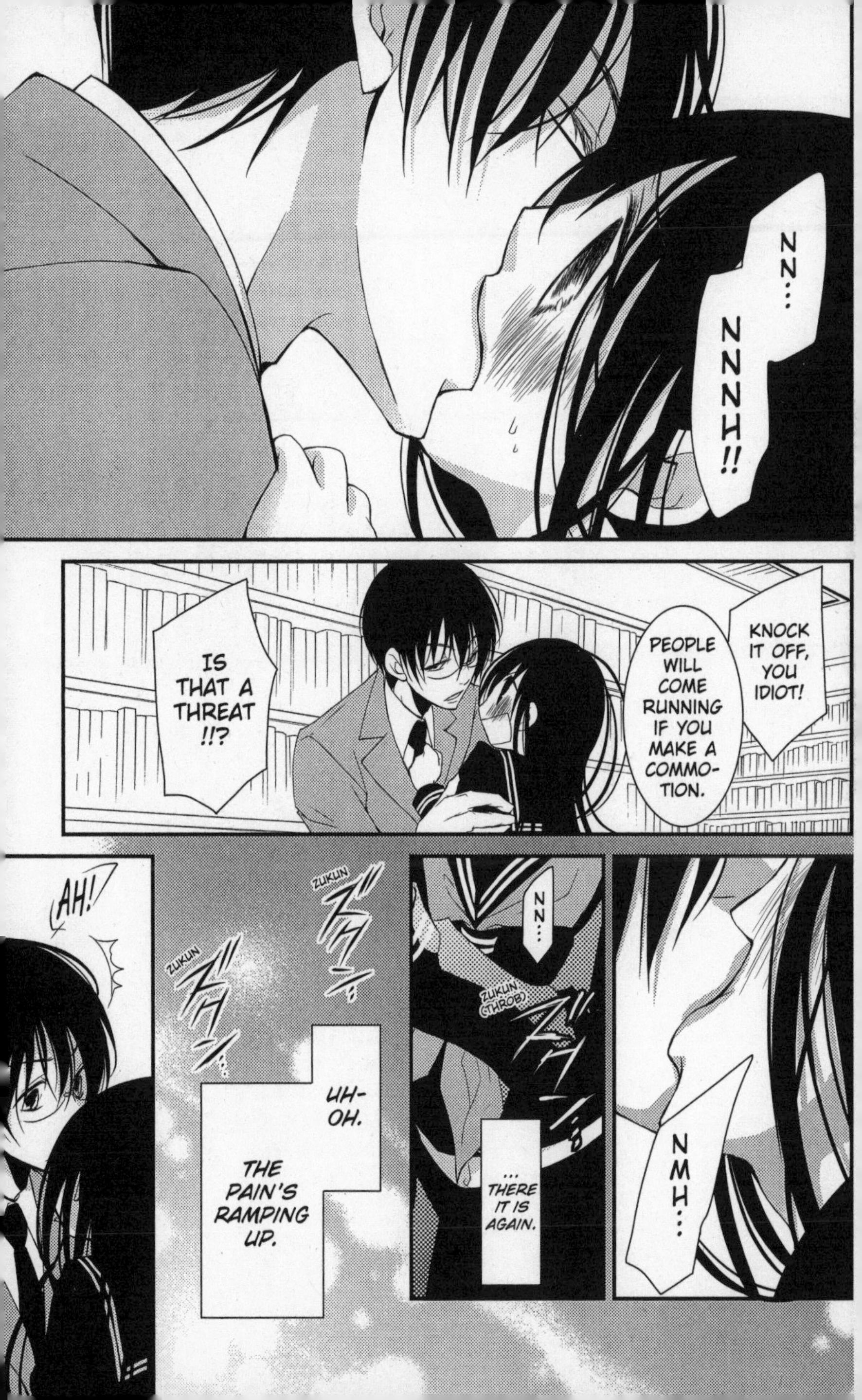
NN...
NNNH!!
KNOCK IT OFF, YOU IDIOT!
PEOPLE WILL COME RUNNING IF YOU MAKE A COMMOTION.
IS THAT A THREAT!!?
NMH...
NN...
ZUKUN (THROB)
...THERE IT IS AGAIN.
ZUKUN
ZUKUN
UH-OH.
THE PAIN'S RAMPING UP.
AH!

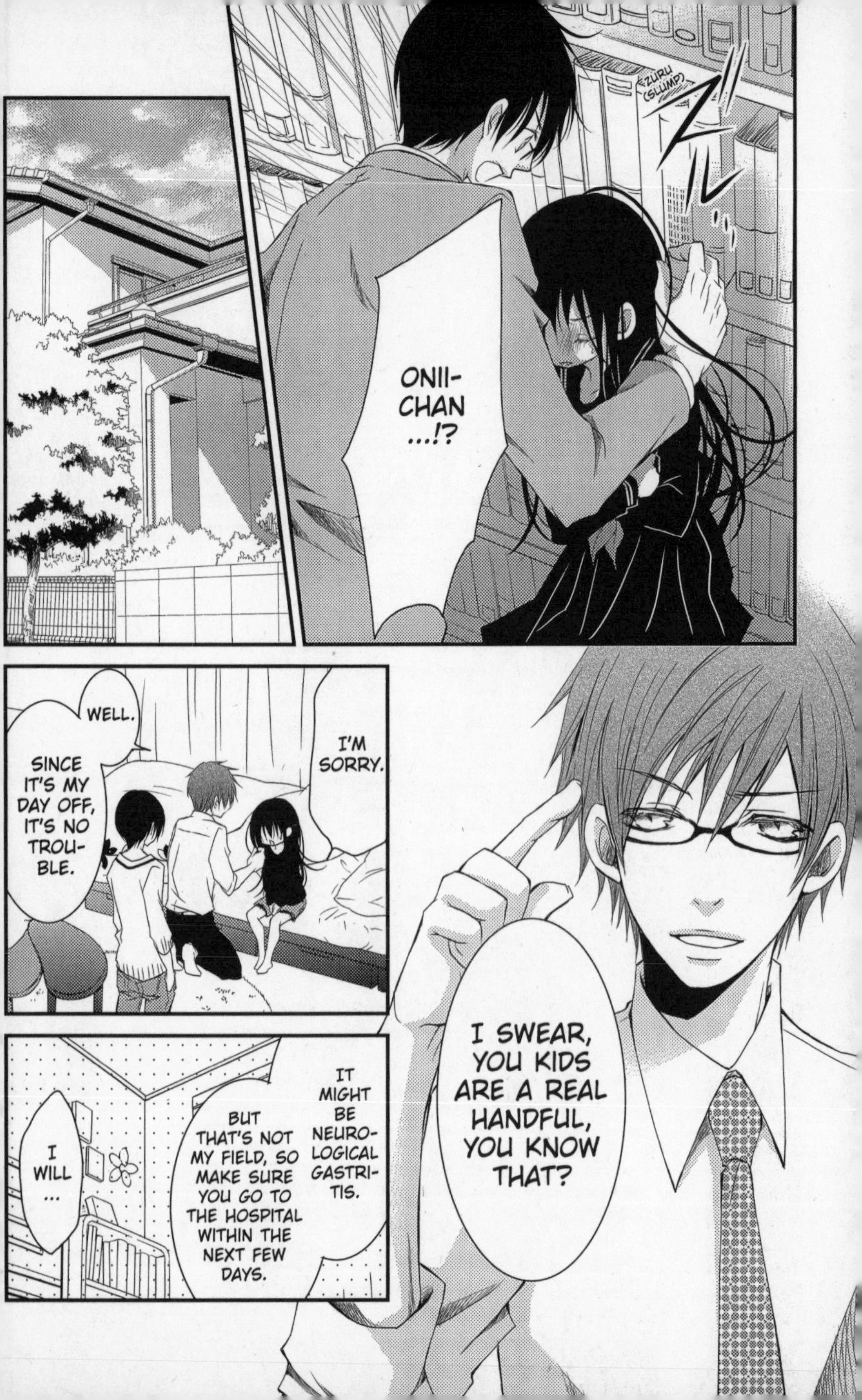
ZURU (SLUMP)
ONII-CHAN ...!?
I SWEAR, YOU KIDS ARE A REAL HANDFUL, YOU KNOW THAT?
I'M SORRY.
WELL.
SINCE IT'S MY DAY OFF, IT'S NO TROUBLE.
IT MIGHT BE NEUROLOGICAL GASTRITIS.
BUT THAT'S NOT MY FIELD, SO MAKE SURE YOU GO TO THE HOSPITAL WITHIN THE NEXT FEW DAYS.
I WILL ...

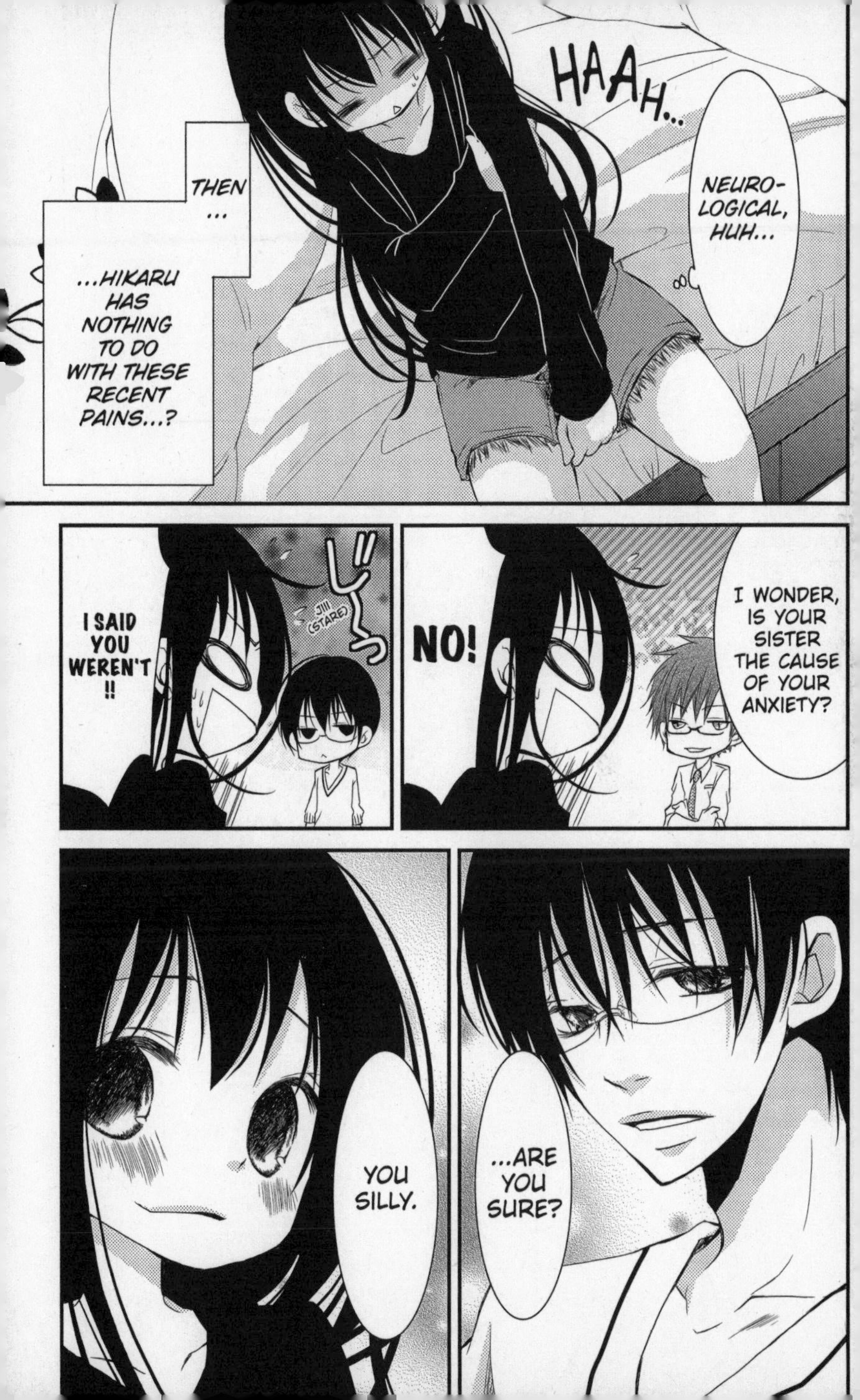
HAAH...
NEURO-LOGICAL, HUH...
THEN...
...HIKARU HAS NOTHING TO DO WITH THESE RECENT PAINS...?
I WONDER, IS YOUR SISTER THE CAUSE OF YOUR ANXIETY?
NO!
じーっ
JIII (STARE)
I SAID YOU WEREN'T !!
...ARE YOU SURE?
YOU SILLY.

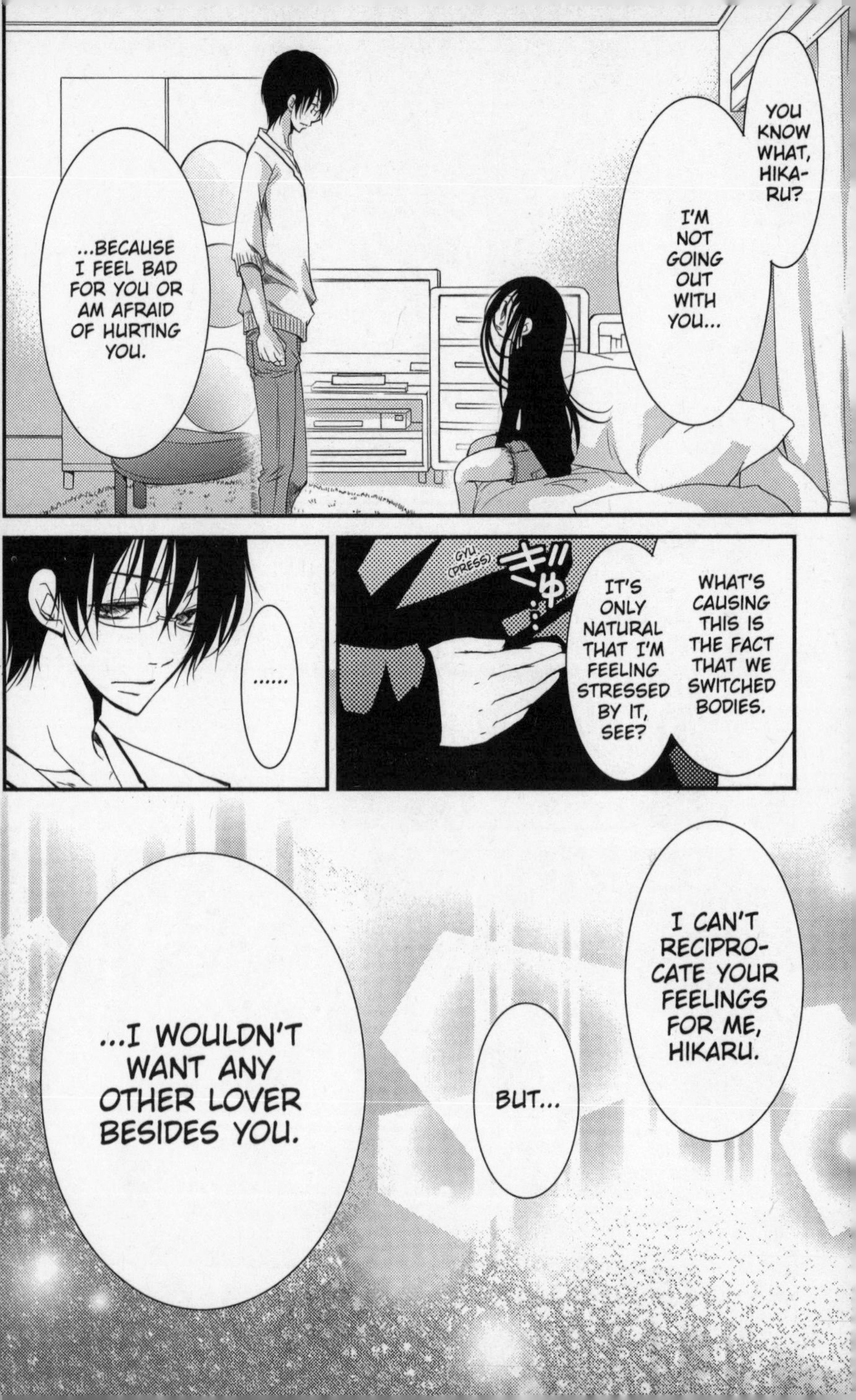
YOU KNOW WHAT, HIKARU?
I'M NOT GOING OUT WITH YOU...
...BECAUSE I FEEL BAD FOR YOU OR AM AFRAID OF HURTING YOU.
GYU (PRESS)
ぎゅ
WHAT'S CAUSING THIS IS THE FACT THAT WE SWITCHED BODIES.
IT'S ONLY NATURAL THAT I'M FEELING STRESSED BY IT, SEE?
......
I CAN'T RECIPROCATE YOUR FEELINGS FOR ME, HIKARU.
BUT...
...I WOULDN'T WANT ANY OTHER LOVER BESIDES YOU.

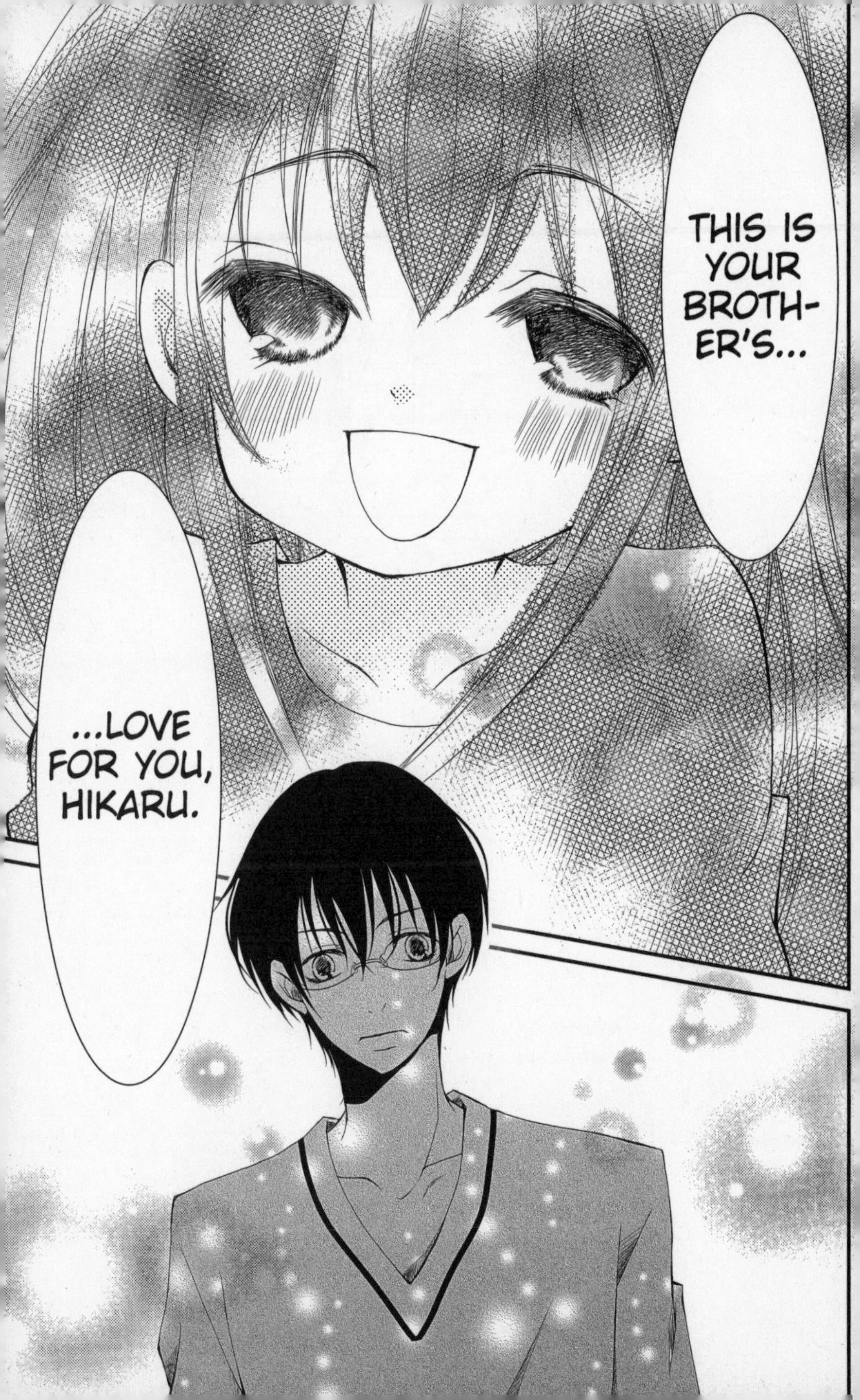
THIS IS YOUR BROTH-ER'S...
...LOVE FOR YOU, HIKARU.

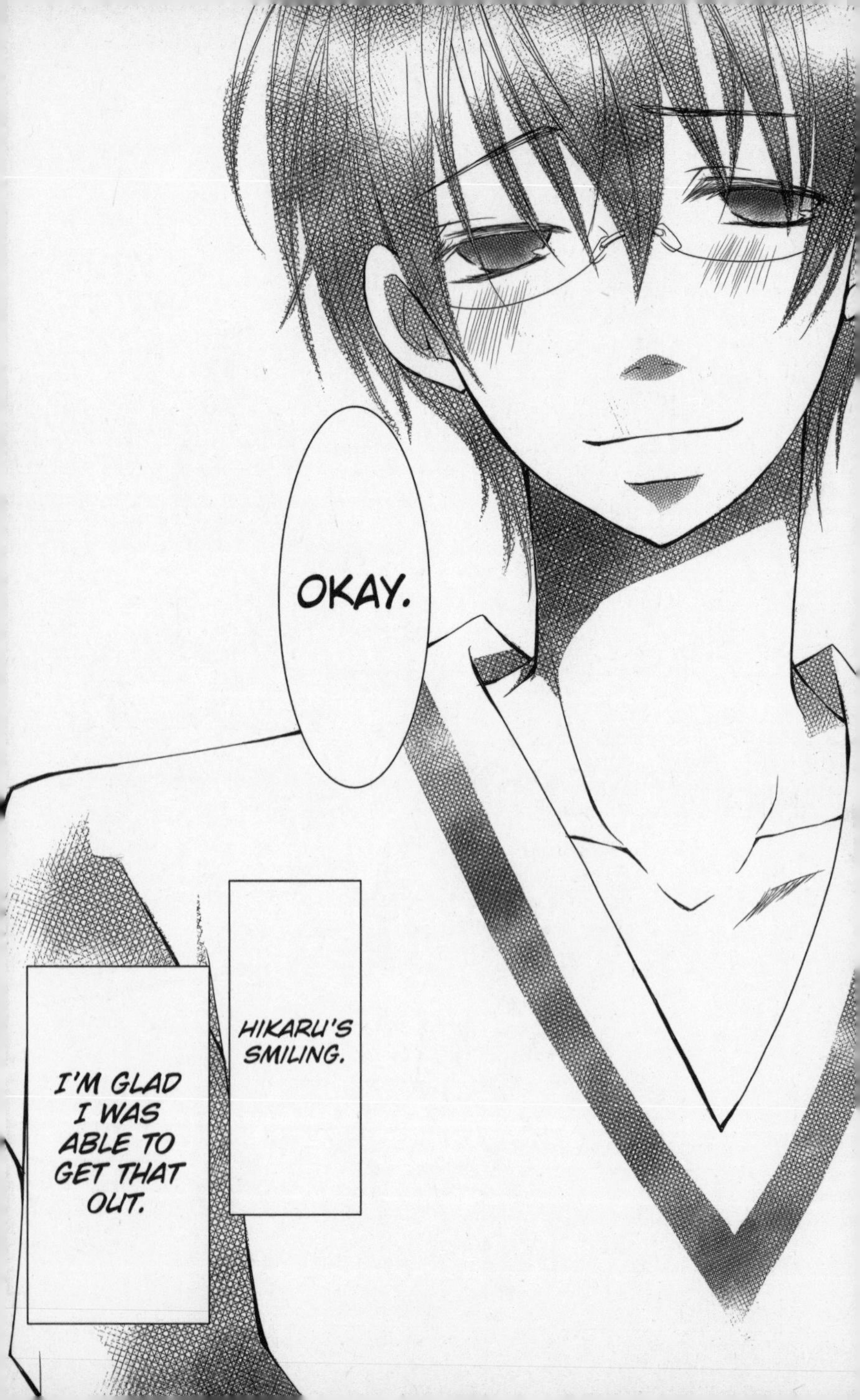
OKAY.
HIKARU'S SMILING.
I'M GLAD I WAS ABLE TO GET THAT OUT.

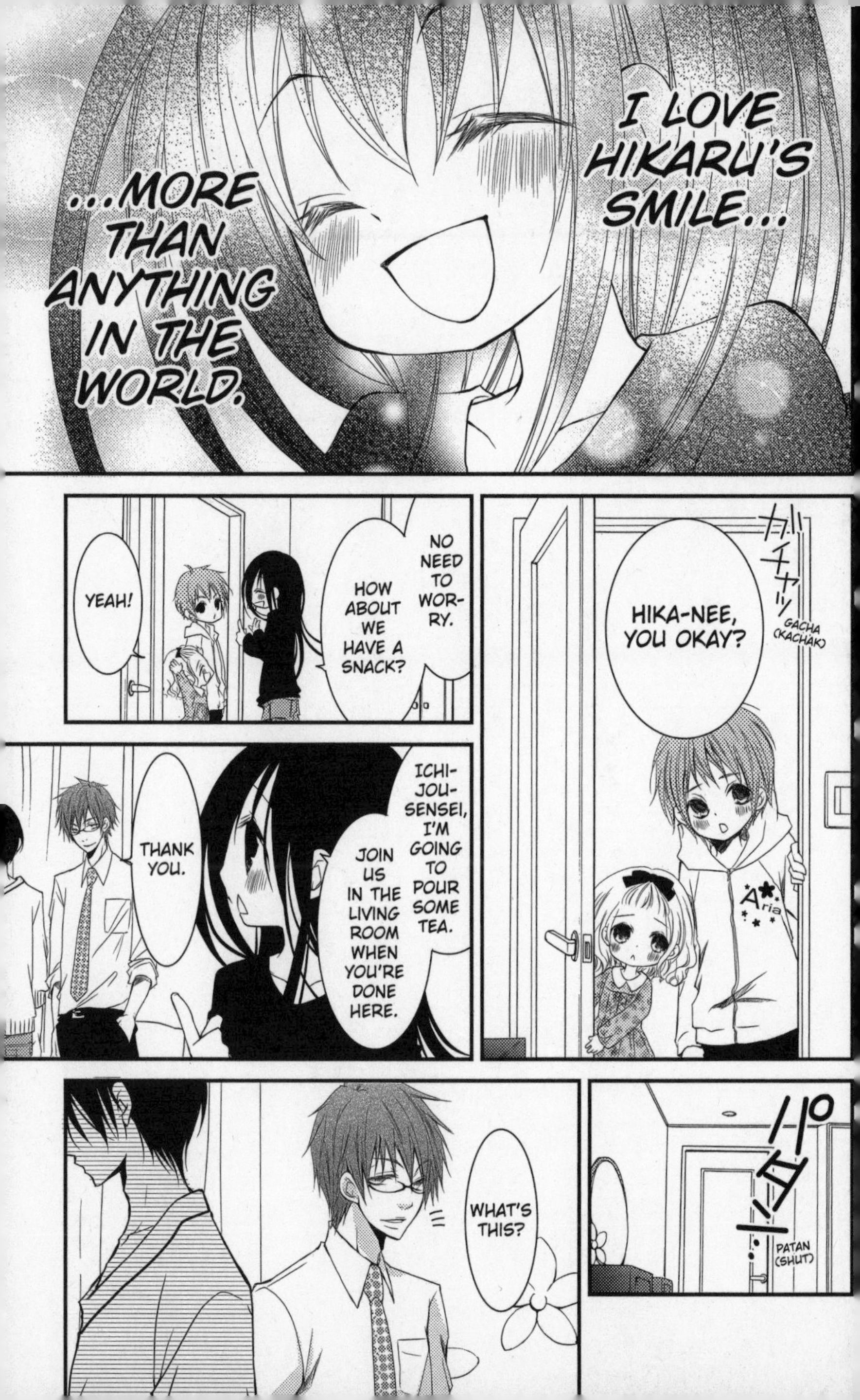
I LOVE HIKARU'S SMILE...
...MORE THAN ANYTHING IN THE WORLD.
ガチャッ
GACHA (KACHAK)
HIKA-NEE, YOU OKAY?
NO NEED TO WORRY.
HOW ABOUT WE HAVE A SNACK?
YEAH!
ICHIJOU-SENSEI, I'M GOING TO POUR SOME TEA.
JOIN US IN THE LIVING ROOM WHEN YOU'RE DONE HERE.
THANK YOU.
パタン
PATAN (SHUT)
WHAT'S THIS?

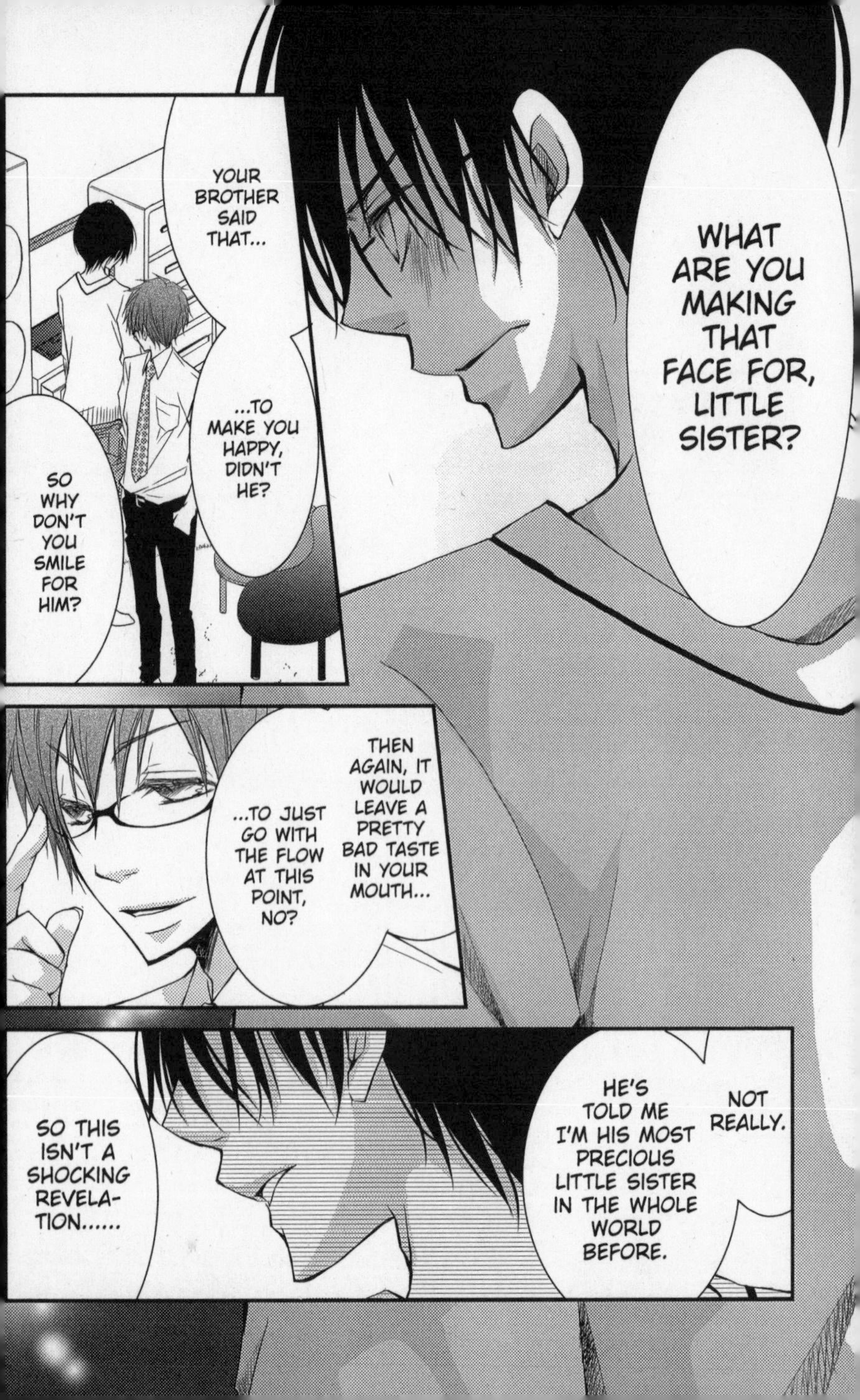
WHAT ARE YOU MAKING THAT FACE FOR, LITTLE SISTER?
YOUR BROTHER SAID THAT...
...TO MAKE YOU HAPPY, DIDN'T HE?
SO WHY DON'T YOU SMILE FOR HIM?
THEN AGAIN, IT WOULD LEAVE A PRETTY BAD TASTE IN YOUR MOUTH...
...TO JUST GO WITH THE FLOW AT THIS POINT, NO?
NOT REALLY.
HE'S TOLD ME I'M HIS MOST PRECIOUS LITTLE SISTER IN THE WHOLE WORLD BEFORE.
SO THIS ISN'T A SHOCKING REVELA-TION......

IT JUST...

...FEELS LIKE I'VE BEEN REJECTED A SECOND TIME.

BUT IT'S OKAY. I KNOW I CAN'T WIN HIM OVER JUST LIKE THAT.

...IF IT WERE YOU, SENSEI...

...WHAT WOULD BE YOUR STRATEGY FOR WINNING SOMEONE'S AFFECTIONS?

I SEE. THEN YOU'LL HAVE TO KEEP PUTTING UP A GOOD FIGHT FROM HERE ON.

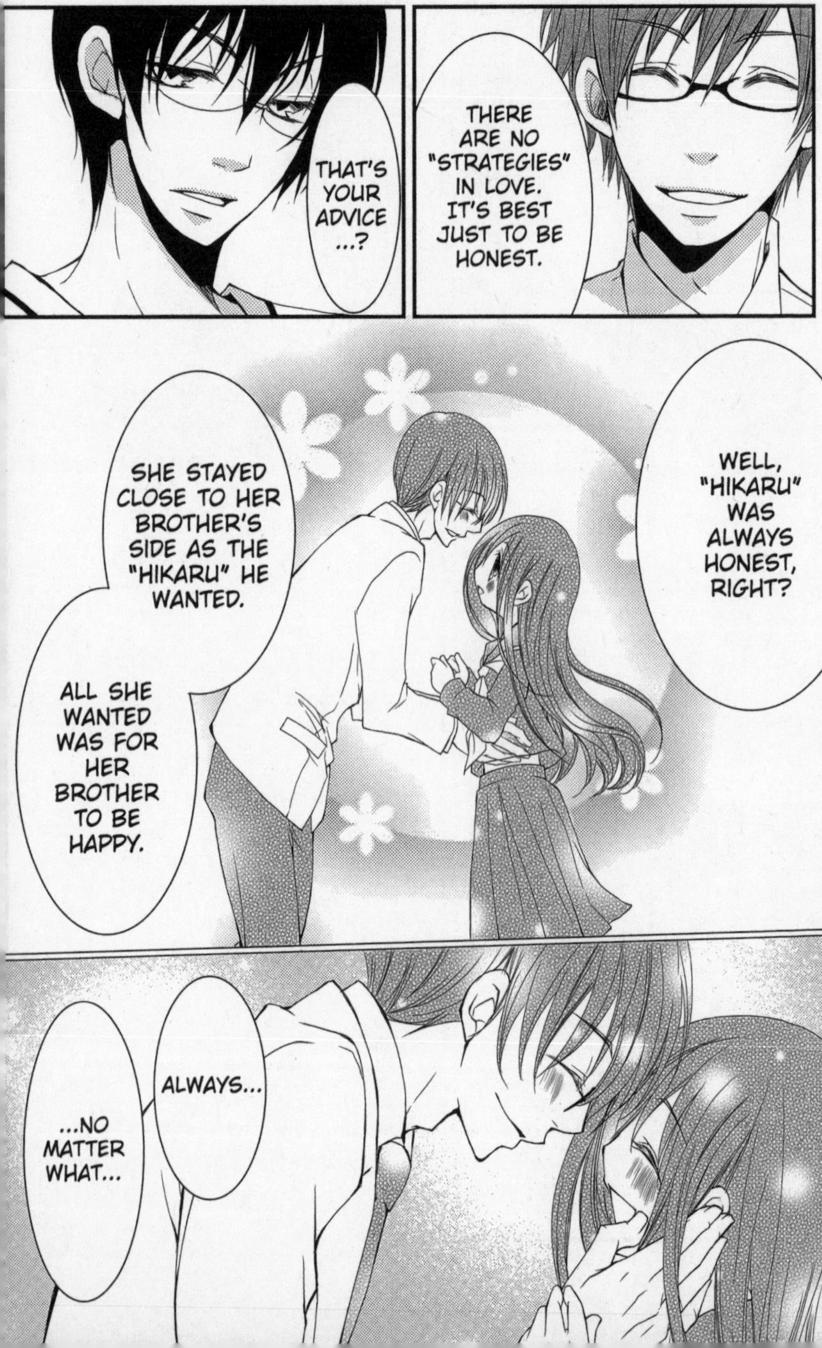
THERE ARE NO "STRATEGIES" IN LOVE. IT'S BEST JUST TO BE HONEST.
THAT'S YOUR ADVICE ...?
WELL, "HIKARU" WAS ALWAYS HONEST, RIGHT?
SHE STAYED CLOSE TO HER BROTHER'S SIDE AS THE "HIKARU" HE WANTED.
ALL SHE WANTED WAS FOR HER BROTHER TO BE HAPPY.
ALWAYS...
...NO MATTER WHAT...

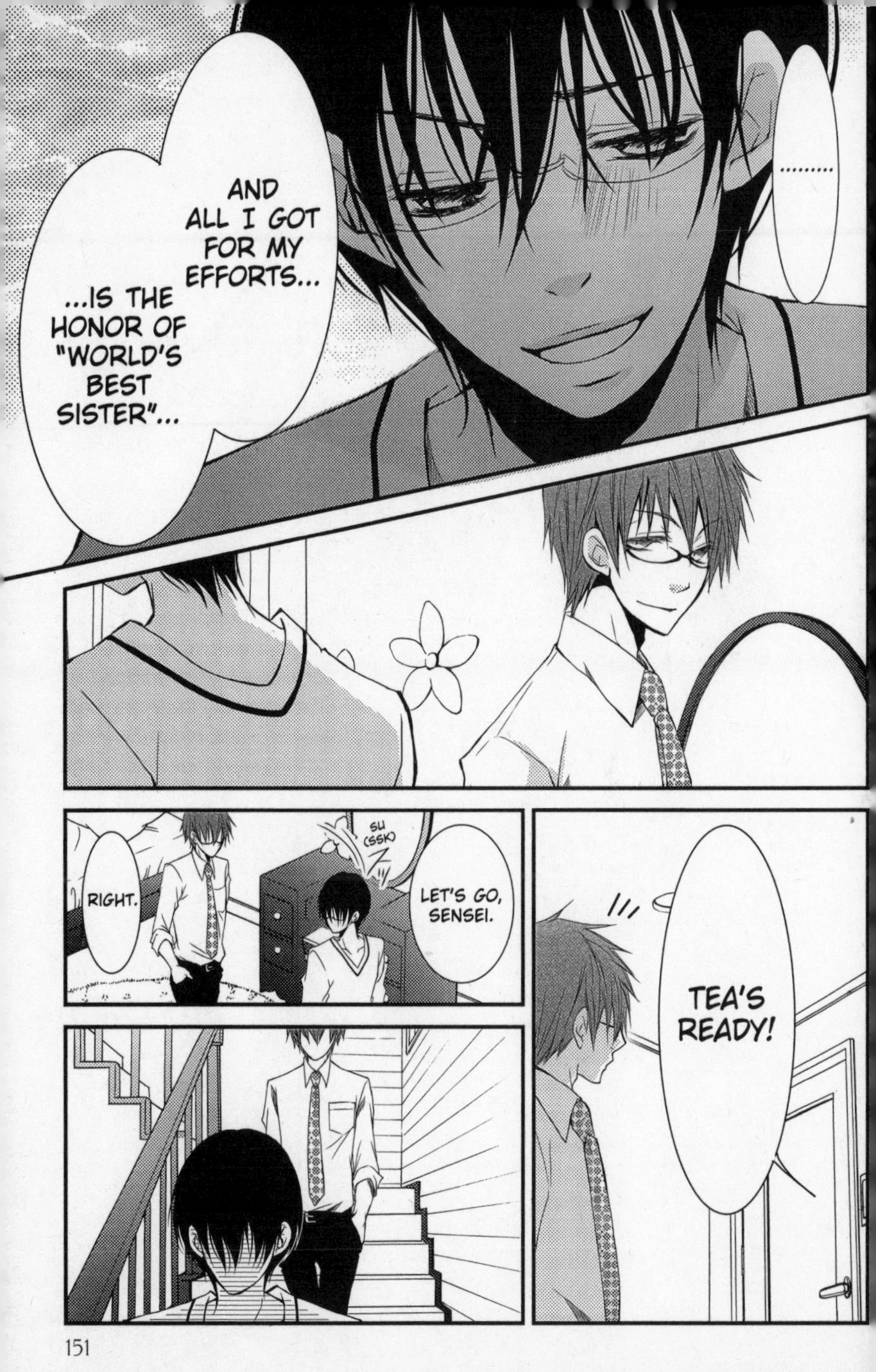
....
AND ALL I GOT FOR MY EFFORTS...
...IS THE HONOR OF "WORLD'S BEST SISTER"...
TEA'S READY!
SU (SSK)
LET'S GO, SENSEI.
RIGHT.

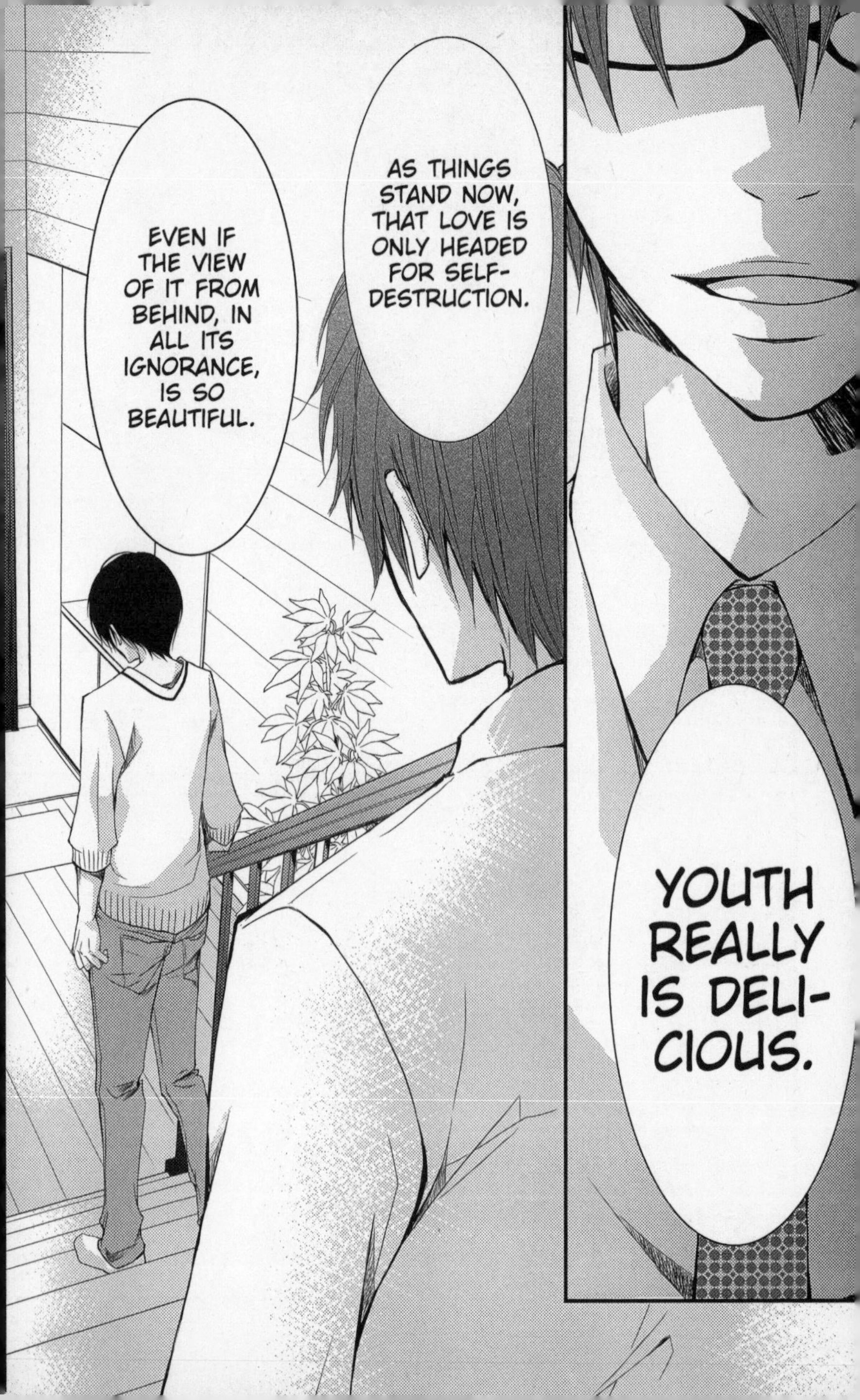
YOUTH REALLY IS DELICIOUS.
AS THINGS STAND NOW, THAT LOVE IS ONLY HEADED FOR SELF-DESTRUCTION.
EVEN IF THE VIEW OF IT FROM BEHIND, IN ALL ITS IGNORANCE, IS SO BEAUTIFUL.

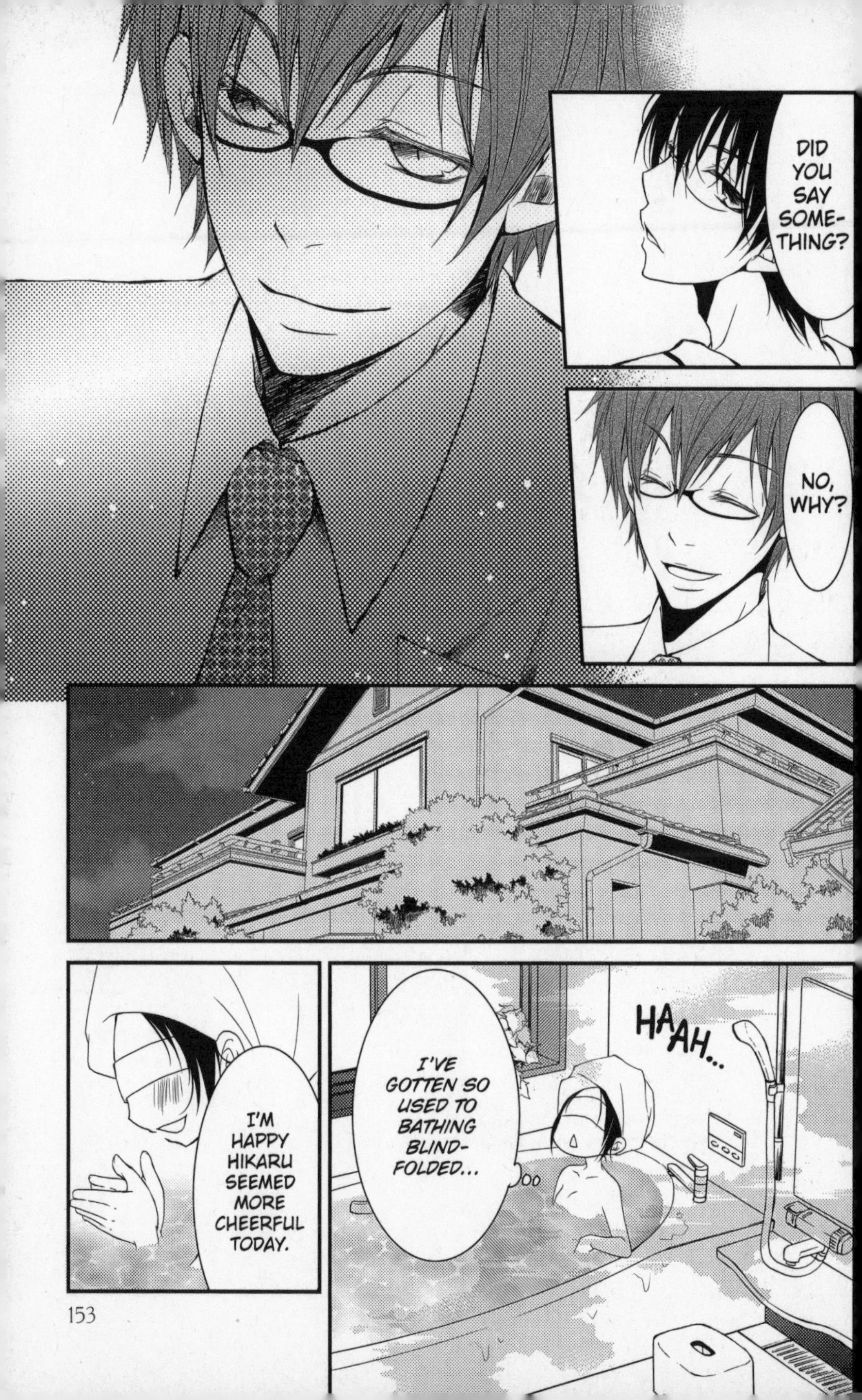
DID YOU SAY SOME-THING?
NO, WHY?
HAAH...
I'VE GOTTEN SO USED TO BATHING BLIND-FOLDED...
I'M HAPPY HIKARU SEEMED MORE CHEERFUL TODAY.

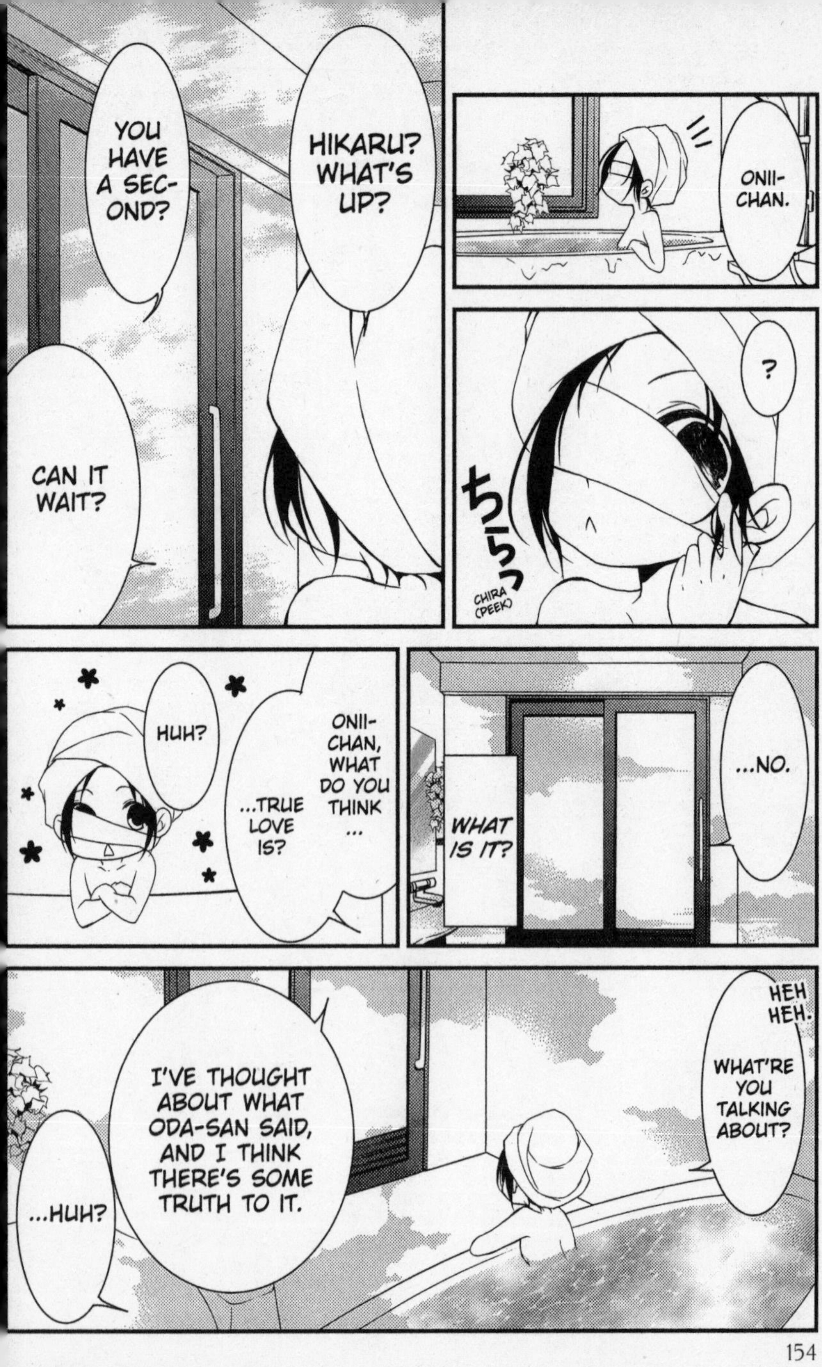
ONII-CHAN.
?
ちらっ
CHIRA (PEEK)
HIKARU? WHAT'S UP?
YOU HAVE A SEC-OND?
CAN IT WAIT?
...NO.
WHAT IS IT?
ONII-CHAN, WHAT DO YOU THINK ...
...TRUE LOVE IS?
HUH?
HEH HEH.
WHAT'RE YOU TALKING ABOUT?
I'VE THOUGHT ABOUT WHAT ODA-SAN SAID, AND I THINK THERE'S SOME TRUTH TO IT.
...HUH?

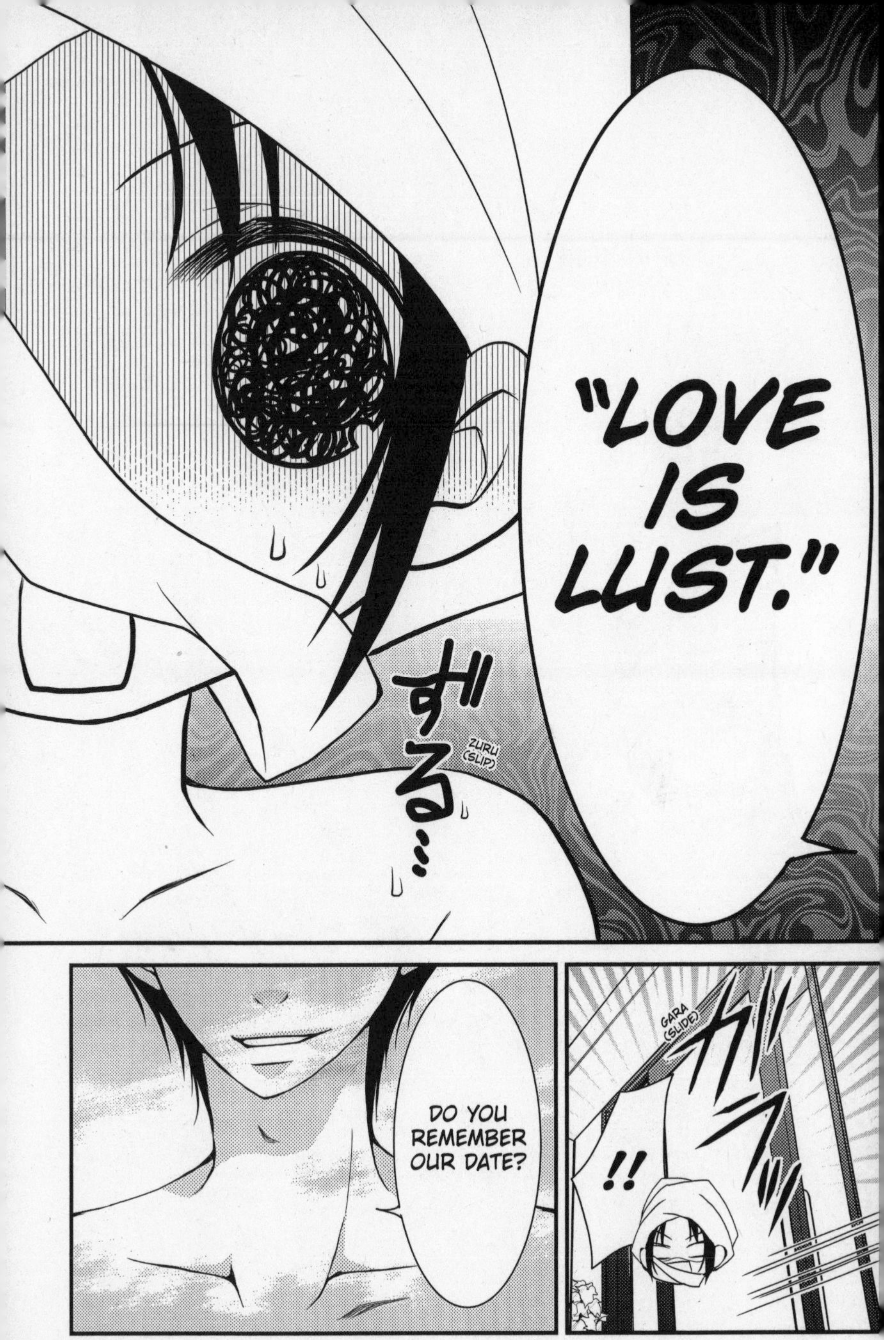
"LOVE IS LUST."
ずる…
ZURU (SLIP)
GARA (SLIDE)
ガラッ
!!
DO YOU REMEMBER OUR DATE?

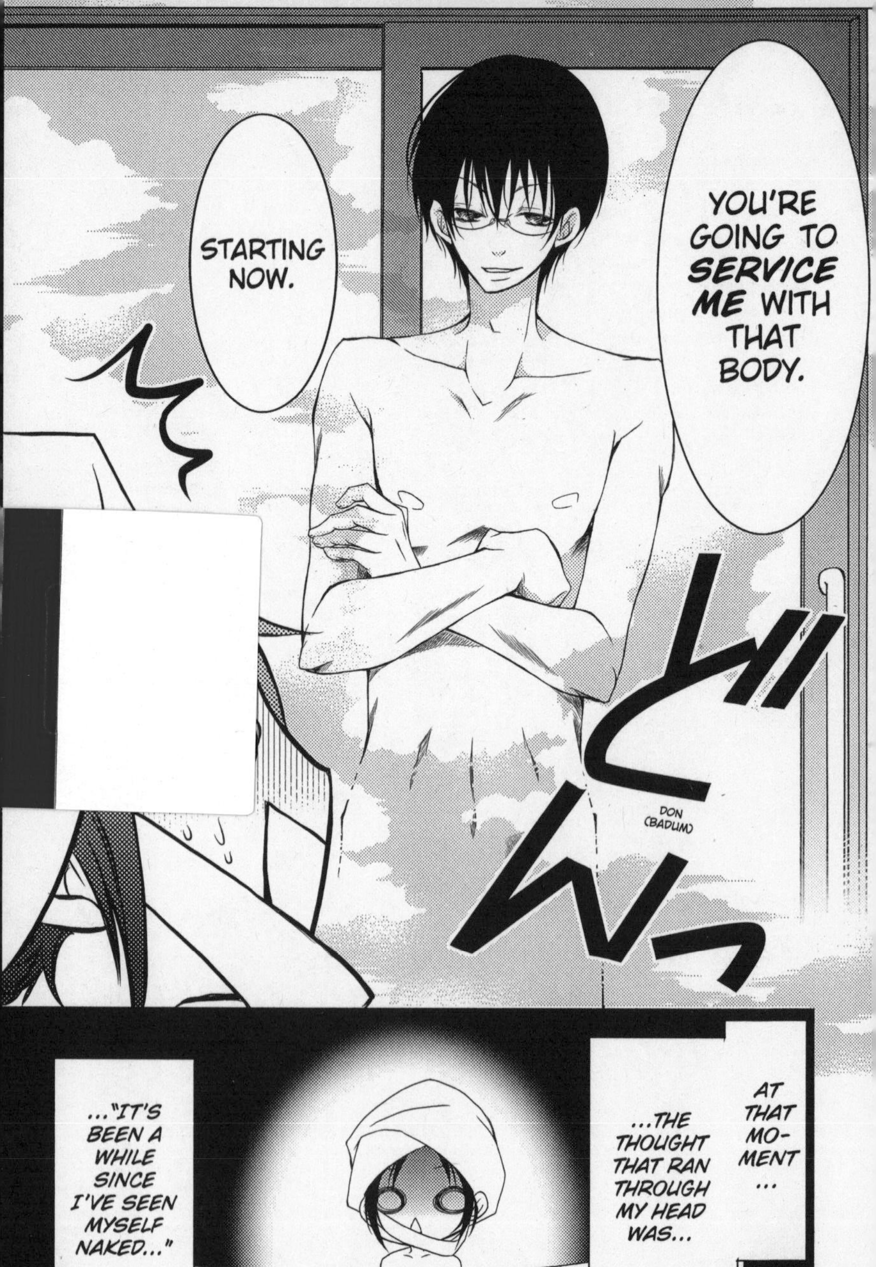
YOU'RE GOING TO SERVICE ME WITH THAT BODY.
STARTING NOW.
DON (BADUM)
AT THAT MOMENT...
...THE THOUGHT THAT RAN THROUGH MY HEAD WAS...
..."IT'S BEEN A WHILE SINCE I'VE SEEN MYSELF NAKED..."

Continued in Volume 3

Translation Notes

Common Honorifics:

no honorific: Indicates familiarity or closeness; if used without permission or reason, addressing someone in this manner would constitute an insult.

-san: The Japanese equivalent of Mr./Mrs./Miss. If a situation calls for politeness, this is the fail-safe honorific.

-sama: Conveys great respect; may also indicate that the social status of the speaker is lower than that of the addressee.

-kun: Used most often when referring to boys, this indicates affection or familiarity. Occasionally used by older men among their peers, but it may also be used by anyone referring to a person of lower standing.

-chan: An affectionate honorific indicating familiarity used mostly in reference to girls; also used in reference to cute persons or animals of either gender.

-senpai: A suffix used to address upperclassmen or more experienced coworkers.

-sensei: A respectful term for teachers, artists, or high-level professionals.

-oniisan, onii-san, aniki, ani etc.: Terms used to address an elder brother or brother-like figure.

-oneesan, onee-san, aneki, etc.: Terms used to address an elder sister or sister-like figure.

[**Ani-Imo**]

Big Brother becomes Little Sister;
Little Sister becomes Big Brother.

DADDY'S PORTRAIT♡

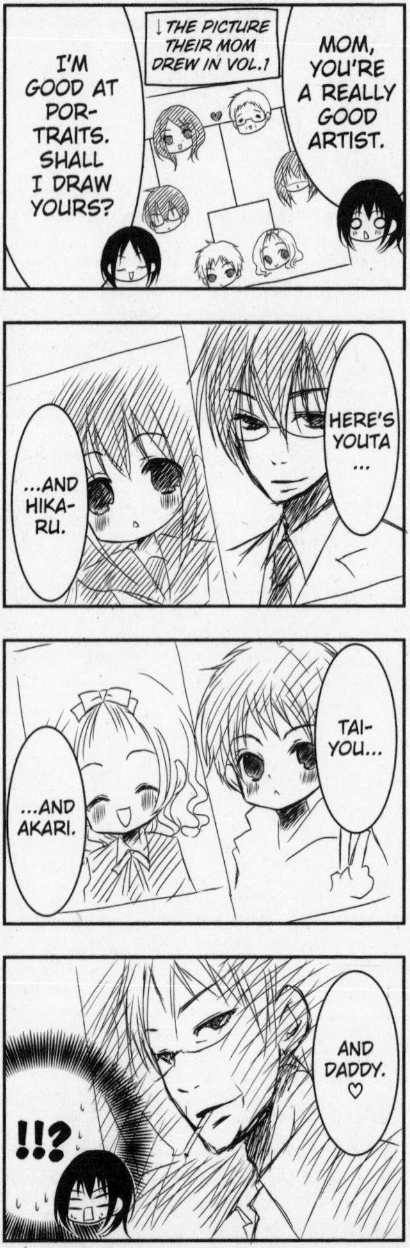
MOM, YOU'RE A REALLY GOOD ARTIST.
↓THE PICTURE THEIR MOM DREW IN VOL.1
I'M GOOD AT POR-TRAITS. SHALL I DRAW YOURS?
HERE'S YOUTA ...
...AND HIKA-RU.
TAI-YOU...
...AND AKARI.
AND DADDY. ♡
!!?

DADDY'S ALBUM♡

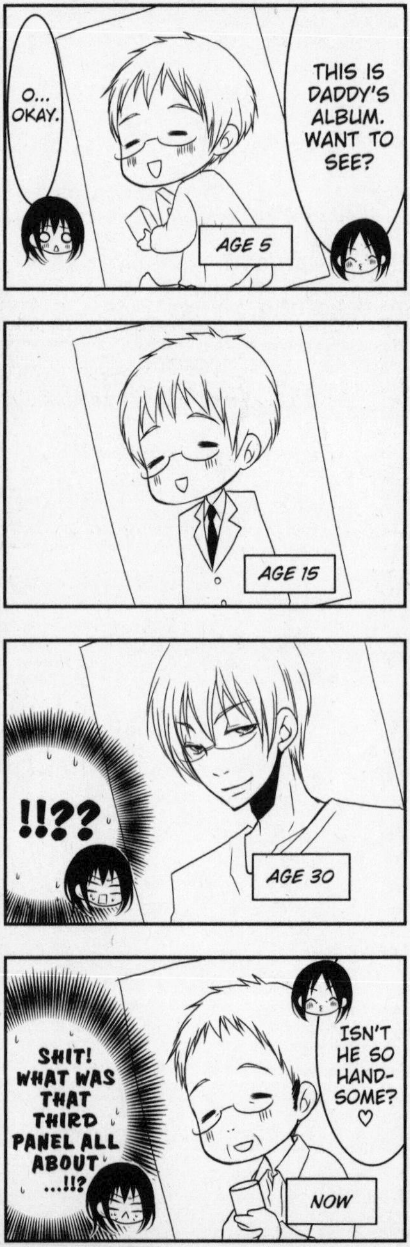
THIS IS DADDY'S ALBUM. WANT TO SEE?
AGE 5
O... OKAY.
AGE 15
AGE 30
!!??
ISN'T HE SO HAND-SOME? ♡
NOW
SHIT! WHAT WAS THAT THIRD PANEL ALL ABOUT ...!!?

HELLO, THIS IS HARUKO KURUMATANI.
THANK YOU VERY MUCH FOR PICKING
UP VOLUME 2 OF *ANI-IMO*.
HOW DID YOU LIKE IT?
I HOPE YOU ENJOYED IT,
EVEN JUST A LITTLE BIT.
AND I'LL BE LOOKING FORWARD
TO SEEING YOU IN VOLUME 3.
PLEASE LET ME KNOW WHAT
YOU THINK SO FAR:
HARUKO KURUMATANI
C/O YEN PRESS
1290 AVENUE OF
          THE AMERICAS
NEW YORK, NY 10104

http://kurumatani.jugem.jp/

Twitter ID: @kurumatani_h

Next Issue

THIS TIME HIKARU IS SERIOUS!?

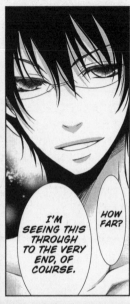

HOW FAR?
I'M SEEING THIS THROUGH TO THE VERY END, OF COURSE.

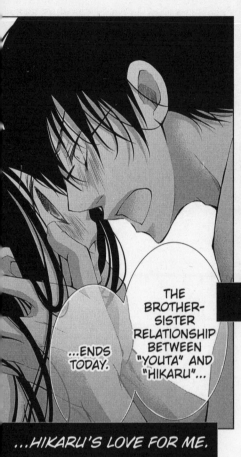

THE BROTHER-SISTER RELATIONSHIP BETWEEN "YOUTA" AND "HIKARU"...
...ENDS TODAY.

I UNDERESTIMATED...

...HIKARU'S LOVE FOR ME.

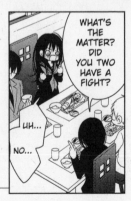

WHAT'S THE MATTER? DID YOU TWO HAVE A FIGHT?
UH...
NO...

AND OUR RELATIONSHIP BECOMES UNCERTAIN...

Available May 2015

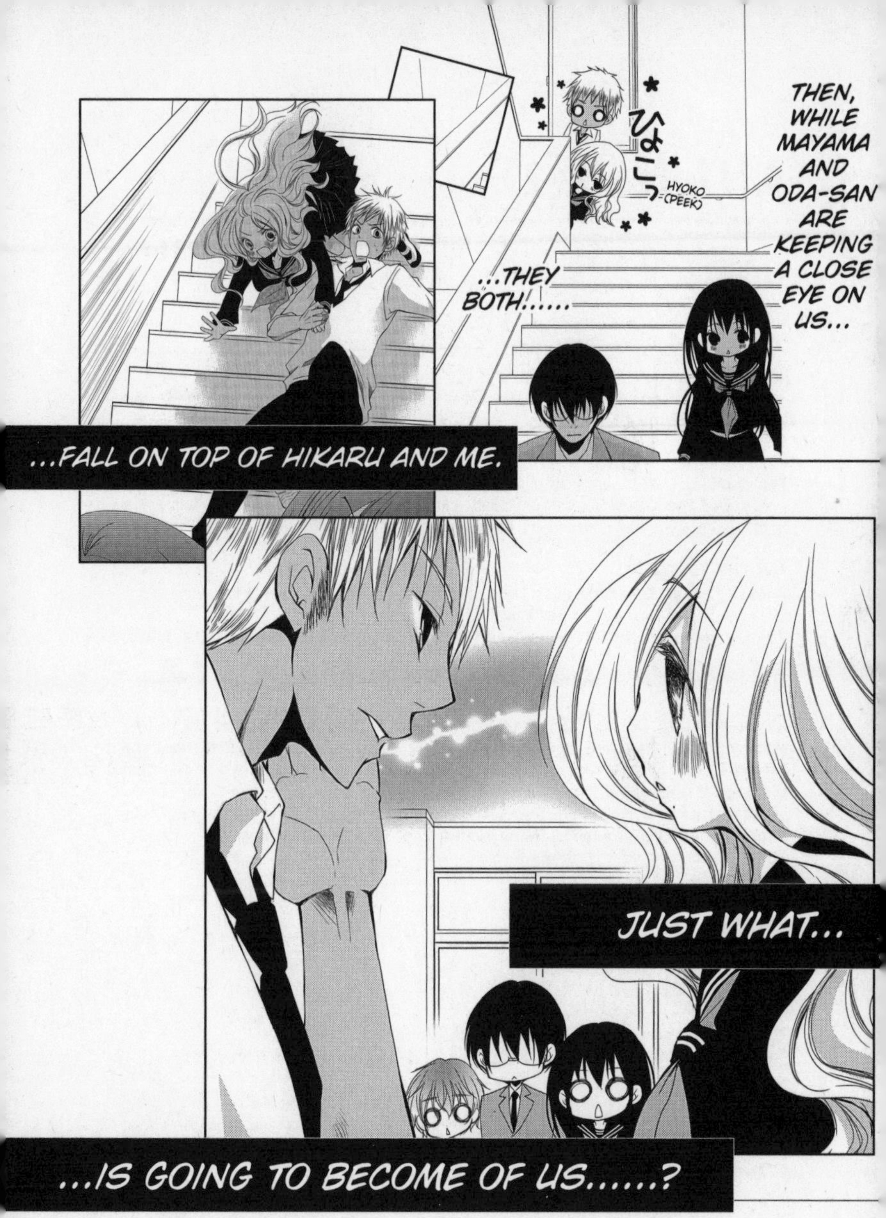
THEN, WHILE MAYAMA AND ODA-SAN ARE KEEPING A CLOSE EYE ON US...
ひょこっ
HYOKO=(PEEK)
...THEY BOTH......
...FALL ON TOP OF HIKARU AND ME.
JUST WHAT...
...IS GOING TO BECOME OF US......?

Ani-Imo (3)

ANI-IMO (2)

HARUKO KURUMATANI

Translation: Christine Dashiell

Lettering: Abigail Blackman

ANI-IMO Volume 2
© 2013 Haruko Kurumatani. All rights reserved.
First published in Japan in 2013 by Kodansha, Ltd., Tokyo.
Publication rights for this English edition arranged through Kodansha Ltd. Tokyo.

Translation © 2015 by Hachette Book Group, Inc.

Yen Press
Hachette Book Group
1290 Avenue of the Americas
New York, NY 10104
www.hachettebookgroup.com
www.yenpress.com

Yen Press is an imprint of Hachette Book Group, Inc.
The Yen Press name and logo are trademarks of Hachette Book Group, Inc.

The publisher is not responsible for websites (or their content) that are not owned by the publisher.

First Yen Press Edition: February 2015

ISBN: 978-0-316-38045-4

10 9 8 7 6 5 4 3 2 1

BVG

Printed in the United States of America